Grün

Günther Grzimek

Planning
Design
Program

With photographs by Karsten de Riese and The Pk. Odessa Co

Regine Keller

HIRMER

Olympic Park, Theatron amphitheater,
and aquatics center, 2021,
photo: The Pk. Odessa Co / Markus Lanz

9	Foreword		
10	Prologue		

11 Anette Freytag
Günther Grzimek: A New Type of Green Urban Planner

13 About the person

15 Timeline
16 Biography

21 Stations

23 Berlin
29 Ulm
35 Kassel
41 Munich

51 Collaborations

54 Otl Aicher and Inge Aicher-Scholl
60 Arnold Bode
62 Günter Behnisch

65 Projects, competitions, engagement

67 Sandfloh: The Sand Flea Campaign
77 Cemetery, Weingarten
87 New Cemetery, Ulm
95 Green Spaces Planning, Ulm
99 School of Engineering, Ulm
103 Green Spaces Planning, Darmstadt
109 New Botanical Garden, Marburg
117 Olympic Park, Munich
165 Munich Airport
175 South Isar Model

177 Günther Grzimek
Seven Theses from the Exhibition
The Appropriation of the Lawn

178 Competitions
180 Teaching

182 Günther Grzimek
The Profession of Landscape Architect

184 Günther Grzimek
Thoughts on Urban and Landscape Architecture
since Friedrich Ludwig von Sckell

196 Biographies
200 Epilogue

203 Appendix
204 Awards
204 List of Works
211 Bibliography
215 Author and Editor / Contributor
216 Colophon / Image Credits

Sketch for book design of *Grün*,
Otl Aicher, undated

Foreword

The volume lying before you is an experiment. It is an attempt to write the book that Günther Grzimek himself wanted to write, but which, regrettably, he was not able to do. In the late 1980s, he and Otl Aicher had the idea to publish his works together in a monograph. Several letters in his archive, as well as some material collected in preparation for such a book, bear witness to this. All of these papers were found in a box that had been stored unopened for many years in the Günther Grzimek Archive of the Chair of Landscape Architecture and Public Space at the Technical University of Munich. Apparently he had already finished the book in his mind, and it "only" had to be written. A mock-up designed by Otl Aicher with a cover and blank white pages, at the intended scale, lay neatly bound in the archive box. Written on it, in large green letters, was the title—the German word for green:

Grün

Template for the book cover of *Grün*, Otl Aicher, undated

Planung
Gestaltung
Programme

Günther Grzimek

Inside the blank volume, loose sheets of A4 paper contained various proposals by Otl Aicher for the book's structure, a hand-drawn layout, and sketches of possible graphics, as well as two pages of placeholder text to define the font and character height: it was to be 9.5-point Rotis Semigrotesk, which has therefore been chosen for this book as well.

On a pile of white index-card-sized papers, Günther Grzimek had also noted down the structure of the book. It was not to be a mere biography, they both agreed, but above all an illustration of his thinking on various topics; in addition, it would include an account of Grzimek's life and work. What a wonderful idea. And what a pity that the two great designers were not able to bring this "beautiful book," as they called it, into reality.

Can one simply take over such a book and finish writing it? No, one cannot. But it is possible to imagine what the contents might have been, and take the ideas found in the articles and lectures by Grzimek as a basis to develop them further. The present volume is something of an imaginary coauthorship between the two designers, who are quoted in original texts and image spreads, and myself, having further developed and interpreted the available material. Grzimek's planned structure was adopted, though it proved extremely complex in the writing process, and it has required flashforwards and flashbacks, like in a play in which montage is deliberately used as a device to create the effect of alienation.

This makes the book a speculative experiment, and I am most grateful to the family members, especially Juliane Grzimek and Florian Aicher, who gave advice on the contents and supported me in this endeavor. Two papers also lay the groundwork for this project. In 1996, Andreas König began his in-depth thesis research by viewing Günther Grzimek's papers and analyzing and interpreting them; the fact that König was able to interview Grzimek himself is of particular interest. A master's thesis by Andrea Mühlmann followed in 2015, which examined and discussed the work in terms of its participatory aspects.

Join me in the experiment, and enjoy the book!

Regine Keller

Prologue

In the context of the world's increasing urbanization and the global climate crisis, the significance of green space in urban agglomerations is now widely understood and has become more relevant than ever. It is all the more surprising, then, that the benefits of open space in cities, particularly if it is green space, have not been given more attention. It is common knowledge that more green space contributes to better climatic and ecological living environments—not only for humans, but also for other species. However, enormous effort is required if landscape architects are to work on the ever-decreasing amount of open space in parallel to increasing urban density. This is no longer primarily about prestigious green spaces, but about effective ecological resources that are an essential part of making life worth living, especially in cities; less green space needs to deliver more. It is also about reclaiming or discovering open space resources that people were previously unaware of, be they former railway sites or spaces on and around buildings. These ideas are not new. They gave impetus to many groundbreaking landscape designs going back two hundred years, for instance by Frederick Law Olmsted in New York's Central Park, Peter Joseph Lenné at the Tiergarten in Berlin, and Friedrich Ludwig von Sckell in Munich-Schwabing.

In this context, a fresh look at the life of Günther Grzimek proves to be a source of myriad discoveries, as it allows us to throw light on the history of landscape architecture in Germany. Spanning a period of more than sixty years, from the 1930s in Berlin to the 1990s in Munich, Grzimek lived in a time when the term "landscape" was ideologically charged under National Socialism, in the era of German reconstruction, at the time when the concept of automotive cities took hold, during the technological emergence of the 1960s, and at the time of the ensuing environmental movement. In his work as the head of the parks department in Ulm, he was committed to reforms in the administration and the planning of green spaces at the municipal level. Similarly, in the context of the student riots at universities, he supported practice-led and academically reformed landscape education. He was deeply committed while teaching at the University of Fine Arts in Kassel and at the Technical University of Munich, but many of his proposals for reform were met by fierce resistance from the conservative management and from the university administrations in Kassel and Munich. His completed works are impressive and timeless. The Olympic Park in Munich is certainly his most noted project, and it remains influential to this day.

We shall rediscover this landscape architect, whose life journey and cooperation with renowned landscape architects, architects, town planners, and designers let us take a detailed look at the professional discourse and the architectural and town planning practices in German cities, as well as the history of modern Germany. The basis for this book is Günther Grzimek's archive, which was entrusted to my predecessor, Professor Christoph Valentien, by Grzimek himself at the beginning of 1995. Valentien had the archive sifted through, sorted, and had an index compiled. This provided a basis for academic work in this archive. This book is a compilation of his life, his career, and his collaborations, as well as his projects and reflections on the profession. It is complemented by photographs of selected projects both from the time of their inception and from the present. This book also contains original texts that express Günther Grzimek's views.

Günther Grzimek: A New Type of Green Urban Planner

The year 1968 was of special importance in Günther Grzimek's career: Günter Behnisch invited him to join the planning team for the Olympic Park in Munich, and Grzimek published a new "Mission Statement for Studies at the Chair of Landscape Culture at the University of Fine Arts in Kassel," where he had been professor since 1965. These two professional moments intersected with each other. Although in 1968 the University of Fine Arts in Kassel was still organized according to so-called "master classes," Grzimek's new curriculum had dispensed with the bourgeois idea of a creative genius who designs landscape based on personal intention and the power of observation. Grzimek wanted to train a "new type of green urban planner": a political person who went beyond formally and aesthetically effective solutions and strove to fulfill social needs and technical functions. The mission statement focused on analyses, processes, discussions, and cooperation between specialists, to develop a "planning idea" derived from the "knowledge of the functioning of different forms of urban nature." Knowledge should not be an end in itself but should be accumulated for the sake of its application in practice. The goal was to train green urban planners to take the role of a mediator between the individual disciplines—to become a "transversal-oriented" and "use-oriented" coordinator. The broad artistic and scientific training in the curriculum included philosophical, sociological, and psychological lectures, joint classes with the chairs of architecture, painting, and sculpture, spontaneous assignments, and participation in competitions and excursions. To help students solve specific planning tasks, they were trained in biology, ecology, engineering, materials science, plant use, photography, drawing, urban design, the history of landscape architecture, and landscape development.

The planning and design of the Olympic Park in Munich represents a constructed manifesto of Grzimek's landmark educational reform. To this day, German landscape architecture remains influenced by both the Olympic Park and the preceding educational reforms. Literally modeled out of the rubble of the Second World War, the Olympic Park was also intended as a platform for a new aesthetic and a liberating pedagogy in response to fascist trauma. Make it green!

The challenge was to plan equally for a mass audience during the Olympics and for meaningful post-Games use. It was to be not only a park for people, and especially for children, but also a sustainable home for flora and fauna. The specific interplay of terrain modeling, pathways, water surfaces, planting, and furnishings achieves just that: the main paths wind between hills that are eight to nine meters high, separating individual areas of use, and from which one can look down with pleasure on the various activities. The overview was intended to encourage people to stop, observe, participate, and freely develop their own use for the park once the Olympic Games were finished. At the same time, there were intimate spaces, shielded from prying eyes, situated in the hollows. The paths range from two to four meters wide, the planner fully aware that during the Olympics a multitude of people had to circulate along them. For this purpose, too, the grass in the flat areas was fixed on both sides to a width of forty meters. The water areas were suitable for boating and skating, the hills for unstructured play and sledding. Since its construction, the Olympic Park has been a vast, unenclosed children's play paradise with swings, seesaws, merry-go-rounds, and countless fruit trees and berry bushes scattered throughout the grounds. To this day, you can still pick fruit in the Olympic Park. The park also represented a liberation from Nazi pedagogy, which sought to eradicate any capacity for relationships and love in young children. The planning team hoped that the city of Munich would continue to use the park after the Olympics with sporting events, concerts, theater performances, and other programming. The futuristic-looking tents by Behnisch & Partners remain a spectacular visual highlight of the park, well-embedded in an expansive landscape that has been modeled exclusively with organic forms.

A sure indicator of good planning and design is whether a site has aged well, or even gets better with the years. As for the Olympic Park, Günther Grzimek's most outstanding work, this is clearly the case. Regine Keller's "beautiful book" is not so much a monument to this green urban planner, educational reformer, and designer as it is an open, living form that continues to evolve his vision. It is a milestone for the study of landscape architecture in the twentieth century because it contextualizes and historically situates Grzimek's works and approach, while offering a rich compendium of ideas that remain relevant today. Regine Keller is a master of precise observation, and her book underscores the importance of designing and building for use—by people, but also by plants and animals, with whom we form a community. At a time when the promotion of biodiversity is writ large and associated with images of arbitrary and rank growth, striking examples of good design are more important than ever.

Anette Freytag

About the person

Günther Grzimek, undated

Timeline

1915	Born in Cologne on November 3 to Dr. Günter Grzimek, attorney, and Emmy, née Jansen, daughter of a merchant
1921–25	Primary school in Königsberg (today Kaliningrad, Russia)
1925–34	Middle and high school in Berlin
1934–36	Apprenticeship as gardener, Bellevue Palace, Berlin
1937	High school diploma from evening school
1937–41	Studies garden design at Friedrich Wilhelm University in Berlin (today Humboldt University)
1941–45	Military service
1942	Marries Ingeborg Dittmann (together they have four children)
1945–47	Prisoner of war in France
1947	Returns to his family in Ravensburg, founds first studio
1947–1960	Head of the parks department in Ulm
1949	Head of the cemeteries office in Ulm
1947	Garden architecture studio in Ulm
1949–54	Lecturer at the community college in Ulm
1953–64	Member of the Board of Trustees of the Ulm School of Design
1960–65	Engineering Office Grzimek in Ulm and later Neu-Ulm, HfG
1965–72	Professor at the University of Fine Arts in Kassel, successor to Hermann Mattern
1969	Foundation of the Development Group for Landscape Culture, EGL
1968–72	Planning and execution of the Olympic Park, Munich
1970	Admitted to the German Academy for Urban and Regional Design
1972–80	Professor at the Technical University of Munich, successor to Ludwig Schreiber
1973	Awarded the Sckell Ring of Honor and admitted to the Bavarian Academy of Fine Arts in Munich
1973	Exhibition *Democratic Green Space* in Munich
1973	Founding of Grünplan GmbH in Freising
1974	Formation of EGL GmbH with Arnim Koch and Jan Michael Runge
1979	Marries Juliana Menzel after divorcing Ingeborg Grzimek
1980	Moves EGL to Landshut
1983	Exhibition *The Appropriation of the Lawn* in Munich
1987	Awarded the Fritz Schumacher Prize
1993	Retires from business
1996	Dies on May 8 in Pfeffenhausen

Biography

Line of people in front of the municipal potato distribution center in Cologne, 1915, photo: Fritz Geus

Rastenburg in East Prussia, postcard, undated

When Günther Grzimek first saw the light of the world on November 3, 1915, in Cologne, the city was in a state of emergency. It was full of soldiers, up to 400,000, who had been stationed in the strategically crucial city since the Rhineland province was taken over by Prussia. And they had to be fed. Responsibility for this was given to the young Konrad Adenauer; as Cologne's "first alderman," he took on such administrative responsibilities. In particular, he was in charge of ensuring the supply of food to Cologne's population, a great logistical challenge. Wheat was not to be found. In this second year of the war, many Cologne inhabitants experienced their first supply bottlenecks: people stood in line for potatoes, and there was no bread at all. But Adenauer, the future first chancellor of West Germany, seems to have been predestined for this task, since he came from a baker's family. He quickly developed a "war bread" out of bran, cornmeal, and rice flour, and in 1915 he took out a patent for his so-called "Cologne bread."

Whether the Grzimek family was familiar with this "war bread" is likely but not known. Everyone received only rationed bread, but privations were perhaps not as dire for the well-off middle-class Grzimek family. The father Günter, an attorney born in Wrocław (Breslau), had come to Cologne in 1910, right after gaining his doctoral degree, to serve his legal clerkship. At the tennis club he fell in love with Emmy Jansen, a merchant's daughter. A year later they became engaged and were wed in Bonn in November 1911. The family grew quickly: the first children were born in 1913 and 1914; the younger Günther Grzimek arrived in 1915 as the third of ultimately six children. Despite his family obligations, the father had to interrupt his legal career to serve in the First World War as a reserve lieutenant in France and ultimately at the front in Kutno in Poland. After being wounded, he was transferred behind the front to the region of Masuria in East Prussia, to the artillery in Rastenburg, today Kętrzyn in Poland, where he saw the end of the war. There he was able to open an attorney's office.[1] After the war, Grzimek senior joined the Freisinnige Partei (Liberal Union Party) and was politically active. The first elections were a success for the Socialist Party of Germany and the Freisinnige Partei. After the Kapp Putsch in 1920, he was promoted by the Prussian state government to senior civil servant, at the level of a government president, and made deputy to Ernst Siehr, the new executive president of the province of East Prussia, where the Grzimek family then settled. Only twenty years later, Hitler's headquarters, known as "Wolfsschanze," was built very nearby in the forest of Rastenburg.

The younger Günther Grzimek thus spent the first years of his life together with his five siblings in Rastenburg in former East Prussia, and a little later in what was then Königsberg (today Kaliningrad). After his father was elected to the Prussian parliament in 1924 as chairman of the German Democratic Party of East Prussia, he moved his family to Berlin, where he set up office as an attorney. Grzimek senior remained a member of the Prussian parliament until 1931. During all the years of his political, professional, and family development, he remained gripped by an intense passion for Mannerist paintings. He amassed a considerable collection, from which he made loans to museums and initiated several exhibitions.[2]

In 1925, Günther Grzimek junior attended the Mommsen and Falk high schools in Berlin. His school career was not very successful. In 1934 he left school and at the age of nineteen decided to complete an apprenticeship as a gardener with the state zoo administration in the Bellevue Palace park. The experience gained during his subsequent work assignments inspired him to study garden architecture. In order to be able to enter the university, he earned his high school diploma at an evening school in 1937. No sooner had he graduated than he was required to do six months of labor service. In the fall of the same year, he was able to begin his studies in garden design at the Friedrich Wilhelm University in Berlin. Here he studied under Heinrich Wiepking-Jürgensmann and experienced how landscape architecture was ideologically molded by National Socialism. From his collaborations with the so-called "landscape advocates" around Alwin Seifert, Wiepking-Jürgensmann is particularly known for the development of the German *Wehrlandschaft*, a landscape designed for military defense. Grzimek did not dare to publicly express his rejection of National Socialism in this environment, as he revealed in an interview with Andreas König in 1995. In 1939 he completed his preliminary exams and was summoned to the front. During the first years of the war, he managed to continue his studies up to the sixth semester while doing his military service. In 1940/41 he was granted examination leave by the military to complete his studies. During this time Grzimek started a family together with his first wife, Ingeborg Dittmann. The intensifying air raids made life in wartime Berlin ever more threatening, so that the family, including the grandparents, left Berlin and found accommodation near Ravensburg on Lake Constance. After war service in Holland, Italy, and Poland, Günther Grzimek was assigned to a research group for camouflage technology as a specialist in defense landscape at the end of 1944. In the course of this assignment, he managed to travel via Berlin to his family in Ravensburg, then under French occupation. His possible discovery moved him to turn himself in to the French commandant, in order to prevent reprisals for himself and his family. As a result, he was sent to southern France as a prisoner of war. There the interned German soldiers were allowed to run a so-called "camp university," in which he actively participated. His father, who had been exonerated politically, was able to practice law again after the war, but did not succeed in getting his son released immediately. Günther Grzimek junior had not joined the Nazi party, and he was released from internment in 1947 and returned to his family in Ravensburg.

Immediately after his return, he established a studio as a freelance garden architect. He completed his first small commissions in Weingarten near Ravensburg. An application for the position of head of the parks department in nearby Ulm was successful. Recommendations from the landscape architects Wilhelm Hübotter and Wiepking-Jürgensmann helped convince the new city planning director, Max Guther, during a visit to Ulm; at the end of 1947, he took up his new post, and he held the office for thirteen years. During this time, he began to restructure the department and established a cemeteries office. In addition to administrative responsibilities, he also introduced planning work in the office. Ulm was heavily damaged in the war and had enormous reconstruction needs. The "Green Planning for Ulm" made apparent Grzimek's expertise not only in landscape architecture but also in urban planning, which had a decades-long influence on the overall planning for the city.

During his time in Ulm, he also met the designer Otl Aicher. The two came to appreciate each other as lecturers at the newly founded community college in Ulm. Their friendship lasted until Aicher's death in 1991.

In addition to his own professional practice as a landscape architect and his work as head of the municipal garden office, Grzimek was also active as an educator. During his time in Ulm, he started teaching at the community college in 1949. Adult education had become a major concern for him. Especially after the war years, he—like Aicher—was aware that education alone could defend people from again becoming politically blind.

The first ideas for participatory procedures and citizen initiatives that promised involvement in the shaping of the city emerged at the community

left: Günter Grzimek senior, painting, undated

right: Günther Grzimek junior, undated

college. The idea for the promotion of new children's playgrounds in Ulm, the Aktion Sandfloh (Sand Flea Campaign), was developed in cooperation with the community college groups "Art and Design" and "Architecture," in collaboration with Aicher and the architect Hans Frieder Eychmüller. In 1953 the Ulm School of Design was founded, initiated by Aicher and Inge Scholl, drawing from the circle of lecturers at the college and others. Grzimek's connection to both founders enabled him to make the acquaintance of formative designers and architects of the time, such as Max Bill and Walter Gropius.

In addition to his work in the garden office, Grzimek was permitted to accept and realize his own planning commissions as a garden architect. Beginning in 1955, he created house gardens and, above all, plans for cemeteries, such as those in Weingarten, Blaubeuren, Crailsheim, Mengen, and Dürmentingen. During this time, he began a long-term collaboration with Lore Kellinghaus, who worked with him in his studio for many years. After unending quarrels in the municipal office—several councilors disagreed with his administration of the parks department and accused him of mismanagement—Grzimek decided to leave civil service in 1960. He founded the Ingenieurbüro für Grünplanung (Engineering Office for Green Planning) in Ulm. His urban planning skills led him naturally to the new urban land use planning that came into force in 1960 with the new Federal Building Code. In addition, he worked on planning for the cities of Weingarten, Biberach, and Ulm.

Also in Ulm he initiated a long and successful collaboration with the architect Günter Behnisch. Initially, they worked together on the Ulm School of Engineering (1961–63) and later also the School of Engineering in Aalen (1965–68). This was followed by major consulting commissions at the level of urban green planning for entire cities, for example Darmstadt, Biberach an der Riss, Aschaffenburg, and Ludwigsburg.

At the same time, Grzimek remained continuously interested in the academic study of the field of landscape architecture, and he hoped to be able to disseminate his findings at a university. Through numerous lectures at various universities, he remained in touch with the academic world, for example with Gerd Albers at the Technical University of Munich, where as early as 1962 he lectured on topics related to green planning. When Hermann Mattern's professorship at the University of Fine Arts in Kassel became vacant in 1961, Grzimek succeeded him in 1965 as associate professor for the chair of Landscape Culture. From the very beginning of his activity as a university lecturer, he was committed to reforming academic education. This included the integration of other fields of study such as architecture and urban planning, a concept that led to the idea of "environmental design."

In Kassel, he became involved in the city's cultural activities, and he participated with Arnold Bode in the committee that organized the documenta art exhibition. He established a new engineering office for green planning in Kassel, which he ran until 1972. Together with students at the University of Fine Arts in Kassel, he founded in 1969 the Development Group for Landscape Culture (EGL in its German abbreviation) as a registered association.

He likewise advocated an interdisciplinary planning approach in his office. On the recommendation of Max Guther, he was awarded the planning contract for the new Botanical Garden in Marburg in 1965, a remarkable project covering twenty-two hectares, with which he was involved until 1970. In parallel, he worked on the development of the Zoological Garden for Münster (1968–71). In 1968, Günter Behnisch summoned him to join the planning team for the Olympic Park in Munich; and from May 1968 until the end of 1972, together with the architects and engineers of the Olympic Park team, he led an office in designing and executing the planning for that project.

In 1972 Günther Grzimek assumed a professorship at the Technical University of Munich. In 1973 he founded the engineering office Grünplan in Freising as a limited liability company.

Grzimek disseminated his broad experiences through numerous lectures and publications, but also in two influential exhibitions: *Democratic Green Space* in 1973 at the Bavarian Academy of Arts, and *The Appropriation of the Lawn* in 1983. The latter show was documented with a catalog of the same name. Less well known are his studies from the 1970s, such as the consulting report for the airport Munich II.

In his work as professor at the Technical University of Munich, he was repeatedly and tirelessly committed to the study of reforms. In 1979 he underwent a further professional and private transformation. The EGL, now renamed Development and Design of Landscape, moved with his office to Landshut. In the same year he married Juliana Menzel.

He continued to teach at the Technical University of Munich until 1981. After his retirement, he remained active in the EGL office as well as in competitions and juries until 1993. In 1996, after a serious illness, Günther Grzimek died at the age of eighty in Holzhausen near Pfeffenhausen, in the Landshut district.

1   Klaus von der Groeben, *Verwaltung und Politik 1918–1933 am Beispiel Ostpreußens*, 2nd ed. (Kiel: Lorenz-von-Stein-Institut 1988), 391.
2   Günther Grzimek, *Manieristensammlung der Familie Grzimek. Vom Aufgang der Neuzeit* (Ravensburg: Drexler, 1966).

Stations

Friedrich Wilhelm University, 1938, photo: Otto Hagemann

Berlin

Günther Grzimek quit high school. He no longer enjoyed school, as his father later noted in his memoirs. He wanted to become a gardener, and in 1934, instead of returning to high school, he began an apprenticeship in the nursery of Bellevue Palace in Berlin. It meant getting up early in the morning, but he did not mind, because now he knew what interested him. During his subsequent period as a journeyman, his desire to study garden architecture grew. In his book *Grzimeks Menschenleben. Erinnerungen eines Urahns* (Grzimek's Human Life: Memories of a Forefather), Grzimek's father reflects on his son's decision:

> My eldest son becomes a gardener:
> In Easter 1934, my eldest son Günther, then eighteen years old, came to my office. He had just passed the eighth year at the high school by the skin of his teeth.... Günther told me frankly that he had no pleasure in earning a diploma and intended to learn a trade as quickly as possible.... He wanted to become a gardener.... He became an apprentice in the Berlin Tiergarten, had to get up at 5 a.m., the work was hard. I never heard a complaint from him. After a few months he told me that the other gardeners thought he was stupid if he didn't get his diploma. Because then he could become a garden architect or a horticultural director.[1]

This argument convinced Günther, and now he began to attend evening school. In 1937, he received his diploma and was able to begin his university studies. A year earlier, his father had informed himself about the possibilities of studying garden design during a conversation with Professor Heinrich Wiepking-Jürgensmann at the Friedrich Wilhelm University (today Humboldt University) in Berlin. Wiepking-Jürgensmann probably made clear to him that he saw a growing political importance in the profession of garden designer. He showed interest in having a large number of graduates, so that it would be easy to obtain a place at university.[2]

How can one imagine Berlin in the 1930s? The entire family, which had lived in Berlin since 1924, experienced firsthand how life in the city visibly changed after Hitler's rise to power in 1933. Berlin, as the capital of the Reich, became the stage for Hitler's monumental building plans. From 1933 onwards, countless administrative and representative buildings were erected at breakneck speed, visibly reinforcing the Nazis' display of power. The city's appearance was rapidly transformed. Not only was the brisk construction activity omnipresent, but so were symbols of the regime; the permanent display of flags at all places made the new political situation visible to inhabitants and visitors. In 1936, the last year of Grzimek's apprenticeship, the whole city had become a symbol of National Socialism, particularly during the Olympic Games. The Olympic Stadium was built on the area known as the *Reichssportfeld* (Reich athletic grounds) by the architect Werner March. Hitler had ordered the new construction of a large stadium, and its appearance alluded to ancient colossal buildings. The building was covered with natural stone from Franconia and Württemberg. The landscape gardener Wiepking-Jürgensmann, Grzimek's future professor at the university, was responsible for the Olympic Village in Berlin-Elstal and the park landscape, along with the architects Werner and Walter March.[3]

The monumental stone architecture of the sports buildings, especially the stadium, and the accompanying autochthonous landscape, whose plantings consist of native woody plants, were intended to emphasize National Socialist ideas. These principles stem not only from a glorification of archaic and ancient buildings, but also of an agrarian ideology. The idealization of rural landscapes and a "natural" way of life led the National Socialists to idealize the landscape and nature, resulting in their legal protection.

As early as 1933, nature conservation associations were forced into line politically, and Jewish members were excluded from them. Until 1935, far-reaching new legal regulations followed in the area of nature and environmental protection. The new Reich Nature Conservation Act introduced, in addition to the category of nature conservation area, that of the less protected landscape conservation area. For the first time, compensation for private building-interventions was regulated, but major state projects such as traffic or military projects were exempted. In 1936, nature conservation and landscape management were subordinated to the Reich Forestry Office thus to Reich Minister of the Interior Hermann Göring as the "Supreme Commissioner for Nature Conservation."

On January 30, 1937, Albert Speer was appointed General Building Inspector of the Reich Capital Berlin. On November 4, 1937, Speer, as the National Socialist Party's Commissioner for Urban Planning, issued the "First Order on the Redesign of the Reich Capital Berlin," at the same time as the Reich Law on the Redesign of German Cities. This marked the beginning of the idea to transform Berlin into the metropolis of "Germania" by 1950.

It was also in 1937 that the Italian dictator Benito Mussolini visited the city. Berlin once again served as the theatrically designed backdrop for a tremendous demonstration of power. Photographs depict the

top: View from the Brandenburg Gate to Unter den Linden, decorated for Mussolini's visit to Berlin, 1937, photo: Harry Croner

bottom: *An Enemy of the People*, film with Heinrich George, 1937

cityscape of Berlin as dominated by Nazi symbols. On November 15, 1937, the film *Ein Volksfeind* (*An Enemy of the People*) starring Heinrich George premiered at Berlin's Capitol Kino. In that same month Günther Grzimek, only twenty-two years old, began his studies at the Friedrich Wilhelm University. He enrolled at the Institute for Garden and Landscape Design, part of the Faculty of Agriculture, directed by Professor Wiepking-Jürgensmann. Eight semesters lay ahead of him. However, due to military politics and the war, the course of studies was accelerated.

Sixty-seven students were enrolled with Grzimek in the program, a significant increase over the years before.[4] The mood at the university was National Socialist and clearly anti-Semitic, as manifested in a statement by the university's rector, Wilhelm Krüger. He wrote in 1937:

> A student who does not consider it necessary to join the ranks of Adolf Hitler's political soldiers shall not be worthy to study at the University of Berlin in the future.[5]

Accordingly, since 1933, massive action was taken against political opponents and Jewish students. To study garden design during the Nazi era at the Friedrich Wilhelm University in Berlin meant also to serve the national idea, by designing gardens and landscapes for the ideological underpinning of the regime. The university's professors submitted to the demands of National Socialism in their research and teaching; if they did not, they were removed from their posts.

How can the growing interest in the academic training of garden architects during National Socialism be explained? The number of enrolled students doubled in a short period of time in the 1930s. The reasons for this development become evident when one looks more closely at the research tasks and political motivations of some of the people involved: Heinrich Wiepking-Jürgensmann was appointed professor in Berlin in 1934, succeeding the garden director and professor Erwin Barth (1880–1933). Barth became the first full professor and director of the Institute for Garden Design in 1929, established as the first scientific educational institution for garden designers at the Agricultural College in Berlin-Dahlem. Barth was a progressive and successful garden designer and, in addition to his professorship, the horticultural director at the Schloss Charlottenburg. Many designs of parks and squares in Berlin, such as the the Volkspark Jungfernheide, Volkspark Rehberge, or Savigny-Platz, were conceived by Barth. In 1933 he took his own life—on account of health problems, but also, it is assumed, in response to the seizure of power by the National Socialists.

His successor at the university, Heinrich Wiepking-Jürgensmann, is today considered by some scholars to be one of the most influential representatives of garden designers under National Socialism, along with the *Reichslandschaftsanwalt* (Landscape Advocate for the German Reich) Alwin Seifert. His mission, according to his own statements, was to equal the great role models in the history of garden design. Like Peter Joseph Lenné, he believed he could create works in the "countenance of the best German spirit." He received his professional training in Bornstedt and in Barnim (Brandenburg). His experience with landscape design is based on the tools of the characteristic North German *Knick*: these are hedge-path landscapes, which he was to further evolve in the following years as strategic landscape elements. The conception of landscape designs that seemingly do not reveal their designer and can "achieve the impression of a mature harmonious landscape" dominated his design approach. When the National Socialists seized power, Wiepking-Jürgensmann envisaged a great future for his activity as garden architect, which strove "no longer to be mere decoration, but a target-defining and trend-setting pursuit."[6]

An important mentor for Wiepking-Jürgensmann was Konrad Meyer, who seems to have been instrumental in his appointment.[7] It is clear from the personal links between Meyer and Wiepking-Jürgensmann that all activities in the scientific-academic field were

Franz Würbel, poster for the Olympic
Games in Berlin, 1936

to be subordinated to the goals of Nazi policy. The teaching and training of students were to support this task. As early as 1940, Wiepking-Jürgensmann was appointed special commissioner for landscape design and maintenance at the "Reich Commission for the Consolidation of the German People," or RKF in its German abbreviation. Together with Meyer, he was to develop a set of rules for the landscaping of the incorporated eastern territories that was "appropriate for the [German] race."[8]

In June 1941, a few days after the invasion of the Soviet Union, Konrad Meyer and his Institute for Agrarian Affairs and Agricultural Policy were commissioned by Heinrich Himmler to draw up a larger general plan in which the settlement program for the eastern territories, referred to in Nazi jargon as "Germanization," was to be specified. Later known as the "General Plan East," the proposal called for the colonization of "neglected" areas in the east.

In 1941 Meyer wrote an article titled "Settlement and Reconstruction Work in the German East" for the Munich student newspaper *Die Bewegung*:

The unique task that has arisen for the German people in our days, above all in the east, extends profoundly into all areas of our lives, and is therefore impossible without the precondition of a total mobilization of all popular and moral, social and economic forces of the entire nation.... In addition, the shaping of the landscape, the forming of this comparatively barren and monotonous area into a German homeland—with forests and gardens, rows of trees and hedges— will have to begin on the first day of peace.[9]

In 1942, Wiepking-Jürgensmann intensified both the tone and the harsh National Socialist racist sentiment when he wrote,

The landscape is always a figure, an expression, and a mark of the people living in it. It can reflect the noble countenance of its spirit and soul, as well as the grimace of unspirituality, of human and spiritual depravity.... It shows us in inexorable severity whether a people is constructive and part of the divine creative power, or whether the people must be numbered among the destructive forces. Thus the landscapes of Germans differ in all their essence from those of the Poles and Russians—like the peoples themselves. The murders and atrocities of the Eastern peoples are carved razor-sharp into the faces of their traditional landscapes. The more neglected and squalid, the emptier a landscape is, the greater is the frequency of crime[10]

Heinrich Wiepking-Jürgensmann

Heinrich Wiepking-Jürgensmann (1891–1973) studied architecture at the Technical College in Hanover but did not complete the degree course. Beginning in 1922 he worked as a "freelance architect for garden and urban planning" in Berlin and Cologne. In 1934 he succeeded Erwin Barth at the Institute for Garden and Landscape Design at the Friedrich Wilhelm University in Berlin. From 1945 to 1958 he was a full professor for Landscape Planning, Garden Design, and Landscape Architecture in Hanover. More on Wiepking-Jürgensmann's biography, see p. 198.

Konrad Meyer

Konrad Meyer (1901–1973) studied agriculture in Göttingen. He joined the NSDAP (National Socialist German Workers' Party) in 1932. After a lectureship in Göttingen, he was appointed to the Chair for Farming and Planting at the University of Jena in the spring of 1934. In the fall of that year, he received a full professorship in Farming and Agricultural Policy at the Agricultural Department of the Friedrich Wilhelm University in Berlin. No search procedure was conducted for the post. At the same time, he was director of an institute under the identical name founded in the Dahlem district of Berlin; in 1941 he renamed it the Institute for Agricultural Studies and Policy. In order to create this position, the head of the Institute for Apiology, Ludwig Armbruster, was forced into early retirement; he was considered an enemy of the regime and *Judenfreund* (Jew-friend). From this position Meyer was able to wield political influence. In 1935–36 he founded the Research Service of the Reich Working Group for Spatial Research and in 1939 he became head of the planning department of the Reich Commission for the Consolidation of the German People, or RKF in its German abbreviation, as well as the Dahlem SS Planning Office.

In 1942, Wiepking-Jürgensmann was assigned responsibility for the subject area "Landscape Conservation Group II—General Provisions, Landscape Protection, and Landscape Design in the New Settlement Areas" in the restructured Supreme Nature Conservation Authority. In agreement with Heinrich Himmler and the "RKF," this department was located respectively in the "Reich Governors" or "General Advisors for Landscape Conservation."

In December 1942, Reich Leader-SS Himmler issued "General Order No. 20/VI/42 ... on the Design of the Landscape in the Incorporated Eastern Territories" in connection with the "General Plan East." Together with landscape planner Erhard Mäding, Wiepking-Jürgensmann formulated its principles:

The Landscape Rules of the Reich Leader-SS are a decisive landmark of German agriculture and German landscape culture. For the first time in the long history of German landscape management, comprehensive guidelines have been issued for the entire field of landscape management and design, guidelines that issue from the overall space and keep its function and shape in mind.[1]

And in a following paragraph:

The landscape in the incorporated eastern territories is in large areas neglected, desolate, and devastated by overexploitation, due to the cultural incapacity of foreign people.... For the Teutonic-German person, however, contact with nature is a deep need of life.... If the new living areas are to become a home to the settlers, then the planned design of the landscape, though close to nature, is a decisive prerequisite. It is one of the foundations for the consolidation of German national identity. It is therefore not enough to settle our people in these areas and to eliminate foreign people. Rather, the spaces must be given a character corresponding to our nature, so that the Teutonic-German person feels at home.[12]

left: Burning of books at the Opernplatz in Berlin, 1933

right: On order of the police, students carry confiscated walking sticks into the university, 1931, photo: Georg Pahl

Diploma of Günther Grzimek, 1941

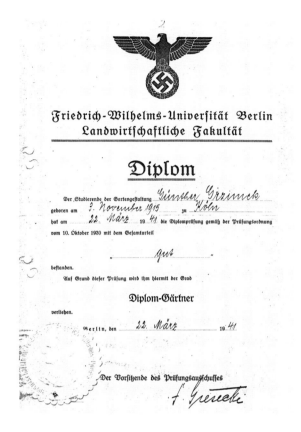

As a student of garden design, Grzimek had to deal with the landscape principles formulated by Wiepking-Jürgensmann. These included the use of native plants in addition to the so-called "German *Wehrlandschaft*"—that is, a landscape designed for military defense. In his *Landscape Primer* of 1942, Wiepking-Jürgensmann describes how landscapes consisting of woods and hedgerows offered "the last means of defense and protection of entire peoples from annihilation." The defense landscape consists of "covered deployment areas and connecting paths." Woodland-like roadside and covering plantings should serve to "protect all wartime transportation facilities, industrial and residential areas." These and other guidelines were to govern landscape design.

The camouflage of the landscape became Wiepking-Jürgensmann's idée fixe, which he pursued during the war as the research topic of a so-called "camouflage group." With the outbreak of war, studying became increasingly difficult. In 1939, Günther Grzimek had just received his intermediate diploma. His semesters were repeatedly interrupted by deployments to the front. Nevertheless, the university continued to function, and Grzimek junior served on the front. In 1941, he managed to complete his studies while on short furloughs.

Berlin was being bombed, and life there was no longer safe for him and his family. The elder Grzimek tried to get the family out of the city around 1941. He recounts in his memoirs:

How could we escape this hell? We, who had long been disliked by the Nazis, would only be allowed to leave for a quieter region if we could present absolutely valid reasons. So from Riedlingen, where a friend of my wife's lived, we looked for a lawyer in the area around Lake Constance, which had been spared from the war, who had been called up for military service and needed a replacement. In April 1944, two Ravensburg lawyers, who were serving as reserve officers in the army and navy, were overjoyed to find a replacement.[13]

Günther Grzimek junior served at the front in Holland, Italy, and Poland. From 1944, he was assigned to a research unit for camouflage affairs. He would never return to Berlin permanently after the war.

1 Günter Grzimek, *Menschenleben. Erinnerungen eines Urahns* (Dorheim: Podzun-Verlag, 1970), 129.
2 Statements by Günther Grzimek (the younger) in later interviews. PQGG Geheft Arbeitsdienst / Militär Politik. Interview on December 30, 1936.
3 Emanuel Hübner, "Olympisches Dorf 1936," *Historisches Lexikon Brandenburgs* (published May 8, 2018), https://www.brandenburgikon.net/index.php/de/sachlexikon/olympisches-dorf.
4 Humboldt University, *Chronik der Friedrich-Wilhelms-Universität zu Berlin* (1937–38), retrieved from https://www.digi-hub.de/viewer/image/1603980265057/1/LOG_0003/.
5 Jörg Pache, "Uni im NS. Die Entfernung unerwünschter Studierender" (2013), https://www.hu-berlin.de/de/ueberblick/geschichte/juedische-studierende/uni-im-ns/entfernung, retrieved from https://www.hu-berlin.de/de/ueberblick/geschichte/juedische-studierende/uni-im-ns/entfernung.
6 Staatsarchiv Osnabrück 2022, Dep. 72B, no. 116 (July 30, 1933).
7 Gert Gröning and Joachim Wolschke-Bulmahn, *Liebe zur Landschaft. Arbeiten zur sozialwissenschaftlich orientierten Freiraumplanung, Teil 3: Der Drang zur Landschaft. Zur Entwicklung der Landespflege im Nationalsozialismus und während des Zweiten Weltkrieges in den "eingegliederten Ostgebieten"* (Münster: Lit-Verlag, 1987) 43.
8 Ursula Kellner, "Landschaftsbilder. Einfluss auf die Gestaltungen von Landschaft bei Heinrich Wiepking (1891–1973)," lecture (Hanover), 6.
9 Konrad Meyer, "Siedlungs- und Aufbauarbeit im deutschen Osten," *Die Bewegung* 8 (1941): 71 (https://www.agrar.hu-berlin.de/de/institut/profil/geschichte/profil/geschichte/leseprobe).
10 Heinrich Wiepking-Jürgensmann, *Die Landschaftsfibel* (Berlin: Deutsche Landbuchhandlung, 1942), 13.
11 Erhard Mäding, *Regeln für die Gestaltung der Landschaft. Einführung in die Allgemeine Anordnung Nr. 20/VI/42 des Reichsführers SS ...* (Berlin: Verlag Deutsche Landbuchhandlung, 1943), 16.
12 Mäding, *Regeln für die Gestaltung*, 51.
13 Grzimek, *Menschenleben*, 155.

Ulm in ruins after the war, 1945

Ulm

During the war, the Grzimek family—or more precisely the Grzimek parents with their three daughters, their daughter-in-law Ingeborg, and five grandchildren—managed to find refuge for four years in the village of Grünkraut near Ravensburg. In 1945, toward the end of the war, the village was occupied by French troops. The younger Günther Grzimek arrived in Grünkraut shortly before and hid in the family's home. But since he still had his lieutenant's uniform with him, the entire family was in danger of reprisal from the occupying forces. He therefore turned himself in at the local commandant's office and was sent to France as a prisoner of war, where he remained until 1947. It was not until February of that year that Grzimek was able to return to his family in Ravensburg.

After the war it was difficult for him to regain a foothold as a garden architect. Grzimek's applications for employment were turned down, whereupon he decided to open his own studio in Ravensburg as a "landscaper and garden architect." His personal archives contain only a few of his work documents from that period; these include plans for a staircase at the Weingarten monastery and a design for an entrance to a nursery. He had put himself forward for the Weingarten monastery, and this seems to have helped him get the commission for the staircase.

On June 23, 1947, Grzimek received a written invitation from Max Guther, the city planning director of Ulm. Guther had just accepted the position and was searching for competent colleagues for his department. They were to aid him in the reconstruction of the city, which had been severely destroyed during the war. His friend, the landscape architect Wilhelm Hübotter, provided Guther with Grzimek's address, and suggested contacting him about a position in garden administration.

After being invited to apply, Grzimek traveled to Ulm for a three-day stay, where he held intensive talks with Guther. The journey required him to make a hazardous journey through different occupation zones, since Grzimek lived in the French zone while Ulm was occupied by the Americans. After the meeting, Grzimek drafted a written statement for Ulm entitled "Thoughts on the Existing Options, and Those to Be Explored, for a Comprehensive Design of the Green Areas of the City of Ulm." In it, he outlines the issues facing the future management of the parks department—but, most importantly, the challenges and importance of open green spaces in the reconstruction of the city. Since his student transcripts had been lost during the war, he asked Heinrich Wiepking for a brief recommendation to confirm his academic training. Wiepking complied with this request, and Grzimek was able to win out over the other applicants. He took over the management of the parks department, and Guther found in Grzimek a like-minded partner who perceived the tasks at hand not only as administrative duties, but also as a challenge for the planning and designing of urban and green spaces. Grzimek's academic background was crucial here.

However, major undertakings lay ahead of him. Eighty-five percent of Ulm had been destroyed—the Royal Air Force raid on December 17, 1944, had left the city in ruins—and his first job as head of the office was to clear the rubble and make the open spaces usable again. Following Germany's surrender, the architect Hans Frieder Eychmüller became provisional director of the city administration. In June 1945, the American occupation forces installed Robert Scholl—a financial auditor from Ulm and father of resistance activists Sophie and Hans Scholl—as mayor. His liberal stance had caused him problems during the National Socialist era: after publicly calling Hitler the "scourge of God" in 1942, he spent four months in prison. The 1943 conviction and execution of Sophie and Hans, who had founded the White Rose resistance group in Munich, also brought further difficulties to the family. Scholl and his daughter Inge were imprisoned several times, but managed to survive the war.

Robert Scholl did not have an easy time as mayor of Ulm. The citizens felt that the clearing of the city progressed too slowly. In 1947, Max Guther became the city building councilor in Ulm. As a modernizer, he had a clear position on the subject of redevelopment. His stance was naturally polarizing, because Ulm's reconstruction was characterized by conflicting concepts and, above all, by controversial discussions among the inhabitants. These were embodied in particular by two civic associations in the city: Alt-Ulm (Old Ulm) and the Gesellschaft 1950 (1950 Society). Grzimek joined the Alt-Ulm association in 1947, probably at Guther's bidding. However, the increasing number of arguments about reconstruction between the municipal planning offices and the association, as well as a campaign against Guther, drove Grzimek to leave it in 1950. The Gesellschaft 1950 was formed to oppose the conservative faction; its members included Guther, Otl Aicher, and Inge Scholl. The coming years were marked by numerous debates between the associations: these primarily revolved around the preservation or rebuilding of old buildings versus new construction. The debates between the

Max Guther

Max Guther (1909–1991) studied under Paul Bonatz, Paul Schmitthenner, and Heinz Wetzel at the Technical University in Stuttgart. Beginning in 1931 he was employed as an architect in Stuttgart and Colmar im Elsass, and as an architect and urban planner in Hamburg and Schwerin from 1934 to 1940. Guther served in the navy from 1940 to 1945; afterwards he worked for Konstanty Gutschow in Wismar.

In 1947, Robert Scholl—the mayor of Ulm and father of resistance activists Hans and Sophie Scholl—invited Max Guther to be head of urban planning in the reconstruction of the city, which had been destroyed in the war. At the end of the same year, Guther brought Günther Grzimek to Ulm.

After his time in Ulm, Guther was appointed professor for urban planning and housing in Darmstadt in 1954. From 1969 to 1970 he was chancellor of the Technical University of Darmstadt.

He brought Ernst May as a visiting lecturer to Darmstadt, as well as Thomas Sieverts as professor for the new chair of Urban Planning II.

At the end of the 1950s, he worked for the professional organization of urban planning and founded the Federation of German Urban Planners together with fifty colleagues; that grew into the Association of City, Regional and State Planners, which Guther headed in its initial phase. In 1973 he gave the honorary speech for Günther Grzimek when the latter was awarded the Sckell Ring from the Bavarian Academy of Fine Arts. After retiring in 1974, Guther continued to work on urban planning from his own Office for Urban Development and Planning for many years.

Otl Aicher, poster for the community college on the Ulm recreational landscape, a course held by Günther Grzimek, Ulm, 1953

characteristic Gothic pointed gables versus modern eaves grew into a major source of conflict between the opposing sides. Andreas Gnahm has dealt with this subject excellently in his book *Giebel oder Traufe* (Gable or Eaves).[1]

The consequences of an automobile-oriented urban redevelopment, as was exemplified in the Neue Strasse, which crosses the historic urban structure diagonally as a new main avenue, were also a point of contention, characteristic of the numerous controversies in urban planning during the postwar period.[2] Grzimek no longer participated in this debate in the associations, but primarily through letters to the editor in the local newspaper (*Schwäbische Donauzeitung*).

During his first year—in his probationary period—Grzimek received a visit from the landscape architect Alwin Seifert, a meeting arranged by Guther. Seifert was to support him in the redevelopment of Ulm with a consultant's report on open-space planning. This fact clearly demonstrates that after 1945 numerous leading figures from the Nazi era were still active in many fields. Seifert's short, rather superficial report proposes only a few, general recommendations for action in the reconstruction of Ulm.

A year before Grzimek took office, in 1946, an adult education center and community college was founded in Ulm. Inge Scholl headed the management of the school, which had the clear-cut political mission of "re-education"—that is, of democratically consolidating Germany and returning it to the "cultural community of civilized nations." Here Grzimek was given the opportunity of participating in the first lectures and courses as an instructor. Working groups on art and design were formed under the direction of Otl Aicher, on architecture under Hans Frieder Eychmüller, and on garden and landscape under Günther Grzimek. In 1952, these working groups led to the founding of an association for the promotion of playgrounds, the Aktion Sandfloh (Sand Flea Campaign), an initiative that supported the construction of children's playgrounds and the development of good playground equipment in the heavily damaged city, together with the participation of parents and committed citizens. For many years, the association was chaired by Ursula Pfizer, wife of the mayor Theodor Pfizer, elected in 1948. The Sand Flea logo designed by Otl Aicher functioned as a trademark and as a kind of mascot (see p. 66).

After 1948, conditions in the office had evolved to such an extent that Grzimek was able to undertake larger planning projects. In the meantime, he was also

Günther Grzimek at the "Progress and Reconstruction" fair in Ulm, 1950, photo: HfG–Archiv

Alwin Seifert

Alwin Seifert (1890–1972) was an architect, a lecturer at the Technical College of Munich, and a member of the Todt Organization (Nazi engineering organization) from 1938 on. In 1940 Hitler appointed him Reich Landscape Advocate. After the war he returned to teaching at the Technical College—now University—of Munich. More on Seifert's biography, see p. 198.

Gerd Albers

Gerd Albers (1919–2015), was born in Hamburg and originally wanted to be a stage designer. He served as a lieutenant commander in the Second World War. After 1950 he studied architecture in Hanover and in Chicago under Mies van der Rohe and Ludwig Hilberseimer, returning to Hanover to earn his PhD. From 1952 to 1954, he worked at the city planning office in Ulm; in 1954 he was head of urban planning in Trier, and in 1959 of Darmstadt. In 1963 he joined the Technical University of Munich, where he was professor until 1987 and was rector of the university from 1965 to 1968. He served as president of the German Academy for Urban Development and State Planning until 1974 and as president of the Academy of Fine Arts in Munich from 1974 to 1983. He detailed his views on urban planning in numerous publications.

put in charge of the cemetery office. His redesign of the old cemetery in the center of Ulm into an "inner park" is an early example of his ideas for open spaces. Here, the green space of the cemetery was not only designated as a place of remembrance in urban-historical terms, but also acquired a new significance as a structural element and recreational space in the city. This type of urban-structural thinking also guided him in future urban developments, such as in Ulm-Eselsberg, where housing had to be erected for the many new residents of the city. The new district was laid out according to a joint design with the urban planner Gerd Albers, who worked in Ulm's office of urban planning beginning in 1952, under the head of the planning office, Ludwig Zimmermann.

The idea of the settlement followed that of the "urban cell" with 16,000 inhabitants as conceived by the urban planners Göderitz, Rainer, and Hoffmann.[3] The principles of an "articulated and dispersed city," as described by the authors in their publication, here guide an urban planning model providing generous green areas between the building zones. They form a network of green spaces that connects the development with the surrounding landscape. Grzimek's experience in Ulm-Eselsberg provided further impetus for a city-wide planning approach. Ulm's rapid growth was to be accompanied and controlled by the deliberate preservation of green zones.

The Ulm School of Design was founded in 1953. Alongside the community college, it was to become a place for modern training in the various fields of design. Grzimek was a member of the advisory board from the start and contributed to the exterior design of the building, positioned in a developable hillside (see "Otl Aicher and Inge Aicher-Scholl," p. 54).

In 1954, Grzimek submitted a comprehensive study to the city administration, the publication *Green Planning in Ulm: Problems of a Growing City*, which deals with the overall urban development on a large and small scale. The publication was the result of three years of work that Grzimek did together with Heinz Ellenberg, a phytosociologist (specialist in vegetative environments). The pamphlet was designed by Otl Aicher.

The city of Ulm was growing quickly, which meant rising costs for maintaining its open areas. This also applied to the green spaces, whose upkeep increasingly required more funds. It fell to Grzimek, in his position as director of the parks department, to justify these costs. The growing financial and personnel costs were met with incomprehension by the city council, and Grzimek found himself exposed to

mounting criticism. In 1956, the projects of the social housing developers were transferred to the parks department, which exacerbated the financial situation of the local government. This prompted Grzimek to work more intensively to address the issue of the cost-effective management of green spaces. In later years this led him to the concept of "functional performance green space," with which he was certainly the first landscape architect to systematically research and present the cost–benefit ratio of open spaces. In 1956–57, he also created memorials for the victims of the Second World War, of which the memorial complex in Ulm's New Cemetery stands out especially (see p. 87).

The hostilities within the city administration did not let up. In 1958, he again had to respond to criticisms by city councilors, which prompted him to demand a report from an external consultant. The result of this report was clear and in his favor—but by then the atmosphere had been poisoned, and in 1960 Grzimek resigned from the post. From then on, he devoted more time to his private planning studio, which he ran as an engineering firm with Lore Kellinghaus, located first in Ulm and then in Neu-Ulm. Numerous construction projects were undertaken, especially cemeteries in communities such as Weingarten and Biberach. In addition to designing buildings, he increasingly engaged in urban land use planning, which had been a focus of his studio since the early 1960s. The green planning for Darmstadt (1964) was the next major milestone (see p. 103).

In 1965, an academic appointment finally materialized. The University of Fine Arts in Kassel appointed him as the successor to the landscape architect Hermann Mattern. Now Grzimek's long-cherished wish that his ideas and activities as a landscape architect should be transmitted in an academic context was finally fulfilled. He had long been involved in teaching, giving numerous guest lectures at universities, and had already attempted to gain a foothold at the Technical University of Munich in Weihenstephan in the mid-1950s. In 1960, he hoped to succeed Gustav Allinger at the Technical University of Berlin. But in neither of those cases had he been offered the position.

Grzimek and Mattern knew each other from their time together in Berlin. In Kassel, Mattern succeeded in convincing the university to consider his colleague as the only candidate. Grzimek left Ulm and began a new chapter of his life in Kassel.

1 Andreas Gnahm, *Giebel oder Traufe, Die Wiederaufbaukontroverse in Ulm nach dem Zweiten Weltkrieg*, Kleine Reihe des Stadtarchivs Ulm, vol. 5 (Ulm: Haus der Stadtgeschichte – Stadtarchiv Ulm, 2008).
2 Thomas Vogel, *Dem "Grab allen Anstandes" entstiegen. Ulm-Entwürfe im ersten Nachkriegsjahrzehnt* (Ulm: Archiv der HfG, 1995), 66.
3 Johannes Göderitz, Roland Rainer, and Hubert Hoffmann, *Die gegliederte und aufgelockerte Stadt* (Tübingen: Wasmuth, 1957).

New Cemetery in Ulm, 2021,
photo: The Pk. Odessa Co / Markus Lanz

University of Fine Arts in Kassel, north building, architect: Paul Friedrich Posenenske, 2017, photo: Cordula Schulze

Kassel

After the end of the war, the landscape architect Hermann Mattern, together with the painters Ernst Röttger and Arnold Bode, became engaged in reestablishing the Academy of Fine Arts in Kassel. It began operating again in 1948 under the name Werkakademie (School of Applied Arts) and from 1960 as the Staatliche Hochschule für Bildende Künste (State University for Fine Arts). Mattern was a professor there from the beginning, working in a section that later became the Department of Landscape Culture.

How is one to imagine Kassel in 1965, when Günther Grzimek moved there from Ulm? Like Ulm, Kassel had been largely destroyed in the war. Its reconstruction was to be based on designs presented by the Reconstruction Task Force appointed in 1943 by the architect Albert Speer (senior); these designs, however, met with strong criticism from the city's inhabitants. An important figure at this phase of reconstruction was the planning department architect Erick Heinicke. Kassel, under American occupation, became the capital of the newly founded state of Hesse after the war, but it was unsuccessful in its bid to become the capital of the newly established Federal Republic of Germany; in 1949 the Parliamentary Council decided in favor of Bonn as the seat of government. The extensive destruction of historical monuments led to widely divergent approaches to reconstruction: the old Orangerie was rebuilt, but the Fridericianum, later the site of the documenta, was only partially reconstructed and restored, while other buildings were demolished and replaced by new structures. Here, too, reconstruction under the concept of a "car-friendly city" would come to characterize the former ducal capital—and does so even today. Yet Kassel gained national attention with its construction of one of West Germany's first pedestrian zones. At the time, the conversion of the Treppenstrasse into a pedestrian zone was measured against models such as the Lijnbahn in Rotterdam. In 1964, German Chancellor Ludwig Erhard visited the pedestrian zone in Kassel.

In 1955, Kassel became the site of the Federal Garden Show. Garden shows have a long tradition in Germany. In 1865, Erfurt was the site of the first International Agricultural and Horticultural Exhibition. During the National Socialist era, the German Horticultural Exhibition, directed by Gustav Allinger, was held in Berlin in 1933. Between 1936 and 1939, three further Reich Exhibitions of German Horticulture were held in Dresden, Essen, and Stuttgart-Killesberg. After the Second World War, a distinction continued to be made between state and national garden shows. In 1951 and 1953 the first national garden shows after the Second World War were held in Hanover and Hamburg respectively.

Hermann Mattern was commissioned to develop the concept of the 1955 show in Kassel. In fact, Mattern's former wife, Herta Hammerbacher, had won first prize in the competition for the Federal Garden Show, but she was only allowed to design plans for the perennial shrubs. Was Hammerbacher, an experienced landscape architect and one of the few female figures in the profession, not trusted with the complex task? She had already been a lecturer at the Technical University of Berlin since 1946, and a professor since 1950.[1]

The garden show concept in Kassel was primarily intended to present solutions for urban planning in the postwar period. The rubble from the buildings destroyed in the war had been dumped at the so-called "Schöne Aussicht" street by the city's baroque park. Mattern was to work out a horticultural solution for the remains left by this action. The exhibition grounds were visited by almost three million people; the grounds provided the first documenta with space in the new Karlsaue Park for the exhibition's open-air objects.

The initiator of the documenta was the artist Arnold Bode. There were 148 artists presenting their work at this first documenta. The focus of the exhibition was not so much on "contemporary art" created after 1945; rather, Bode primarily wanted to introduce visitors to the works of those artists whose work had been vilified during the National Socialist era as "degenerate art" (a reference to the notorious 1937 exhibition of that name in Munich) and also to present those works of classical modernism that had not been shown in Germany between 1933 and 1945.

Thus, when Grzimek came to Kassel in 1965, he found a city that already offered a vital cultural environment. It had been ten years already since documenta was established in Kassel, and it was held for the third time in 1964. Grzimek's brother, the sculptor Waldemar Grzimek, exhibited at documenta III.

The Museum Fridericianum, which had been partially rebuilt after World War II under the direction of Arnold Bode, was the center of an active art scene as well as a new exhibition venue. Günther Grzimek was appointed to the documenta council in 1966 by Bode, who taught painting at the University of Fine Arts in Kassel. It can be assumed that the inspiration he received from his work on the documenta council impacted his work at the university and on his planning projects, right up to the later idea of the "visitor park" in the Olympic Park. At documenta 4 in 1969, artistic reactions to events in politics and society were particularly visible. Among other topics, student turbulence and the accompanying demands for other forms of communication and participation in decision-making processes had an impact here. The artist and activist Bazon Brock announced that he would set up a "visitors' school" in which those interested would be "taught appropriation techniques and reception practices." This event was integrated into the documenta concept.

Grzimek worked intensively at the university to reform the course of studies. Reforms were welcomed in the context of student protests, but Grzimek realized that they could only be developed through intensive dialogue. Grzimek began to integrate other disciplines into the degree program. Biology and ecology, gardening technology, and sociology had to become integral parts of the course of studies, according to his experience. The issues he addressed went far beyond the previous traditional curriculum of a landscape architect, demonstrating the new responsibility of integrating into horticultural design issues of technology, the environment, and society. Planning came to the fore, while artistic and design skills were seen as secondary. In this way, he opposed the traditional curriculum of his predecessor and the goals of an art academy. However, this also meant that the process of designing was henceforth considered a team effort, rather than as the original achievement of an individual. In addition, students were to develop their skills by working on practical, real-life tasks. New development groups were seen as the format for such tasks, which represented a new aspect in the course of studies and for which Grzimek designed a systematic concept. In publications such as a special issue of the magazine *Garten + Landschaft* in April 1968,[2] which dealt exclusively with the new curricula of the Chair of Landscape Culture in Kassel, he made a strong case for this reformed training of landscape architects. The reform of 1968 was pioneering, and other universities eventually followed suit. At first, Grzimek was solely responsible for this in Kassel, alongside the dialogue with students, and did not have to coordinate the course of studies with a review board, unlike in other eductional institutions in Germany. In addition to the necessary reforms in the pedagogical area, a consequence of the 1968 movement was also the demand to eliminate the ideological prejudices of the profession and its practices, especially those from the times of National Socialism. The model for this was not least the School of Design in Ulm. The demands for an integration of the above-mentioned curricula led to the renaming of the subject to "environmental design": architecture, landscape architecture, and urban planning were united under this heading. In 1969, Grzimek and his students established the Developmental Group for Landscape Culture and Planning of Open Spaces. The purpose was to establish an alternative planning office in which students would have the opportunity to gain practical experience in planning. Non-hierarchical democratic decision-making cultures were laid down as goals in a manifesto, which were to achieve socially and politically responsible results in the planning practice. The association existed until 1973 and was then transformed into an independent planning office.

In 1970, the Werkkunstschule Kassel (School of Applied Arts) merged with the University of Fine Arts. One year later, the latter was integrated into the Comprehensive University Kassel. The course of study was renamed Landscape Architecture and an integration with architecture was considered. In the following years, Grzimek actively shaped the process of reorientation and the understanding of the connection between architecture, urban planning, and landscape planning. He was jointly responsible for the evolution of the University of Kassel as the first "reformed" university in West Germany, which celebrated its fiftieth anniversary in 2022.

Arnold Bode
Arnold Bode (1900–1977) studied at the Kassel Art Academy from 1919 to 1924. In 1926 he set up his own studio, and in 1929 joined the SPD ("a Social Democrat with heart and soul"). He was appointed lecturer in a municipal handcrafts department in Berlin in 1930, residing in the "Onkel Toms Hütte" housing development in the Grunewald district. He was removed from office in 1933 on account of his political convictions and progressive teaching methods. After being banned from his profession, he worked "in the dark," according to his own statement. In 1945 he was a prisoner of war under the American army. In 1948 he launched the revival of the Kassel Art Academy. He founded Club 53 with the aim of comprehensively presenting "Western art of the twentieth century on the occasion of the Federal Garden Show in 1955" and ultimately organized the first documenta exhibition in Kassel, together with a committee of artists, politicians, landscape planners, art historians, and creative people from various other professions. He succeeded in establishing this format of a "100-day museum" as an exhibition series, transforming it into one of the world's leading art exhibitions. Bode died in Kassel in 1977, one day after the end of documenta 6.

Almanac of the Federal Garden Show, Kassel, 1955

Hermann Mattern
After finishing his studies, Hermann Mattern (1902–1971) oversaw the planning department in the office of Karl Foerster and Herta Hammerbacher, whom he later married. From 1935 on he was one of the "landscape advocates" for the Reichsautobahn (Reich highway system). He played a major role in the reconstruction of the Werkakademie (School of Applied Arts) in Kassel. In 1961, Mattern was appointed professor at the Technical University of Berlin. More on Mattern's biography, see p. 198.

Grzimek's dedicated teaching activities made it almost impossible for him to continue his activities in Neu-Ulm. Starting in 1968, a new planning studio was established in Kassel, whose staff consisted primarily of graduates of the "Landscape Culture" class at the University of Kassel. Lore Kellinghaus was once again involved.

In the meantime, Grzimek had built up a reputation that opened up many contacts with local authorities as well as with renowned architects and urban planners, including Günter Behnisch, Walter Schwagenscheidt, Tassilo Sittmann, Friedrich Spengelin, and Erich Kühn. His main activities in the studio during this phase were related to horticultural development and green space plans for urban land-use planning in municipalities and cities, such as Darmstadt-Kranichstein, Frankfurt-Kelsterbach, Bad Godesberg, and Münster.

However, he also worked on notable building projects during the Kassel period. Among them, the New Botanical Garden of the Philipps University in Marburg (1965–70) must be mentioned, as well as the All-Weather Zoo in Münster (1968–71), which resulted from a competition won together with the architect Harald Deilmann. Grzimek had met Deilmann on the Am Berg Fidel project in Münster and continued his collaboration with him on the new building for the Westdeutsche Landesbank in Münster. The Münster Zoo had allegedly become too small by the end of the 1960s and was to be relocated. However, in reality the Münster city administration needed the zoo's property for the headquarters of the Westdeutsche Landesbank, fearing the city would otherwise lose the Landesbank, an important institution. For this reason, they provided the zoo with a larger area opposite the Aasee lake. Grzimek was advised in the planning for the zoo by the director of the Frankfurt Zoo, his great-uncle Bernhard Grzimek. He had been able to gain his first experience with the needs of keeping wild animals in captivity in Ulm, during the construction of the bear pen in the Friedrichsau. In 2004, the Ulm bear pen was filled in and the animals moved to an open-air enclosure.

The idea of the all-weather zoo was realized by shielding from the elements all the paths between the large animal houses. By shielding the paths, which had a total length of one kilometer, the zoo could be used in all weather conditions. Due to various disagreements, Grzimek stopped work on the zoo in 1971, before it was completed. The architect Bernd Kösters finished the architectural planning. After the completion of the Münster enclosures, the zoo animals

Bernhard Grzimek

Bernhard Grzimek (1909–1987) was a second cousin of Günther Grzimek. Bernhard was son of an attorney in Neisse and studied veterinary medicine in Leipzig in 1928. In 1933 he was employed as a specialist in the Prussian Ministry of Agriculture, and until 1937 as a consultant in the Reich Food Society. He was a Nazi party member and belonged to the SA paramilitary wing. During the war he was employed as a veterinarian. Suspected of having given food to Jews living in hiding, he was targeted by the Gestapo and fled from Berlin to Detmold and later to Frankfurt am Main. There he was appointed director of the zoological garden in 1945. Grzimek achieved fame through his trips to Africa, his books, films, and ultimately a television show. His film *Serengeti Shall Not Die* won an Oscar. Together with Horst Stern and others, he was one of the founding members of BUND (German Federation for the Environment and Nature Conservation) in 1974.

Waldemar Grzimek

Waldemar Grzimek (1918–1984), younger brother of Günther, began modeling clay figures at the age of eleven. As a child he met the sculptor Hugo Lederer, who taught him art and sculpture. At first, Grzimek worked mainly on animal motifs, which he exhibited as early as 1933. After an apprenticeship as a stonemason, he pursued academic training at the Berlin Academy of Fine Arts, which he had to abandon in 1941, due to the war. He was appointed to a teaching position in Halle at the Burg Giebichenstein University of Art and Design in 1946. From 1948 to 1951 he was professor for sculpture at Berlin-Charlottenburg College, and from 1956 to 1961 at the Fine Arts College in Berlin-Weissensee. In 1964 he exhibited at documenta III. From 1967 until his death, Grzimek taught sculpture at the Technical University of Darmstadt.

were transported in an ark across the Aasee lake in 1973—a spectacular event. The zoo's motto promised that one can "experience animals up close" here. To this day, parts of the zoo remain as originally designed by Grzimek, who employed a lot of exposed concrete in the design developed with Deilmann.[3]

The Botanical Garden in Marburg was planned in 1965, and with twenty hectares it occupied a much larger area. Originally located in the city center, the Botanical Garden was to receive a larger property at the Institute of Biology due to the relocation of the Philipps University to the northeast of the city (see p. 109).

The completion of both major building plans already overlapped with the beginning of what was for Günther Grzimek the largest project of his career, the Olympic Park. For the planning period from 1968 to 1972, Grzimek set up his own planning office in Munich. The completion of the Munich Olympic project also marked the end of Grzimek's time in Kassel. After being appointed to the Technical University of Munich in 1972, he moved his office to Bavaria and, at the age of fifty-seven, left Kassel.

1. Go Jeong-Hi, *Herta Hammerbacher (1900–1985). Virtuosin der neuen Landschaftlichkeit*, Der Garten als Paradigma (Berlin: Universitätsverlag der Technischen Universität Berlin, 2006).
2. Günther Grzimek, *Hochschule für Bildende Künste Halle, Lehrstuhl für Landschaftskultur* vol. 1968a (Munich: Callwey, 1968).
3. Henning Stoffers, "Über den alten Zoo und was aus ihm wurde," Münster, Menschen, Geschichten und Erinnerungen, https://www.sto-ms.de/bildgeschichte/über-den-alten-zoo-und-was-aus-ihm-wurde/.

Germany's first pedestrian zone, Kassel, undated, photo: Günther Becker

Elevated road over Ludwigstrasse in Munich, 1966, photo: Kurt Huhle

Munich

What was Munich like when Günther Grzimek began work on his Olympic Park in 1968? It was a city on the go. The awarding of the Olympic Games accelerated many projects in Munich, transforming the city from a traditional royal capital to a pulsating, modern metropolis in only a few years. A glance back at the important developments in the years prior to the Olympic Games will spotlight some of these milestones.

Munich had followed its own path in its reconstruction after the Second World War. The question in all German cities was: reconstruction or a new beginning? In Munich, as in Ulm, the decision was made to rebuild the historic city center, 60 percent of which was in ruins, according to its former ground plan. Under the planning direction of Karl Meitinger, however, the historic center was not cut through by expressways, as was the case in Ulm. Instead, a broad ring road encircled the city center.[1] In 1946, Meitinger proposed a first route for the so-called "Middle Ring" to complement the inner ring road. An "Outer Ring" was also planned, but only the sections of Fürstenrieder Strasse, Frankfurter Ring, and Föhringer Ring were realized. The war debris was transported from the historic city to areas that were still vacant, such as Luitpoldpark, Fröttmaning, the high bank of the Isar near Neuhofen, and Oberwiesenfeld, where a sixty-meter-high hill was created.

In the city center, the architecture of the reconstruction years in Munich interpreted the historic buildings according to the design canons of postwar modernism. Where historic ornaments, paintings, and stucco once characterized the buildings, new patterns and structures, predominantly in the sgraffito technique, now adorned the façades. The new face of Munich's city center was emerging. Little attention was paid to Munich's green planning in the postwar period. Many avenues and individual tree plantings were created, but no larger green spaces. Munich relied entirely on its existing feudal greenery, such as the Englischer Garten and Nymphenburg Park.

In 1948, the renowned garden architect Alfred Reich of Munich ventured to "See the Bigger Picture," the title of his radio program on Radio München, in which the longing for a little bit of greenery was accompanied by practical advice on the subject. While Munich residents dreamed of having their own garden, the city was characterized by a flurry of construction activity. In the city center, but especially on the outskirts, numerous housing developments were erected for the rapidly growing population and the many refugees who still lived in barracks such as the Frauenholz camp. Developments for residential areas such as those at Hasenbergl or Milbertshofen were pushed forward.

Life in Munich also picked up again culturally. In 1949, the Haus der Kunst once again hosted the Grosse Kunstaustellung art exhibition, and a show on the Der Blaue Reiter displayed artists who had been labeled "degenerate" by the Nazis.[2]

A newspaper report of April 21, 1950, claimed that Munich was the most successful city in clearing away war rubble. Out of the five million cubic meters of rubble, four had already been removed.

On October 8, the Munich Kammerspiele theater celebrated its premiere. Therese Giehse played the leading role in *Mother Courage and Her Children*, directed by Bertolt Brecht himself, who wrote:

Courage, together with her friends and guests and almost everyone, recognizes the purely mercantile nature of war: that is precisely what attracts her. She believes in war to the end. It does not even occur to her that you need to have a very big pair of scissors to get your cut out of war. After all, onlookers at a catastrophe wrongly expect that those affected will learn from it. As long as the masses are the object of politics, they cannot regard what happens to them as an experiment, but only as fate; they learn as little from the catastrophe as the experimental rabbit learns about biology.[3]

Internationally celebrated stars came to Munich again, such as the American dancer Josephine Baker, whose first appearance in Munich in 1929 was banned by the police department for fear that Nazis would riot. At Prinzregentenstrasse 1, the US Army set up an officers' club in a wing of the Haus der Kunst; the soldiers called the club "P1"—and it remains there to this day. In any case, the American military left its mark on many areas of the city in these years. In particular, the former military barracks were occupied by the US Army after the end of the war; as a result, many families of military personnel needed additional living space.

In 1955, the McGraw Settlement celebrated its completion as the most modern residential district of the postwar period. "Little America," as the development was called, boasted continuous lighting, wide streets, and large parking lots. Here, the city took its cue from US housing development models, car-friendly with lots of green. That same year, the first parking meters were introduced in Munich.

As early as 1954, Alwin Seifert, who had been appointed *Reichslandschaftsanwalt* (Reich Landscape Advocate) by Hitler, was given a chair for Landscape Conservation, Landscape Design, and Road and Water

Hans-Jochen Vogel

Hans-Jochen Vogel (1926–2020) was born in Göttingen. From 1943 to 1945, he served as a soldier in the Second World War. Beginning in 1946 he studied law in Munich and Marburg, and in 1952 he began his career as an assessor at the Bavarian Ministry of Justice. In 1958 he became a city council member and leader of the legal department for the City of Munich. He was a member of the federal leadership committee of the Social Democratic Party (SPD) beginning in 1970. From 1960 to 1972 he was mayor of Munich. In December 1972, Chancellor Willy Brandt appointed him minister for Land Use Planning, Building and City Planning. From 1972 to 1977 he was regional chairman of the Bavarian SPD and he was a member of the German parliament in 1972–1981 and 1983–1994. He was mayor of Berlin in 1981, and from 1983 to 1991 he was chairman of the SPD parliamentary group. In 1987 he succeeded Willy Brandt as chairman of the SPD, a position he held until his resignation on October 28, 1991. He was founding chairman of the bipartisan initiative "Against Forgetting—For Democracy" from 1993 to 2000, and he was a member of the National Council on Ethics from 2001 to 2005. Hans-Jochen Vogel died in Munich on July 26, 2020.

The Munich delegation with the first competition model for the International Olympic Committee in Rome

Engineering at the Technical University of Munich, after he succeeded in presenting himself as politically "exonerated." In July 1955, the Building Law Committee, together with the Municipal Building and Art Committee and the State Building Law Committee, decided against the proposal for a forty-six-meter-high Siemens administration building in the south of the city, instead proposing a maximum height of thirty-six meters. The incident was characteristic of the debates about building heights that have raged in Munich for decades.

In the same year, the Munich courts moved to the Neue Maxburg, built by Sep Ruf and Theo Pabst. The design of this building complex was considered an example of architecturally uncompromising reconstruction. At the same time, the tracing service of the German Red Cross was still occupied with tracking down missing persons—ten years after the end of the war. For many, the horrors of the war were still not over.

Munich in 1957 was driven by innovation: thanks to the presence of major technology companies, universities, and research institutions, the city evolved rapidly. The first research reactor was begun and built at the Technical University. It was located in Garching, its architect was Sep Ruf, and the object was known as the "Atomic Egg." Today, the "Egg" has been declared an architectural monument and has not been in operation since 2000.

In 1958 Munich celebrated its 800th anniversary. The city council adopted a general transportation plan and, together with the German railroad company, decided on the last section in the reconstruction of the main train station, the track hall. In the following year a competition was held for this project, which was won by Krupp Rheinhausen with Professor Franz Hart of the Technical University of Munich. On July 12, a memorial for Professor Kurt Huber and Hans and Sophie Scholl was inaugurated at Ludwig Maximilian University. The philosopher of religion and university preacher Romano Guardini spoke at the ceremony.

In 1960, the new central station was almost completed and a new mayor was elected: Hans-Jochen Vogel. He succeeded the Social Democrat Thomas Wimmer and took office at the young age of thirty-four. One of his first acts in office was to bring urban planning under his purview. In the same year, on the initiative of the SPD, the city council commissioned an urban development plan to serve as a guideline for construction and transportation development in Munich for the next thirty years. The development of infrastructure, in particular the construction of a

Hans-Jochen Vogel at Oberwiesenfeld, 1963, photo: Hans Enzwieser

metropolitan train system and subway, were also part of the program.[4] In 1963, the planner Herbert Jensen became head of the Munich Urban Development Plan Working Group. This embryonic vision for Munich is later referred to as the "Jensen Plan" and was approved by the city council in 1963. The plan laid the central basis for many further housing and transportation projects. The construction of the Middle Ring was pushed ahead, and the realization of the subway and metropolitan train system was based on these urban expansion and development ideas.

On February 1, 1965, construction of the subway began with a ceremony at the City Hall, a car convoy to the corner of Ungererstrasse and Schenkendorfstrasse, and the symbolic beginning of construction: an eighteen-meter-long steel profile girder was sunk into a pre-drilled hole, the governor of Bavaria was allowed to ring the bell, and then lunch was served at the Schwabingerbräu brewery.[5]

On April 5, the first Spring Festival was held on the Theresienwiese. Bavarians again celebrated. The city became attractive, not just for the people of Munich, for whom an impressive 10,525 new apartments were constructed in 1965. The rising number of overnight stays in the city was a telltale sign: the tourist industry reported four million that year, the highest number in all of West Germany. And on May 20, the Queen of England visited Munich, followed by the Rolling Stones.

In August, plans for the new Kaufhof building on Marienplatz were unveiled, designed by Josef Wiedemann, a professor at the Technical University of Munich. The building's appearance was radical, almost cubist in its formal language, and it was right in the midst of the recently reconstructed historic center and within sight of the neo-Gothic New Town Hall. Diagonally opposite the Town Hall, Hans-Jochen Vogel was sitting in his office on October 28 when he received a surprise visit from Willi Daume, president of the National Olympic Committee. Daume proposed that Munich bid to host the 1972 Olympic Games. Vogel is said to have spontaneously replied "Well then!" —and thus Munich's Olympic history was launched.

Although Munich did not have any facilities appropriate for the Games, Willi Daume, as Vogel writes in his memoirs, was confident. The decision was not an easy one, since shortly before in Madrid there had been a dispute regarding sports between West and East Germany. An all-German Olympic team was no longer conceivable. It was decided that two separate teams for the Federal (FGR) and Democratic (GDR) Republics (West and East Germany respectively) should participate. Would the East German team compete in the Munich Games? This question was in the foreground of the bidding process for a long time.

Other considerations related more to the precarious financial situation of the city in the mid-1960s. From a marketing point of view, the Games stood to benefit Munich. A trip to Berlin and a visit to Willy Brandt was intended to provide Hans-Jochen Vogel with the necessary backing from the West German government—and he got it, as well as the support of the Bavarian state government. The news of Munich's intention to bid caused a sensation in the city. It was now the end of November 1965, and the application deadline was December 31. Before the required city council decision could be made, all the relevant asso-

Willi Daume

Willi Daume (1913–1996) came from a family of entrepreneurs in Dortmund and was himself a businessman, but above all he was a sports official at the national as well as international level. An active sportsman, he left his studies to take over the iron foundry of his father, who died in 1938. Daume was a Nazi party member. After the war he utilized his contacts in sports associations to become president of the German Sport Association in 1950. In 1956 he joined the International Olympic Committee, and in 1961 he became president of the German National Olympic Committee. Munich's bid to host the Olympics was successful in large part due to his intense commitment, and he remained engaged with sports throughout his life. Daume died in 1996 in Munich, spending the last years of his life in the Olympic Village.

Munich, construction of the pedestrian zone, 1969, photo: Erika Groth-Schmachtenberger

ciations were heard from, and all were in favor of the application. On December 20, the city council then also unanimously approved the bid. The costs were estimated at 47.7 million Deutschmarks. One third was to be borne each by the federal government, the state of Bavaria, and the city authorities.

The rush to submit the Olympic bid and the preparations for a concept were in full swing by the end of 1965. A site for the Olympic stadium had already been found, the Oberwiesenfeld.[6] On December 31, Munich submitted its application to host the 1972 Olympic Games to the International Olympic Committee (IOC).[7]

In 1966, Hans-Jochen Vogel was re-elected Munich's mayor with 78 percent of the vote. From March 25 to 27, he traveled to the United States together with his deputy Georg Brauchle and other city representatives. On the agenda was a meeting with IOC President Avery Brundage in Chicago. The Munich delegation presented the selling points of its bid. It is interesting to note that Brundage was particularly interested in how athletes from East Germany would be dealt with. The political aspects of the East–West conflict applied to sports as well. The world was heading into the highpoint of the Cold War conflict in those years. The Munich delegation tried to make clear that the Games would be open to all participants. Munich presented its concept as the "Games of Short Distances," with the idea of concentrating all of the venues on one site. Competing with Munich for the bid were Detroit, Madrid, and Montreal.

On April 26, the decision-making body of the IOC met in Rome. A delegation from Munich had prepared the presentation of the bid in the form of an exhibition. Huge black-and-white photographs were used to illustrate the history of the city. In addition, a model of the stadium by the architects Henschker and Deiss was presented. A panorama of the city, 17 meters long and 2.7 meters high, formed the background of the presentation. On the day of the decision, representatives of the cities once again gave speeches to support their bids.[8]

It was not until the second round of voting that a decision was made in favor of Munich, which received thirty-one votes; Montreal received fifteen and Madrid thirteen votes. Munich thus became the venue for the 1972 Summer Olympics. A telegram was sent to Munich: "Munich Olympic City 1972, *please inform the Chancellor.* Signed, Daume-Vogel-Brauchle-Danz-Wülfing."

The victorious delegation returned to Munich. The exhibition presented in Rome was shown in the Stadtmuseum for Munich's inhabitants. On June 3, the Olympic Committee for Munich was founded with National Olympic Committee President Willi Daume, Federal Minister of the Interior Paul Lücke, Bavarian Minister of Culture Ludwig Huber, and Hans-Jochen Vogel.

On June 23, 1966, the Beatles made a guest appearance in Munich, accompanied by wild storms of enthusiasm. The city was now able to prove for the first time that it could handle new mass events. The de-escalating effect of the so-called "Munich Policy," which relied on prevention and psychology in police work, was put to the test here. Munich police chief Manfred Schreiber was chosen to oversee security at the Games.

In 1967, the first subway section, 2.8 kilometers long, was completed. On February 1, the planning for the Olympic Games buildings took off with the announcement of an urban planning ideas competition and a building competition for Oberwiesenfeld. The foundation stone for the new Neuperlach commuter suburb was laid on May 12.

On May 17, 1967, students protested on Leopoldstrasse against the new higher education laws and the "reactionary education policy of the CSU," referring to the conservative Christian Social Union party. Contemporary teaching curricula and equal social opportunities were demanded by the students, who also rebelled against outdated university structures. Better learning conditions and the removal of teachers with a Nazi past were vehemently demanded. At the same time, the demonstrators expressed solidarity with the protests in America against the Vietnam War.

An even that provoked additional unrest was the visit of the Shah of Iran to Munich on May 27, 1967. This caused a tense situation in many places, and on June 5 the student Benno Ohnesorg was murdered during protests in West Berlin.

On July 3, 1967, Otl Aicher wrote, "The Munich Olympic Games should have the character of informality, openness, lightness, and relaxation."[9] In spite of the turbulent times, 101 entries were submitted on July 3 to the competition for the buildings for the Olympic Games. Three exhibition halls with a total of 10,000 square meters were required to display the works for the jury. Then, from September 4 to 8, nineteen judges assessed the competition entries: the jury was chaired by the architect Egon Eiermann, Karlsruhe, and was made up of the professional experts Gerd Albers, Munich; F. W. Kraemer, Braunschweig; Herbert Jensen, Braunschweig; Ernst Maria Lang, Munich; Edgar Luther,

Olympic Park, August 1972, photo: Karsten de Riese

Munich; Roland Rainer, Graz; Johannes Rossig, Berlin; Walther Schmidt; and Clemens Weber. They were assisted by the administrative judges National Olympic Committee President Willi Daume, Deputy Mayor Georg Brauchle, Minister of Culture Ludwig Huber, State Secretary Anton Jaumann, Paul Lücke, Heinz Noris, Konrad Pohner, Ludwig Störl, as well as Minister-President Franz-Josef Strauss and Mayor Hans-Jochen Vogel. After four days, twenty-three works were shortlisted.

A second meeting was held from October 11 to 13. Behnisch & Partners emerged victorious from the competition with their tent-roof design. Second prize went to the team Klaus Nickels, Timm Ohrt, and Anke Marg from Hamburg. Erwin Heinle and Robert Wischer from Stuttgart received the third prize.

In 1968, the team led by Behnisch & Partners was finally awarded the planning contract after all doubts about the construction of the tent-roof had been cleared up. Behnisch was now able to put together his team of planners for the Olympic Park. He brought Günther Grzimek on board, whom he already knew from their collaboration in Ulm. Grzimek received his own commission and immediately began with the first planning (see "Olympic Park," p. 117).

The first earthworks on Oberwiesenfeld began as early as spring 1968. Construction work quickly took shape. Building on all the Olympic buildings was carried out almost simultaneously. The group of buildings in the central area consisted of the Olympic Stadium, the Olympic Hall, and the Olympic Aquatics Center. In addition to the buildings on the overall site, the Olympic Press City was also erected to the west of the university sports complex.

In that same year, 1968, Hans-Jochen Vogel founded a communication forum for urban development. He called it a kind of "laboratory" for testing planning ideas in the city. The participants came from the entire spectrum of the inhabitants. In June, the city council approved the founding of the Munich Forum, an institution that still exists today and where urban planning is discussed and commented from outside the administration.

In 1968, student riots again shook Munich as well as Berlin. The organizers of the Olympic Games feared the riots, which could no longer be ruled out in view of the political mood. Troublemakers were expected, as was demonstrated by a law passed by the German parliament on June 31, 1972, protecting the "Olympic Peace," which, contrary to Article 8 of the German Constitution on the freedom of assembly, allowed a temporary ban on assemblies in the vicinity of the Olympic facilities.[10]

Construction activities surrounding the Olympic Games now included not only transportation planning but also the redesign of many public spaces in the city. After a decision passed by the city council in 1966, the city center was provided with a pedestrian zone according to plans by the architects Bernhard Winkler and Siegfried Meschederu. The first draft envisaged a 900-meter-long and in parts thirty-meter-wide auto-free zone in Munich's historic center. New fountains and concrete planters, known as "nuts" because of their hexagonal shape, adorned the former street, which was covered with uniform concrete slabbing. To visually rhythmize the paths, the architects chose a banding of black cobblestones. Metal chairs were also placed about, inviting people to rest and enjoy.

The concept worked. Contrary to the fears of local residents that the pedestrian zone would become inhospitable, it has enjoyed great popularity since its opening. It is only today's store vacancies, caused by the Coronavirus pandemic beginning in 2020, that have caused problems for the pedestrian zone.

In February 1969, Otl Aicher suffered a heart attack, right in the middle of the grueling work of the design commission, which was also accompanied by numerous conflicts. Werner Wirsing resigned as chairman from the visual design committee. Work immediately continued, as the official laying of the foundation stone for the Olympic buildings was scheduled for July 14. In addition to Willi Daume and Hans-Jochen Vogel, it was attended by German Finance Minister Franz-Josef Strauss.

By the end of the year, the first subway line from Münchner Freiheit to the Fröttmaning depot was operational. In 1970, due to excessive costs, the project had to be reduced from four to three main lines that were to run through the city center. In the same year, planning commissioner Edgar Luther's term ended, prompting Hans-Jochen Vogel to create the post of director of urban development alongside that of the building department. After an extensive selection process, Uli Zech was chosen as the new city planning commissioner.

Just six days later, the world was preoccupied with a completely different event: on July 20, 1969, the capsule of the Apollo 11 space mission landed on the moon. While Neil Armstrong and Buzz Aldrin walked on lunar gravel, the American artist Michael Heizer created his work *Munich Depression* in the gravel of Munich-Neuperlach, a pit thirty meters in diameter that was excavated to a depth of 4.9 meters. Once at the bottom of the hollow, the newly erected sky-

Exhibition catalog for *Democratic Green Space*, 1973

spaces, limited to guests of honor. The majority of visitors—on peak days of the events, an estimated 74,000—were to use subway and metropolitan rail.

On May 8, 1972, the subway line to the Olympic Park was opened and the last plantings were completed there. Preparations for the opening were in full swing. The Games became a great attraction and an international success. The joy of the sports festival and its relaxed atmosphere came to an abrupt end on September 5, 1972, with the attack on the Israeli Olympic team. The taking of eleven Israeli team members as hostages ended with the death of the athletes, five of the terrorists, and a German policeman. The Games continued and ended on September 11. The following day, a mourning ceremony was held with 80,000 participants. The victims of the attack are commemorated to this day with a memorial in the Olympic area.

While the Olympic Park was still being completed, Günther Grzimek was offered a professorship at the Technical University of Munich. There he succeeded Ludwig Schreiber from the Faculty of Agriculture and Horticulture at the Weihenstephan campus, heading the garden and landscape design course. Schreiber had become emeritus professor in 1971, having been responsible for the course since 1956. The delay in filling the chair resulted from the appointment at equal rank of two candidates by different authorities. The other applicant, the garden director in Essen Helmut Klausch, ultimately retired from the selection process, whereupon Grzimek accepted the appointment.

Grzimek was considered by the appointment committee, which included Professor Wolfgang Haber and Professor Gerd Albers, to be the most creative and experienced of the German garden architects and horticultural planners. It is interesting that Alwin Seifert, a former lecturer at the Technical University of Munich, also intervened in this process and, contrary to the recommendation of the commission, proposed to the Ministry of Culture the garden architect Ludwig Römer as a Bavarian candidate. Theoretically, as a private lecturer and German citizen, Römer would have been entitled to the privilege of a professorship (Article 131 of the German Constitution, 1951, Chapter 1: Ousted Members of the Public Service). Römer himself, however, rejected the recommendation.[11]

Günther Grzimek's appointment meant the Weihenstephan campus would have a professor who had already implemented teaching reforms in Kassel. In his first years at the Technical University of Munich

scrapers in Neuperlach disappeared from view for the pedestrian on the ground, and only the sky and the moon were visible to the observer.

In 1970, the tunneling of the Prinz-Carl-Palais at the Englischer Garten clearly demonstrated that even in Bavaria the days of the car-friendly city were not yet over. One year later, Munich was once again completely concerned with mobility: the official inauguration of the Munich subway took place on April 27 and the last section of the Middle Ring went into operation. The building department completed construction of the ring with the opening of the Donnersberger Bridge. This meant that the Olympic roads were completed according to plan. The expansion of the metropolitan rail connection was also completed, and with it a concept that prioritized public transport for the Olympic Games. This was also expressed in the provision of only 7,300 parking

he likewise sought to introduce and develop these ideas (see "Teaching," p. 180). He established a new office in Bavaria called Grünplan GmbH, together with his long-time colleague Lore Kellinghaus and with Eberhard Krauss. The office was the equivalent of the Development Company for Landscape Architecture (EGL according to its German initials) previously founded in Kassel (but without including students in the concept). The office operated in proximity to university education, combining practice and teaching. Many students are given the opportunity of participating in the planning practice through internships at EGL.

In Munich, the landscape architect Grzimek gained visibility via the exhibition *Demokratisches Grün* (Democratic Green Space), held at the Residenz Palace in 1973. After receiving the Friedrich Ludwig von Sckell Honorary Ring from the Bavarian Academy of Fine Arts in 1972, and after being appointed to the Academy, he suggested an exhibition on the development of open spaces in Munich. The Academy enthusiastically took up the idea. Grzimek enlisted his long-time friend Arnold Bode for the design of the exhibition. Together with Gerda Gollwitzer, the editor of Callwey Verlag, he developed the concept for the show. Grzimek took the 150th anniversary of the death of the director of Munich's Oberhofgarten, Friedrich Ludwig von Sckell, as the occasion. The exhibition's subtitle was "From Palace Garden, to Public Park, to Recreational Landscape." These themes were used to discuss the differences between the gardens of feudalism and those of a democratic society, illustrated with numerous images (see the text of Grzimek's lecture, p. 182).

In addition to university teaching, the following years in Munich were marked in Grzimek's career primarily by his involvement with large-scale planning projects in the office. Numerous landscape development plans were created, for example for Bad Birnbach or Markt Oberstaufen. Probably the most interesting project of that time, "the framework and program planning for Munich Airport II," dominated his activity in 1975. In this study, Grzimek, supported by opinions from environmental experts, dealt with the possibility of integrating a large spatial structure into a landscape. In doing so, he used the existing formative landscape elements to create the image of a meaningful landscape concept for the airport site (see "Munich Airport," p. 165). Here, too, he again collaborated with Otl Aicher and his colleague Eberhard Stauss and for many years accompanied the Munich Airport Company on its design advisory board.

Grzimek continued his studies of the evolution of Munich's open spaces at the university. He was especially interested in the user behavior of the city's inhabitants. Together with the landscape architect Werner Nohl, he investigated this topic using the example of the South Isar in Munich. Here, in the gravelly floodplain of the river, especially at the so-called "Flaucher" riverbank, he developed his theses for a new publication, presented in the exhibition and book of the same name, *The Appropriation of the Lawn*, in 1983. The exhibition, shown in rooms at the Munich reinsurance company, may be understood as an antithesis to the International Garden Show in Munich, held that same year in the Westpark. This urban park was designed by Peter Kluska, who successfully won the competition in 1976. A long-lasting debate emerged between the approaches of the two landscape designers Grzimek and Kluska (see "South Isar Model," p. 175).

In 1979 Grzimek left Munich and moved with the office from Freising to Landshut. He moved to Pfeffenhausen in the same district, from where he commuted to Freising and Landshut. In his small house—which, however, had a large garden—he drafted out many a design idea after his retirement in 1981.

1   Lutz Hoffmann, "Aufstieg aus den Trümmern 1945–1960," in *München wie geplant. Die Entwicklung der Stadt 1158 bis 2008*, Referat für Stadtplanung und Bauordnung Landeshauptstadt München, exh. cat. Stadtmuseum München (Munich: Schiermeier, 2004), 112.
2   Irene Meissner, "Der Umgang mit den Bauten des Nationalsozialismus," in *Landeshauptstadt München, Referat für Stadtplanung und Bauordnung Lokalbaukommission, Untere Denkmalschutzbehörde*, Denkmalschutz in München. 40 Jahre Bayerisches Denkmalschutzgesetz (Munich: Landeshauptstadt München 2013, 3rd ed. 2018), 42.
3   "Bertolt Brecht und die Münchner Kammerspiele," https://mkammerspiele.wordpress.com/2015/05/20/bertolt-brecht-und-die-munchner-kammerspiele/.
4   Hans-Jochen Vogel, *Die Amtskette. Meine 12 Münchner Jahre. Ein Erlebnisbericht* (Munich: Süddeutscher Verlag, 1972), 34.
5   Stadtarchiv München, 1965.
6   Stadion Wettbewerb München, Baumeister, vol. 5., 1964.
7   Landeshauptstadt München, Kulturreferat, Kulturgeschichtspfad Milbertshofen, vol. 11, 2015; p. 26.
8   Simone Egger, *"München wird moderner." Stadt und Atmosphäre in den langen 1960er Jahren* (Bielefeld: Transcript-Verlag, 2013), 186.
9   Stadtarchiv, StAMü/Olympiade 1972/117, Aicher Olympische Spiele München.
10 Gesetz zum Schutz des Olympischen Friedens, 48, 31.05.1972 C.F.R. (1972), *Bundesgesetzblatt* 48 (June 3, 1972), 865.
11 Andreas König, *Günther Grzimek*, Diploma Thesis (Technical University of Munich–Weihenstephan), 88.

Collaborations

Sports Design Symposium, Rotis, 1973,
photo: Karsten de Riese

Otl Aicher and Inge Aicher-Scholl

In 1947, Günther Grzimek met the Aicher-Scholl couple in Ulm, marking the beginning of a lifelong friendship. Otl Aicher and Inge Scholl both came from that city, and Otto, known as Otl since the 1950s, was born in the Ulm neighborhood of Söflingen. He grew up in a Catholic working-class family. His father, Anton Aicher, was a master plumber, his mother Anna a housewife. In 1932 his father opened his own electrical installation business. Otto had two siblings, Hedwig and Georg. The family occupied an unequivocal political position during the Nazi period, and neither Anton nor Anna were members of the Nazi party. Otl never forgot the silent resistance against Nazism present in his family, and their courage in protecting others was a lifelong inspiration. Aicher became interested in literature and art early on, learning what he could whenever possible. He developed his craftsmanship skills while learning his father's trade. His desire to practice design developed early on. Eva Moser recounts in her book on Aicher that he once redesigned the office at home while his parents were on vacation, proudly presenting it to them on their return.

His own stance against National Socialism was clear. "i was not in the hitler youth and consequently—and not so illogically—was an enemy of the state."[1] This led him to the point of renouncing admission to the high school diploma examination.[2] He wrote, "i was the only one in the whole state—along with the daughter of the former zentrum party minister president bolz and a stuttgart student—who refused to join the hitler youth and therefore could not take the high school diploma examination."[3] In 1941, despite his father's personal efforts to secure admission for his son from the Stuttgart Ministry of Education, he was excluded from the final examination. By this time Otto Aicher had become friends with Werner Scholl, who was a classmate of his from school. Anton Aicher asked Werner's father, the tax consultant Robert Scholl, who was himself opposed to the Nazi party, for support in Otto's affair, but Scholl placated him and said that he should be proud of such a son.[4]

The children of the Scholl family, on the other hand, had all joined the Hitler Youth, which displeased Otto. His acquaintance with the Scholl siblings grew stronger after 1939, when he grew closer with his schoolmates Werner and Elisabeth Scholl as well as Willy Habermann and Fridolin Klotz. He accepted an invitation to a reading at the Scholl home and there met the other siblings, Hans, Sophie, and Inge. The siblings began to distance themselves from the Hitler Youth. Aicher probably contributed much to the new community of the Scholl family with his erudition and religious-ascetic stance, and this group soon grew into a circle in which opponents of the Nazis could exchange ideas. His courageous position impressed them, as Inge Scholl later reported, and seemed to fit well with the internal resistance that the Scholl siblings initially engaged in. Close friendships developed between him and the sisters Sophie and Inge.

As a young Christian, Aicher sought ways to intellectually reconcile his faith, which differed from that practiced in the official church. "reason is the point of acceptance of faith. not only is nothing credible that contradicts reason, thinking is what creates the platform for belief in the first place. i've always been a protestant and a catholic, so how do you believe then in that?"[5] He grew closer to the efforts of reform Catholicism and became acquainted with the journalist Carl Muth and the writings of the cultural critic Theodor Haecker. When Muth invited him to Munich, probably in 1941,[6] he connected with a group of theologians engaging in resistance, concealed under the topics of philosophy and theology. A student group emerged around Carl Muth, regarding itself as an intellectual group. The publication of texts produced by this group, beginning in 1941 under the title *Windlicht* (Wind-light), led to the arrest of Inge Scholl by the Gestapo in 1942. Only through fortunate circumstances did she escape being sent to prison.

In 1941, despite an injury he had deliberately inflicted on himself the previous year to avoid conscription, Aicher was drafted into the army and underwent training in Alsace for the campaign in Russia. There he took part in several frontline missions, interrupted by stays in military hospitals in Bad Hall and on the Moselle. In 1942, he was able to see Sophie and then Inge Scholl.

Some of the authors of the *Windlicht* publications also belonged to the White Rose.[7] This resistance group, founded in 1942 by Hans Scholl, Alexander Schmorell, Christoph Probst, and Willi Graf, was formed during their student days at the University of Munich. Sophie Scholl later joined the group. The six texts written by the White Rose and the distribution of leaflets at the Ludwig Maximilian University in Munich led to the arrest of the group's members. Family members Robert, Magdalena, Elisabeth, and Inge Scholl were likewise imprisoned in Ulm for five months since they were considered guilty of participating in the publications. On

Otl Aicher with manuscript, 1969

In November, Aicher wrote a letter to the *Schwäbische Donauzeitung*: "Nazism ... was not only a matter of political opinion, but of the whole person. It took total possession of the human being. So today it also requires a completely new human being.... A new spiritual education is needed."[8]

While Aicher was only able to develop his design skills through self-study during wartime, he hoped to enroll at the Munich Art Academy after the war. Inge Scholl also wanted to enter the university, but she did not have a high school diploma. Aicher's studies in the sculpture class with Anton Hiller lasted only two semesters. Making sculptures did not seem to him to be the right way to transform social conditions; moreover, the atmosphere at the academy, where the majority of the master artists had been appointed under the Nazis, was not acceptable to him.[9] His motto, "creativity in the technical field is more important than in the studio," shaped his entire professional career.

Back in Ulm, he continued his activities and organized lectures as early as 1945, for example on the reconstruction of Germany, and a series of talks to which he brought Romano Guardini, the philosopher of religion. The American military forces and the Ulm city administration offered him the directorship of a planned community college (*Volkshochschule*), which he declined; instead, he suggested Inge Scholl for the post. Thus the community college in Ulm was opened under the direction of Inge Scholl in 1946. Working together, Aicher and Scholl developed the teaching program and selected lecturers. Aicher also created the graphics for the posters and program booklets, which today are regarded as design classics, traded at top prices in antiquarian bookshops.

A Thursday series of lectures at the community college featured prominent speakers. For Aicher and Scholl, it was vital to refill the "overturned receptacle of man." Alongside philosophical issues, Aicher was primarily concerned with the issue of technology and humans. He organized numerous events under the title "Technology as Mission and Risk." The lecture series "Reconstruction," launched in 1947, was dedicated to urban planning issues, bringing renowned architects such as Hugo Häring and Rudolph Schwarz to the lectern. For the topic of garden and landscape, he engaged the recently appointed head of parks department, Günther Grzimek, who aside from delivering lectures also quickly took on supervision of several working groups. The Aktion Sandfloh (Sand Flea Campaign)

February 22, 1943, Hans and Sophie Scholl, as well as Christoph Probst, were sentenced to death and executed the same day.

In 1945 Aicher managed to escape military service. He deserted to the Black Forest, where he hid with the surviving members of the Scholl family. They had taken shelter there at the Bruderhof community in Ewattingen after their release from prison. Aicher was twenty-three years old at the end of the war and returned to Ulm with the Scholls. There, Robert Scholl was appointed mayor by the American military administration on June 6, 1945.

an initiative for the construction of playgrounds in Ulm, was only one of the projects resulting from these working groups. It was for that initiative that Aicher designed the striking figure of the Sand Flea. In 1950 the topic of Ulm's reconstruction was once again included in the program, now with the question, "How do we want to live?" The theme can be regarded as laying the groundwork for the Ulm School of Design. The designer Wilhelm Wagenfeld lectured on the subject of "Even Small Things Can Shape You." His talk focused on everyday objects, a topic that Aicher made the core subject of the working group "Art and Design" in 1951. By this time he had opened his own graphic studio in Ulm.

His idea of the Studio Null (Zero Studio) represented the next step in infusing all areas of life with a clear design concept. Here Aicher conceived of a sort of academy. The original ideas regarding Studio Null arose in 1947–48 and are well documented in the Aicher Archive. He developed the concepts together with his friend Fritz Hartnagel. "Studio Null is a free community of workers who have decided to pursue together all the energies of life and contribute to their design. Each worker can choose the area of work that he believes he can work in positively."[10] In 1948 Studio Null was disbanded. It had a lasting effect, however, for the Studio Null period is when Otto became Otl and when he decided to write exclusively in lowercase.[11]

Aicher formulated ideas for a school of design as early as 1946. While they worked towards its realization, Aicher and Scholl strove to bring back to Germany former members of the Bauhaus from their exile in the United States. To this end, Inge Scholl established contact in 1952 with Max Bill, whose exhibition *Good Form* had been shown in Ulm in 1949. As a site for the new school, the Kuhberg area was proposed in 1949 by the mayor, Theodor Pfizer, and Max Guther, the head municipal architect. Underlying all discussions for the school of design was the intention to construct it in the spirit of Hans and Sophie Scholl. This foundational idea was expressed in 1949 in its provisional name, the "Scholl Siblings School." The various efforts to focus the school's syllabus on either politics or on design did not make the beginnings any easier. The primary advocates of these options were the freelance journalist Hans-Werner Richter, from the circles around the Gruppe 47 literary group, and Max Bill, whom Aicher and Scholl consulted in 1948. Bill's concept was preferred by Aicher and Scholl, and it became apparent that Richter's ideas, which could be described as a humanistic socialism, would not be accepted by the American occupation forces, who were to sponsor the school. Nevertheless, contact with Gruppe 47 was maintained. The author Ilse Aichinger needs to be mentioned in this regard, as she was active at the School of Design in the early years as an assistant to Inge Scholl.

Max Bill ultimately argued against the name "Scholl Siblings School," making it a fundamental condition for his participation that the name be changed. Ultimately the name Hochschule für Gestaltung (School of Design) was chosen.

For the school's founders, maintaining its independence was paramount. Open to everyone, this school, as a non-governmental institution, was to further develop ideas that had already existed at the Bauhaus. For this reason, it was to be privately financed. Scholl set about recruiting American sponsors. The Americans were primarily interested in reform projects, which they were willing to fund. Half of the financing came from American and half from German sponsors. Ultimately, one million Deutschmarks was donated by the McCloy Fund, named after the then US High Commissioner to Germany, while the other half was raised by industry and the state. In 1953, construction began on the buildings designed by Max Bill and Otl Aicher on the Upper Kuhberg. Until building was completed in 1955, classes were held in the community college.

In 1954, Grzimek issued his first publication, *Grünplanung in Ulm* (Green Planning in Ulm), a pamphlet designed at the School of Design by Otl Aicher and Hans Conrad. Here, Aicher's clear graphics help convey the complex subject of urban planning in a striking manner. The pamphlet, printed in black and white, has a square format and is made extraordinarily spare by the addition of just one color in the layout. It has the same format as the *Ulmer Monatshefte* (Ulm Monthly), a journal (now a collectors' item) designed by Aicher: square, reduced graphics, with a maximum of three colors. The two designers would maintain this principle in numerous joint documentations of designs. Grzimek continued his collaboration with Aicher in the publication of design concepts until the last years of his career. Otl Aicher also influenced Grzimek's plan representations and graphics, which differ from the common representations of landscape architecture of the time due to their abstract and reduced style.

The Ulm School of Design opened in 1955, with Walter Gropius giving the opening speech. In the

left: Otl Aicher, poster for the community college in Ulm, November 1953

right: Otl Aicher, logo for the community college (*Volkshochschule*, hence "vh") in Ulm, 1948

following years, it became one of the best regarded design schools in West Germany. Leading architects, designers, and other artists were active as instructors or lecturers there; in addition to Max Bill and Otl Aicher, these included Josef Albers, Hans Gugelot, Johannes Itten, Tomás Maldonado, Alexander Kluge, Werner Wirsing, Nicolaus Sombart, and Konrad Wachsmann, to name but a few. Günther Grzimek did not teach there but served on the board in an advisory capacity.

Otl Aicher and Inge Scholl were intensively involved in the organization of the School of Design, yet they did not succeed in preventing its closure. The portion of funds contributed by the German government was canceled in 1967; the reason given was that the university did not conduct research, an objection familiar to many arts schools today. The design process and design itself have not been recognized as a research discipline in the academic world during the past few decades and continue to be debated in universities. Only after the concept of "design thinking" found its way into research did the perception of the design disciplines change. In 1968, the Ulm School of Design had to close its doors. The Scholl Siblings Foundation, on the other hand, remained alive.

Many parts of this success story were the fruits of Inge Scholl's tireless work. It was Scholl who successfully set up the Ulm community college and convinced the Americans to finance the School of Design. She encountered personal difficulties when she had to admit her past membership in the Bund Deutscher Mädel (Association of German Girls, the female counterpart to the Hitler Youth) during denazification proceedings before the Ulm tribunal in 1946. But the death of her siblings Hans and Sophie also left a political mark on her for the rest of her life. She felt obliged to keep the memory of them and of the White Rose alive, and her activities remained directed toward this goal. In 1952 Otl and Inge, who was five years older, were married. The couple resided on the Upper Kuhberg, in the midst of their work environment, and raised five children there.

When the School of Design era came to an end for Otl Aicher, he could look back on successful designs for furniture and for the corporate identity of major enterprises. In 1968, a new, appealing task lay just around the corner for him. In 1966 Willi Daume proposed Aicher, as a representative of the Ulm School of Design, to the International Olympic Committee as design commissioner for the 1972 Olympic Games in Munich. Aicher delivered an initial concept in March 1966. The personal relationship between Aicher and Daume fostered the collaboration on the Olympic team with Günter Behnisch and Günther Grzimek, both of whom he already knew from the construction of the School of Engineering in Ulm.[12] Otl Aicher exerted a lasting influence on the visual image of the Munich Olympics. Not only were the orientation and color system derived from his designs, but he created the entire visual language of the Games. The pictograms of the Olympic sports, still famous today, became information bearers that were internationally comprehensible to all. The more than seven hundred characters made it the most comprehensive pictorial work of its kind. The copyrighted *otl aicher pictograms* were structured according to uniform design rules and followed their own grammar, which is why they are also known as syntactic pictograms. A separate design manual was fashioned for the Olympic Park, which defined the essential design guidelines for the appearance and visual communication of the Games. Typography, architecture, and landscape played an essential role in the specifications here, along with color and pictograms. In 2015, Kilian Stauss, in collaboration with the architects Auer and Weber and on behalf of the City of Munich, reissued the design manual based on the work of the design group headed by Otl Aicher.[13]

During the construction of the Olympic site, Otl Aicher decided to relocate his office to the Allgäu region. He had several studio houses erected on an old farm with a mill in Rotis near Leutkirch, where Aicher moved his family and office.

The subject of sport continued to link Günther Grzimek and Otl Aicher. Aicher organized symposia in Rotis, and in September 1975 he invited an illustrious group to a seminar on the subject of sport and design. Along with Otl Aicher, the group included the architects Günter Behnisch and Fritz Auer, photographer Karsten de Riese, fashion designer Jochen Kampf, industrial designer Herbert Lindinger, graphic designer Anton Stankowski, and ski racer and designer Willi Bogner Jr., as well as Grzimek. All of them gave presentations that are still preserved in the Grzimek archive.

> Aicher stated that:
> *even the "charter of Athens" accords play and sport a subordinate importance to work. le corbusier divided life in the city into the primary sectors of work, recreation, and sleep. sleep and recreation were assigned to work. today, recreation is so important that a different ideological distortion can occasionally take hold: people work in order to recover, in order to use and enjoy their free time. it is quite possible to avoid karl marx's statement that only work produces culture, without having to fall into the opposite trap. perhaps the conventional system of values and the valuation of sport and play as an exclusionary dualism, as opposites, is out of date.*

And Grzimek wrote the following:
the old, lost culture, which united sport, play, joy, art in a beautiful landscape, because it allowed free spontaneity, is one measure. the other is an arena, in which tension and relaxation are united for all involved, for the athlete as much as the observer. in this arena, a grove, a fountain, niches with protection from the sun, wind, rain, and gazes of others, would be a matter of course. we can demand for society that it be allowed to use landscape again, landscape that was conceived out of impulses and goals, like farmers once did with the rural landscape for their benefit. today, these landscapes are production landscapes and largely obsolete. problems arise like in old cities. ecologists discover them like the conservationists did before them, to discover that, for example, the "limes divergens," the collision of different ecotopes highly qualified by diversity, is from the perspective of landscape analysis a highlight of the natural sciences. all these ecotopes are anthropogenically influenced, even initiated, without the result having been preconceived, as seen from today's viewpoint. what has emerged is a diversity of plant, animal, and beauty that is greater, at least more humane, than nature could have intended or would have been able to create there. so we have to try to create landscapes, as the farmers previously did in their own way. in these landscapes there are new bodies of water: lakes, ponds, streams, marshes. there is enough water after all. we have to "hold it in our hands," as farmers used to say—that is, not channel it away, but stop it—keep it here—manage it for people who are looking for flora and fauna, for the diversity of living things. and in this landscape with bodies of water, forests, trees, and broad accessible areas, games can be played, competitions can be held. then society—in all age groups—would cohabit with the athlete's action. with this, i try to sketch a utopia; utopia of the gross product landscape, into which the usable sports surface—more specifically, the sports field—is to be inserted.

He had already implemented these principles in the Olympic Park and here, in 1975, Grzimek formulated what we believe we are reinventing today under the term of "sponge city."

Grzimek and Aicher remained linked in many joint projects, be it collaborations in building or in exhibitions and publications. They also authored

Portrait Otl Aicher, 1984, photo: Timm Rautert

joint publications, such as on the subject of urban communication.

Every year a circle of friends gathers in Rotis for the *Martinsgansessen*, a meal of goose on St. Martin's Day, a ritual that always welcomes new members while nurturing and establishing valuable contacts. Aicher created his own stationery for this, as well as for the Rotismühle, the mill building where his studio was located. He continued to hold numerous seminars there, in his "temple," as his friend the architect Norman Foster called it.

In 1991, Aicher, backing out of the property driveway, left the "temple" on a riding lawn mower and collided with a motorcycle. He did not survive the tragic accident and died, only 69 years old, from severe injuries. Thus ended the collaboration between Aicher and Grzimek. The "beautiful book" they had planned together had not yet been written.

1. otl aicher, *innenseiten des kriegs* (Frankfurt am Main: S. Fischer, hardcover edition, 1985), 28.
2. Eva Moser, *Otl Aicher. Gestalter* (Ostfildern-Ruit: Hatje Cantz Verlag, 2011), 15.
3. aicher, *innenseiten des kriegs*, 36.
4. Moser, *Otl Aicher*, 27.
5. aicher, *innenseiten des kriegs*, 40.
6. Moser, *Otl Aicher*, 31.
7. Markus Rathgeb, *Otl Aicher* (London: Phaidon, 2006), 16.
8. Moser, *Otl Aicher*, 72.
9. Winfried Nerdinger, "Fatale Kontinuität. Akademiegeschichte von den zwanziger bis zu den fünfziger Jahren," in *Tradition und Widerspruch. 175 Jahre Kunstakademie München*, ed. Thomas Zacharias (Munich: Prestel, 1985).
10. Estate of Otl Aicher, Findbuch 09, Ai AZ 530, 2015, https://hfg-archiv.museumulm.de/wp-content/uploads/2020/06/09_aicher-neu.pdf.
11. Moser, *Otl Aicher*, 2012, 107
12. Moser, *Otl Aicher*, 189.
13. Kilian Stauss, Fritz Auer, and Carlo Weber, *Olympiapark München. Gestaltungshandbuch 2015* (Munich: Landeshauptstadt München, 2015).

Arnold Bode

Arnold Bode, signature

Günther Grzimek met Arnold Bode in 1965 at the University of Fine Arts in Kassel Grzimek's predecessor, Hermann Mattern, had revived the former Werkakademie (School of Arts and Crafts) together with Bode. Bode himself came from the vicinity of Kassel, and his parents had a carpentry business in Kassel's Nordstadt district. He was born in 1900 and did military service during the First World War, after which he studied painting at the Kassel Art Academy. While he graduated as a drawing teacher, his brothers Theo and Paul studied architecture and practiced this profession in their joint studio. The youngest brother Egon became a civil engineer. In his own studio, Arnold Bode worked as a freelance artist beginning in 1926. In 1929 he joined the Social Democratic Party. After lecturing in Berlin at the Städtisches Werklehrer-Seminar, a seminar for training teachers in handcrafts, he became its deputy director. The University of Fine Arts in Kassel was closed in 1931 by emergency decree of the Prussian government for budget reasons.[1]

In 1933, Bode was removed from office in Berlin because of his progressive teaching methods, which prompted him to return to Kassel in 1934. In 1939 he was drafted into military service and was employed in building soldiers' quarters. In 1945 he became an American prisoner of war near Salzburg. After his release, he traveled back to Kassel on foot and re-established contact with the artists he knew from his time at the academy in 1920. His biographer Heiner Georgsdorf discovered during his research that by 1947 Bode had already developed the idea of a large international art show in Kassel, including an organizational concept. In 1948, he became a member of the Hessian Secession and, together with artist friends, re-founded the former art academy.

Starting in 1953, Bode organized a private artists' salon that he called Club 53. Mattern, a colleague of Bode's, was probably a frequent guest. It was in this circle that the initial ideas for documenta, which first took place in 1955 parallel to the Federal Garden Show, were born. Outdoor exhibits, sculptures by the artists, were displayed in the show's gardens. One of the artists exhibiting at documenta III in 1964 was Grzimek's younger brother, Waldemar (1918–1984), who had by then become a renowned sculptor.

Upon meeting at the academy in 1965, Bode and Günther Grzimek probably got along well from the beginning, and their work expanded to include various activities together in addition to their academic collaboration. For example, Grzimek became a member of the documenta council in 1966 and worked intensively with Bode on the idea of the so-called "documenta urbana" from the same year. Both succeeded in convincing the city council and the head of the planning office, Petereit, to hold an international urban planning ideas competition in connection with the following documenta. Nothing less than a developmental planning perspective for the city of Kassel was meant to be formulated by a select number of architects. Two planning zones in Kassel, the Fulda-Ufer and the Weinberg areas, formed the planning perimeter. In addition to the documenta society, the construction company Neue Heimat, the German Werkbund (chaired at the time by Werner Wirsing), and the Association of German Architects were also involved. As early as the end of 1966, Bode and Grzimek began talks with the representatives from Neue Heimat, Hofmann and Konwiarz—the same Hans Konwiarz who had become famous in 1966 with his futuristic design for the Alsterzentrum district in Hamburg. Construction on the so-called Weinberg would provide 300,000 residents with new homes in "family-, child-, and leisure-friendly" developments. There were also plans to build east of the Karlsaue and to relocate the train terminal: big ideas to be addressed in a competition. Bode and Grzimek presented these at a meeting on July 7, 1967, and stated in their drafting of the task:

> The guiding principles formulated in the Athens Charter require rewriting. The various stages of development in urban planning and regional planning have not yet led to clarification that could be evaluated in terms of an international agreement for the basic principles of urban planning. After the realization that the "dispersed, thoroughly greened city" has led to degenerative results, the topics are to be addressed in the competition and worked out in planning proposals.[2]

For years to come after 1977, numerous developments by renowned urban planners and architects were formulated in Kassel under the title of "documenta urbana." Bode and Grzimek were the pioneers of these initiatives.

Neither of the two men ever tired of initiating artistic and experimental projects on different levels. This also included cooperation with the industrialist Philip Rosenthal. Rosenthal's porcelain production facility was located in Erkersreuth near Selb. The art lover installed himself in the Baroque Erkersreuth Castle, which had belonged to the family since 1953. From then on, he asked artists and intellectuals to reinterpret the rooms of the castle with porcelain art. Salvador Dalí, Luigi Colani, Friedensreich Hundertwasser, and Andy Warhol all had their say there. Walter Gropius planned and built part of the factory. Bode and Grzimek advised Philip Rosenthal, among others, on the establishment of the "Rosenthal Relief Series" and the "Circle Walks" in the vicinity of Selb, intended to offer opportunities to experience the landscape.

Beginning in 1964, Bode worked together with renowned sculptors and designers to organize *ars porcellana*, a symposium on porcelain that produced wonderful white artifacts; participants included Luigi Fontana, Hap Grieshaber, Michael Croissant, Bernhard Heiliger, Fritz König, Gio Pomodoro, and Victor Vasarely.[3] Rosenthal was not only interested in art and design but also in architecture and landscape. In 1984 Grzimek authored an article for Rosenthal in the company's annual report, commenting on the interplay between the architecture of Gropius and the landscape: "In Selb, Rosenthal provides an impressive example of how a factory can be inserted into a landscape by reclaiming its footprint for the vegetation that was initially lost" (by greening the roofs).[4] Green roofs are a positively effective structural measure that has yet to be realized on many factory buildings, even today; this is a crucial improvement in times beset by the consequences of climate change.

The design of the 1973 exhibition *Demokratisches Grün* (Democratic Green Space) in the Bavarian Academy of Fine Arts is another—and probably one of the last—joint works between the Grzimek and Arnold Bode. The latter devised the architectural spatial sequence of the exhibition in the royal rooms of the Munich Residenz palace—which were difficult to work with. Huge black-and-white photographs of Munich's feudal parks were juxtaposed with images of the Olympic Park—the symbol of a society's path to democracy, a path that was always of great concern to both of them.

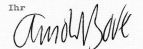

Letter from Arnold Bode to Günther Grzimek, 1967

1. Wikipedia, Hermann Nollau (2022).
2. "documenta urbana," AGG, no. 49.
3. "ars porcellana," in *Rosenthal Relief Reihe*, A. K. Kunstverein (Kassel: Rosenthal AG, Selb).
4. Günther Grzimek, "Mit Grün gegen die Versteinerung," in *Naturraum Menschenlandschaft* (Munich: Meyster Verlag, 1984), 59.

Günter Behnisch

Born in 1922 in Lockwitz near Dresden, Behnisch was conscripted into the army in 1939 when only eighteen years old. As submarine commander he surrendered his vessel and crew to the British in Scapa Flow in May 1945. After returning from war imprisonment, he began to study architecture in Stuttgart in 1947. Immediately after his studies he worked for Rolf Gutbrod in Stuttgart in 1951. The next year he opened his own studio there together with Bruno Lambart.

Günther Grzimek was connected to Behnisch through a productive collaboration stretching over many years, which began in 1960 with a personal recommendation. Before construction on the School of Engineering began, the public works service suggested to Behnisch that he contact the landscape architect Grzimek, who had just left his post as director of the parks department in Ulm. Grzimek had had enough of being accused of mismanaging finances, even having to defend himself against slander. Opening his own office offered a better option, while postwar urban green planning in Ulm had already been significantly guided by him. Now he was able to turn to other tasks. A new university campus for the School of Engineering, today the Technical University of Ulm, was envisioned on Prittwitzstrasse. Günter Behnisch with Bruno Lambart won first prize in the architectural competition in 1959. He followed the advice and sought out Grzimek. This resulted in a building project in which architecture and landscape design were intrinsically integrated from the beginning. The successful university building led to a subsequent project, a State College in Aalen, jointly erected by the two between 1965 and 1968. In between they built a middle school in Rothenburg in 1966.

Letter from Günter Behnisch to Günther Grzimek, 1995

In 1966 Behnisch founded a partnership with Fritz Auer, Winfried Büxel, Erhard Tränkner, and Karlheinz (Carlo) Weber. With this team he took part in the competition for the construction of the Munich Olympic buildings in 1968, which they won. This led to the next collaboration with Grzimek, now for the design of the Olympic grounds. In 1967 Behnisch was appointed professor for Design, Industry Buildings, and Building Design at the Technical University of Darmstadt.

The two forceful personalities did not always see eye to eye. Employees recalled that fiery arguments exploded again and again. Yet they always addressed each other with the respectful and formal "Sie." Their collaboration continued until the end of Grzimek's professional career. Together they erected the Parliament Buildings in Bonn in 1973 and took part in numerous other competitions. Even after Grzimek retired, he continued to consult Behnisch & Partners, as in the competition for the realization of the Biozentrum for the University of Frankfurt in 1987, where they won first prize. The last joint projects were a Montessori school in 1995 and the Münsterpfarrei kindergarten, both in the Hollerstauden district of Ingolstadt.

Günter Behnisch at the laying of the foundation stone for the Olympic Park, 1969

Honorary podium, laying of the foundation stone for the Olympic Park, 1969

Projects, competitions, engagement

Otl Aicher, The Sand Flea,
drawing, India ink on paper,
undated

Sandfloh:
The Sand Flea Campaign

The idea of building new types of playgrounds came about in a work group at the Ulm community college in 1951. In collaboration with the parks department, the goal was to design green play islands within the town and away from traffic, and to furnish them with inspiring play equipment. The idea was well received among the citizens, and led to the formation of a non-profit association chaired by the mayor's wife, Ursula Pfizer. The association was to collect donations of money and goods in order to promote the development of these new playgrounds in Ulm. The "garden and landscape" and "architecture" work groups at the community college, under the direction of Günther Grzimek, Otl Aicher, and the architect Joachim Kimpel, developed initial concepts in many joint discussions; the name *Sandfloh* (Sand Flea) was coined there, and a so-called "menu" of play equipment was formulated. Aicher created the cartoon-like character of a sand flea as a logo, and wrote many adventure stories for it; the sand flea came to vividly embody the campaign. Thus the activities of the campaign were reported in a child-friendly way through comic-strip stories.

> *Who is the Sand Flea?*
> *Profile: Small, stocky figure, ostensibly simple physique, extremely agile, with a smile on his face that can almost be described as a grin. Most of the time he is lugging about some larger or smaller piece of play equipment. His grin becomes especially broad when he is given money, but the corners of his mouth turn down all the way when his efforts are not appreciated. He is the chief of the "Sand Flea Campaign" and represents all playing children. He wants to build playgrounds – more precisely, green play islands, away from traffic, large enough and furnished with much colorful play equipment.*[1]

The work groups designed new play equipment and developed it in models. The items: climbing frames, balance balls, swinging ropes, and roundabouts were all prototypes developed by observing the play instinct of a child. The development of the equipment was to provide a range of possibilities for each type of movement. Soon some of this tried-and-tested equipment went into serial production in collaboration with Albin Grünzig & Co. in Eystrup/Weser.

As the head of the parks department, Grzimek was responsible for allocating the sites and their further design. He distinguished the play areas into different types. Play areas for children up to the age of six years, for school children up to the age of fourteen years, and areas for older children. Many sites combined both types for the first two age groups. For older children, movement was more important, which could take place on roller skating areas and lawns. Grzimek considered the requirements of children at play in some detail, a topic that he pursued throughout his life with his active involvement in associations, lectures, and continued development of concepts. This shows in his later work, such as the Olympic Park and open spaces at schools. Play areas always had a place in his deliberations on town planning. In the landscape plan for Ulm, he introduced them as a part of the overall concept.

The development of new play equipment was time-consuming, and it had to stand out clearly from the standard equipment already commercially available. Equipment depicting, for example, boats, trains, or animals was disapproved of. These analogies, it was believed, in no way promoted creative play and appropriation. The search for "well-designed equipment" stood in the tradition that had started at the Bauhaus or Werkbund. Additionally, there were demands for a high standard of precision in the manufacture of the items, which ultimately should not be "colorful," but produced in two, or at the most three, colors.

Each playground was to be designed individually and to have a distinct appearance. An insight gained from the campaign that was important for its success was the opportunity for citizens to participate in such developments, to become involved, and to share the responsibility. The first result of the Sand Flea Campaign was the Römer-Insel (Romans' Island) playground in Ulm. The site is about half a hectare in area and contains a central playground and a large sandpit with a shade structure. Climbing trees and arches, roundabouts and turning logs stimulate exercise, while a circular path with seats provides a place for people to linger.

As early as 1957, Callwey Verlag published a whole journal dedicated to children's play. It also featured the Sand Flea Campaign.[2] The publication shows that much of the inspiration for the new development of children's play in Germany originated in Scandinavia. Examples from Denmark and Sweden are cited. It even ventures a glimpse towards America in the context of activation and appropriation of open spaces. In the issue, the sports psychologist Liselott Diem writes about the "revolution of mothers" and describes how women opposed plans to transform a stand of trees into a parking lot in New York's Central Park.[3] The lack of playgrounds in the years after the Second World War seemed immense.

---

1 Günther Grzimek, *Grünplanung in Ulm* (Ulm: Stadtverwaltung Ulm, 1954), 27.
2 Günther Grzimek, *Die Aktion "Sandfloh" der Stadt Ulm/Donau* (Munich: Callwey Verlag, 1957), 52.
3 Liselott Diem, "Warum so viel Diskussion über den Spielplatz?" in Grzimek, *Die Aktion "Sandfloh,"* 8.

Otl Aicher, "The Sand Flea – Street Stories," five drawings, pencil and black chalk on paper

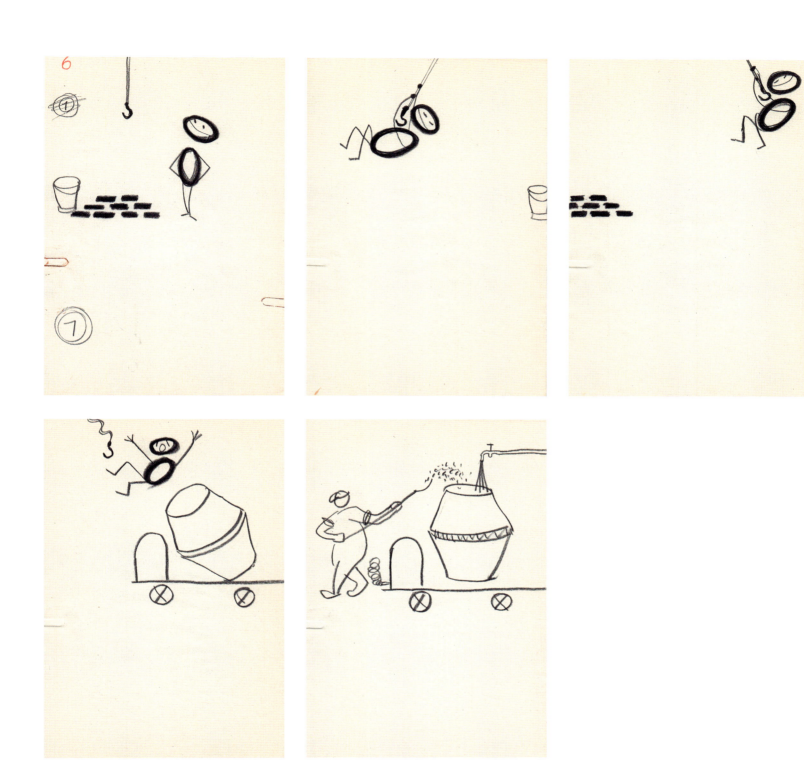

Otl Aicher, "The Sand Flea – Construction Site Stories," five drawings, pencil and black chalk on paper

Sandfloh

Dreifachschaukel
(DBGM 1 693 286)

Nr. 36

Höhe: 2,8 m   Länge: 4 m   Breite: 8 m

Das aus Stahlrohr hergestellte Schaukelgerüst wird mittels Steinschrauben auf Betonfundamenten festgehalten. Es hat eine besonders gefällige Form und ist für verschiedene Altersklassen geeignet.

Die Sitze sind mit den Gehängen starr verbunden. Die an den Querträgern befestigten Gelenke haben Sintermetallbüchsen, laufen auf Stahlkernen und sind mit Schmiernippeln versehen. Dieses Gerät kann auch für eine oder zwei Schaukeln gebaut werden.

Die Verstellung der Gelenke mit Kugellagern und Simmeringen erfordert einen Aufpreis, gibt aber die Gewähr einwandfreien Laufes ohne Wartung während der ganzen Spielzeit.

Preis auf Anfrage

Catalog of playground equipment,
Ulm, 1954, three pages, designs:
Joachim Kimpel, photos: Joachim Kimpel

Baumschaukel
Nr. 35

An einem starken Baumast wird das Schwingseil gelenkig aufgehängt und ist nach allen Seiten drehbar. Der halbmondförmige Sitz aus Eschenholz ist an einem vernickelten Halterohr befestigt.
Gebrauchsmuster 1 693 287)

Ulmer Schwingturm
Nr. 38

Gerüsthöhe 6 m. Gesamtflächenbed. 12 m ⌀
Dieses Gerüst wurde in der Reihe der „Sandflohgeräte" aus der beliebten „Baumschaukel" (DBGM 1 693 287) entwickelt. Es ist ein Schmuckstück für jeden Spielplatz und wirkt auf die Kinder aller Altersklassen wie ein starker Magnet.

Das kräftige, formschöne Stahlrohrgerüst ist nach den Regeln der Statik und Dynamik berechnet und absolut standsicher.

Die halbmondförmigen Reitsitze sind aus bestem astfreiem Holz hergestellt und bilden mit dem Griffrohr eine starre Einheit. Die Schwingseile sind gelenkig aufgehängt und nach allen Richtungen ausschwingbar.

Sandfloh

STÜTZENLOSE RUTSCHBAHN
Nr. 54

Höhe: 2 m Bahnlänge: 4,7 m Platzb. 7x1,5 m
Diese Rutschbahn ist aus Stahlrohr hergestellt und steht auf Fußplatten, die mit Steinschrauben auf Betonfundamenten befestigt werden.
Die Rutschfläche besteht aus Eschenholzleisten, ist muldenförmig und wird durch Flachstahltraversen am Trägerrohr gehalten. Die Treppe hat Stahlrohrwangen, Stufen aus hartem, gut imprägniertem Holz und einseitiges Rohrgeländer.

Playground equipment, the "swinging tower," Ulm, design: Joachim Kimpel, photo: Joachim Kimpel

top: Günther Grzimek, playground equipment, the wooden pile, Ulm, photo: Wolfgang Siol

bottom: Günther Grzimek, Römer-Insel playground, Ulm, photo: Wolfgang Siol

HANGELSTEG
"Sandfloh"   Nr. 073

DREIFACHER KLETTERBOGEN

Größte Länge: 7,9 m — Größte Breite: 2,4 m

Höhe: 2,2 m und 2 m — Platzbedarf: 8 x 2,5 m; Gew. ca. 250 kg

Die Kletterbögen aus Stahlrohr greifen so ineinander, daß sich verschiedene Bahnen des Kletterns und Hangelns ergeben. Die ungleichen Abstände der Sprossen erfordern einen höheren Grad von Geschicklichkeit.   (Gebrauchsmuster 1 693 282)

Kleine Drehwippe
Nr. 88

Länge: 2,5 m
Drehkreisdurchmesser: 2,5 m
Auf einem Dreifuß aus Flachstahl sitzt eine aus 2 Stahlrohren bestehende Wippe, die auch Drehbewegungen zuläßt. Vor den 2 Sitzen sind Haltebügel angeordnet.

Sechsarmige Drehwippe Nr. 87
(DBGM 1 693 288)

Durchmesser: 4 m   Platzbedarf 5 m ⌀

Die Drehwippe hat 12 Sitze und gestattet gleichzeitig Wipp- und Drehbewegungen. - Die Holztragarme sind mit einem schweren Stahlkörper verbunden, der mit seiner gehärteten Pfanne gelenkig auf einer Stahlkugel liegt. Diese Kugel wird auf einer feststehenden Stahlachse gehalten, die im Fundament einbetoniert ist.

Großes Schrägkarussell Nr. 67
(DBGM 1 693 190)

Durchmesser: 6,1 m
Dieses Gemeinschaftsgerät erhält durch die Schräglage der Achse bei Gewichtsverlagerung eine Drehbewegung. - Die Drehplatte läuft auf Kugellagern, besteht aus kräftigen Stahlprofilen, hat einen starken Holzbelag und ist mit einem Rohrgeländer versehen.

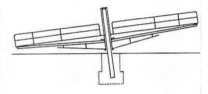

Kleine Drehscheibe Nr. 68
(DBGM 16 97 891)

Durchmesser: 2,5 m
Die Plattform besteht aus einem Stahlprofilrahmen, ist mit Holzbohlen belegt und bewegt sich mittels Kugellagern auf einer schweren Mittelachse, die in einer Bodenhülse befestigt ist. Für kleinere Kinder besonders geeignet.

Playground equipment catalog showing Günther Grzimek's „Sandfloh" designs, Ulm, 1954, three pages, photos: Wolfgang Siol

Balancier-geräte

"SEILKUNSTLER" NR. 147
ist ein zwischen 2 Rohrböcken mittels einer Doppelverschraubung straff angespanntes Drahtseil.
Länge: 6 m
Höhe über der Erde: 63 cm
Platzbedarf: 7,5 x 0,8 m
Ein sehr beliebtes und gern benutztes Balanciergerät.
(DBGM 169328)

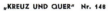

"KREUZ UND QUER" Nr. 148
Dieses Gerät besteht aus 6 straff gespannten Kunststoffbändern mit Stahlseileinlagen, die sich im spitzen Winkel kreuzen. Diese Balancierbänder laden zu einem reizvollen Begegnungsspiel auf federnden Laufstegen ein.
Länge der Bänder je 8,5 m
Höhe über dem Boden: 40 cm
Platzbedarf: 8 x 3,5 m

"ZICK-ZACK" 149
ist ein an mehreren Gabelbogen federnd aufgehängtes schmales, endloses Laufband, das mit Mipolan überzogen ist.
Es kann von mehreren Kindern gleichzeitig benutzt werden.
Höhe: 58 cm
Platzbedarf: 7 x 1,5 m

Playground catalog showing „Sandfloh" equipment, Ulm, 1954, three pages, designs: Joachim Kimpel, photos: Joachim Kimpel

Tauziehgerät „Ulmer Kraftmesser"
(DBGM)   Nr. 143

Höhe: 3 m   Platzbedarf: 11 x 2 m

An diesem Tauziehgerät können größere Gruppen von Kindern gleichzeitig ihre Muskeln stärken. Es erzieht zur Gemeinschaftsleistung.

Das über eine Rolle laufende starke Hanfseil ist in der Ruhestellung zwischen den Holmen des Bockes aufgehängt, während die beiden Enden unten festgehalten werden.

Ziehen die Kinder am Seil, so senkt sich die Rolle, bis das Seil waagerecht nach beiden Seiten gezogen werden kann. Ist die schwächere Gruppe bis an das Gerät herangezogen, dann ist der Kampf entschieden. - Lassen die Kinder das Seil los, so wird es durch Gegengewichte wieder hochgezogen.

Balancierkugeln

Sandfloh

Durchmesser der Kugel: 50 cm, aus Aluminium gegossen.
Das Gerät dient zu Gleichgewichtsübungen, erzieht zur vollendeten Körperbeherrschung und wird auch gern von Erwachsenen benutzt. Es gibt drei Ausführungen:

Nr. 144
Die Kugel wird auf festem Rasenboden ohne Laufbahn verwendet und ist auch für den Privatgarten geeignet.

Nr. 145
Die Kugel bewegt sich auf einer geraden, ca. 5 m langen Laufbahn und ist gegen seitliche Verdrehungen durch Führungsketten gesichert.
Platzbedarf: 7 x 1 m
Auf Wunsch m. Aufstiegstreppe.

Nr. 146
Die Laufschiene aus Stahlrohr, die spiralförmig nach dem Mittelblock verläuft, ist im Fundament so befestigt, daß nur eine schmale Fläche über dem Boden steht. Die Kugel wird durch ein Drahtseil am Mittelblock gehalten und bleibt beim Umlauf stets auf d. Laufkante. Dieses sehr beliebte Gerät wurde auf der Bundesgartenschau 1957 in Köln gezeigt und fand große Beachtung. Platzbed: 5 m ⌀

Nr. 147 Die Kugel wird durch ein Drahtseil an einer Mittelachse gehalten und bewegt sich auf einer Kreisbahn aus Stahlrohr.
Platzbedarf: 5 m ⌀

Rolling beam in a „Sandfloh" playground,
Ulm, design: Joachim Kimpel,
photo: Joachim Kimpel

Cemetery Weingarten

Weingarten, St. Mary's Cemetery,
walkway of the Funeral Hall, 1961

Weingarten, St. Mary's Cemetery, walkway of
the Funeral Hall, 1961

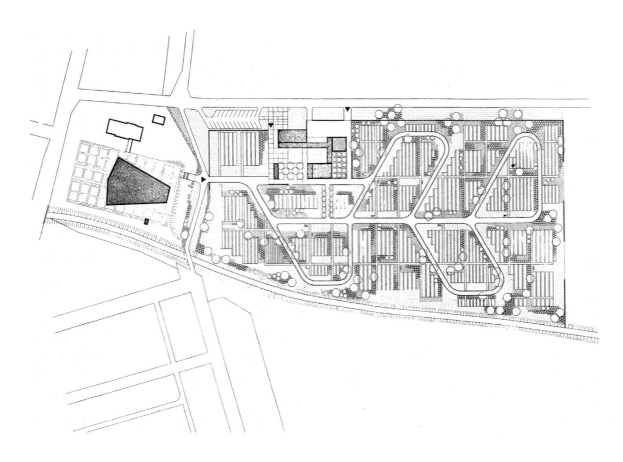

Weingarten, St. Mary's Cemetery, plan drawing, site plan, without scale, 1961

The Marienfriedhof is a cemetery situated on the western periphery of Weingarten. The town with its cathedral, the significant High Baroque Basilica of St. Martin, became the first area of activity for Günther Grzimek after the Second World War. He designed the flight of steps to St. Martin's forecourt in 1947, the extension to the cemetery in 1952, and the grounds of Weingarten Abbey between 1962 and 1965.

The Marienfriedhof was built in 1961, as the cemetery at Kreuzberg had become too small. In the Weingarten project, Grzimek was commissioned to develop the overall plans, including the design for the cemetery chapel. He collaborated with the architect Hans Frieder Eychmüller, as he had done on other projects in Ulm.

The complex consists of three buildings: a cemetery chapel-cum-funeral hall, a room for viewing, and the cemetery offices. Covered walkways connect all components. The concept is based on a 3.6 x 3.6 meter grid. The chapel is entered from a forecourt and through a tripartite portico. The space is 10.8 meters wide and 18 meters long. Opposite the entrance, a large glazed wall in three sections opens up views onto the planting and trees. Inside, the congregation of mourners sits in front of this ceiling-high window. The coffin is laid out in front of the window.

The materials inside the chapel and in the exterior space are exposed concrete with planed formwork, glass, and natural-colored pine. "In order to achieve a roughly similar surface texture, the dimensions of the shuttering boards used were exactly the same as the width of the boards for the timber surfaces."[1] In the forecourt, Grzimek designed a strict network of paths, complemented with trees planted on a grid.

The architecture suggests that at that time Grzimek was intensively studying sacred buildings and cemeteries in Scandinavia. The architectural style of Gunnar Asplund and Sigurd Lewerentz, for example at Skogskyrkogården cemetery in Stockholm, was frequently adapted in Germany in the 1960s. In a 1965 issues of the journal *Kunst und Kirche*, Grzimek published an article presenting his Weingarten project. The same issue features numerous Swedish cemeteries from the 1960s.

1 Günther Grzimek, "Friedhofskapelle in Weingarten / Württemberg," *Kunst und Kirche* 28, vol. 2 (1965): 74.

Weingarten, St. Mary's cemetery, forecourt, 2021, photo: Regine Keller

Weingarten, St. Mary's Cemetery, view from the Funeral Hall, 2021, photo: The Pk. Odessa Co / Markus Lanz

Weingarten, St. Mary's Cemetery, Funeral Hall,
2021, photo: The Pk. Odessa Co / Markus Lanz

Weingarten, St. Mary's Cemetery,
walkway of the Funeral Hall, 2021,
photo: The Pk. Odessa Co / Markus Lanz

New Cemetery Ulm

New Cemetery in Ulm, white stones, photo: Wolfgang Siol

As the director of the parks department in Ulm, Grzimek was also able to integrate the cemeteries office into his area of responsibility, beginning in 1950. In the years before his time in Ulm, he had designed cemetery expansions in cities such as Weingarten. In Ulm, he was then able to incorporate these large open spaces into his landscape plan for the whole city.

First he worked on the redevelopment of the New Cemetery in the city center, a cemetery dating back to 1905, and later on its expansion. He took great care to retain the existing structure and some of the many mature trees. He was able to design the expansion in the style of a cemetery park. An old quarry was the basis for the redevelopment. After the Second World War, memorials for war victims were developed in conjunction with cemeteries, a task within his responsibility and one to which he was especially committed.

At Ulm, he placed large steles made of white concrete in the landscape, like slabs one behind the other, all facing the same way: "white stones." The steles are of different sizes and are surrounded by a field of protruding metal crosses. Metal letters are fixed to the slabs. The dimensions of the individual slabs correspond to the number of fallen soldiers, the missing, or the victims of air raids on Ulm.

New Cemetery in Ulm, 2021,
photo: The Pk. Odessa Co / Markus Lanz

New Cemetery in Ulm, 2021,
photo: The Pk. Odessa Co / Markus Lanz

New Cemetery in Ulm, 2021,
photo: The Pk. Odessa Co / Markus Lanz

Green spaces planning in Ulm, pamphlet, 1954

Green Spaces Planning Ulm

Green spaces planning in Ulm, pamphlet, 1954

Problems of a Growing City is Grzimek's subtitle for a pamphlet he wrote in 1954 as a summary of his work heading the parks department in Ulm. The layout for the pamphlet was devised by Otl Aicher and Hans Conrad at the Ulm School of Design. The report's clear graphics reinforce the structured contents of the designs documented by Grzimek. The initial conditions of the city, which had been destroyed in the war, have already been described. The report offered a new vision of necessary planning controls for the rapidly growing city, and in particular its open spaces. Controls would have to be in place before Ulm grew into a large city. At that time, Grzimek and many others were engaged with the concept of the high-density and low-density city, which planners such as Hofmann and Göderitz had developed from ideas in the Athens Charter and presented as a new paradigm for town planning. Grzimek saw green space as having potential for adding spatial structure, limiting sprawl, developing well-proportioned neighborhoods, and providing recreation areas. Based on a detailed analysis of Ulm's historical conditions and its morphological and natural features, he formulated a landscape plan that prepared the way for a network of open green spaces.

Existing parks, cemeteries, and urban woodlands formed the basis of the network. An urban green promenade along the course of the Danube, as it traverses through the city from the northeast to the southwest, was to link up the open spaces. Additionally, allotment gardens and sports grounds were incorporated into the network. In his pamphlet, Grzimek clearly describes the functions of the green areas, which still apply today. He highlights the significance of the proposed open space and its potential to eliminate various deficits, such as lack of light and lack of ultraviolet rays, mainly to benefit the health of the population; lack of contact with the ground, due to people being far removed from vital processes and experiencing nature; and a lack of the color green, which has a calming effect on people according to the psychology of color. In addition to these health aspects, he also worked with the plant sociologist Heinz Ellenberg on ecological findings, which he intended to apply to his landscape concepts. The landscape projects not only put forward proposals at an urban development scale, but also at a detailed design scale. Allotment sites, playgrounds, cemeteries, and open spaces in housing areas, such as the Eselsberg neighborhood, were selected as examples, and designs were presented for them. The Römer-Insel (Romans' Island) playground is an example of this (see "Sandfloh: The Sand Flea Campaign," p. 67).

Grzimek began to publish his work early in his career and presented it to his professional colleagues for discussion. Time and again, he succeeded in having whole issues of the journal *Garten + Landscnaft* devoted to topics related to his work. This was the case in 1954, when the journal published an issue on "Landscape in Ulm." At the same time, he organized symposia of specialists, where he presented his findings for discussion.

Ulm lost its old town in the Second World War, except for a few remnants, and thus lost much of its former beauty. What is left is a diverse townscape with hills, valleys, and the rivers Danube, Iller, and Blau. Ulm can become a beautiful and healthy city again if it succeeds in resolutely implementing the current plans and designing its open spaces to befit modern urban living. The proposals shown are not interchangeable with open space elsewhere in the city. The residential and industrial areas in the preparatory land use plan are arranged within the network of green spaces, making its impact as large as possible. Essentially, no new open spaces should be created, but the existing ones retained and adapted according to the needs of a growing city. If the significance of green space within the city is recognized and, despite myriad problems and a shortage of land, the necessary measures are implemented, future generations will live in a beautiful and healthy urban environment. This makes our generation's obligation a thankful task.[1]

A glance at Ulm's current green open spaces shows that Grzimek was not able to realize all of his ideas. The 2030 Regional Garden Show will mark a new attempt to develop Grzimek's concepts and continue to weave together the much-publicized network of green spaces.

1 Günther Grzimek, *Grünplanung in Ulm* (Ulm: Stadtverwaltung Ulm, 1954).

Green spaces planning in Ulm, chapter of pamphlet, 1954

School of Engineering Ulm

School of Engineering in Ulm, 2021,
photo: The Pk. Odessa Co / Markus Lanz

Günter Behnisch won the competition for the construction of the School of Engineering—today the University of Applied Sciences—in Ulm, and his proposal was implemented in 1959. The landscape architect Günther Grzimek was recommended to him, and this was their first project together. They soon found a common design approach.

Prittwitzstrasse in Ulm, the site of the former School of Engineering and the current University of Applied Sciences, is in the neighborhood of the historical Veste Wilhelmsburg fortress. The existing sloping terrain with a stand of large Scots pines provided a good landscape setting for Behnisch's strictly functionalist building. The grounds are reminiscent of the Ulm School of Design on the Kuhberg, one of the hills surrounding the city. In contrast, the School of Engineering in Ulm is the first public building constructed of prefabricated components. Grzimek set the building complex, which was designed on a strict grid, in a carefully contoured landscape with a few strong clumps of trees and shrubs. He turned the intricate topography into a dramatic play of landform that allows the building to be entered at different levels, with large staircases and gently curving paths providing access to the campus. Here he started to experiment with different materials; in the "green" parking lot, for instance, he used grass block pavers to reduce soil sealing.

Today, the site is a protected historic monument. The university's size and protected status leave little room for expansion, a fact that has led to years of debate in Ulm.

Carlo Weber, School of Engineering in Ulm
1959–1963, perspective sketch, 1962

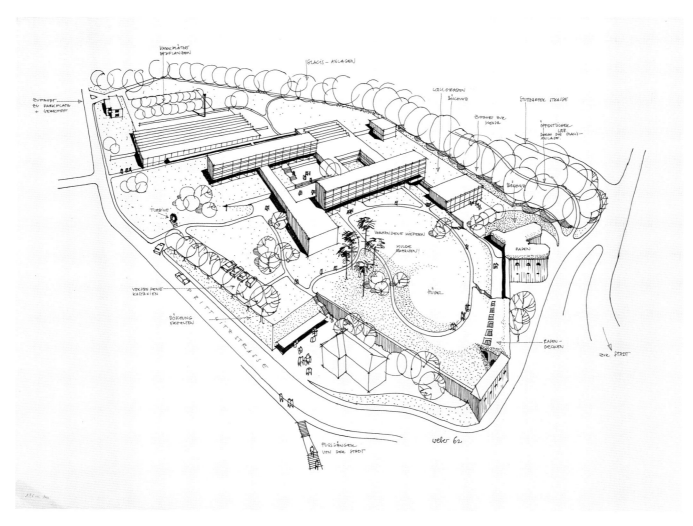

School of Engineering in Ulm, 1970,
photo: Helmut Watter

School of Engineering in Ulm, lawn parking lot,
1970, photo: Helmut Watter

Green spaces planning for Darmstadt,
book cover by Otl Aicher, 1963

Günther Grzimek
Grünplanung Darmstadt

Green Spaces Planning Darmstadt

Between 1960 and 1963, Grzimek worked under the commission of the Darmstadt municipal authority to prepare a plan for the city's green spaces as part of the preparatory land use plan. In 1965, following some revisions, the proposal was also published in a book entitled *Grünplanung Darmstadt* (Green Spaces Planning in Darmstadt). After leaving his position at the planning department in Ulm in 1960, Grzimek had founded his own landscape architecture practice, and in the wake of the new German Federal Building Act, he recognized a need for urgent action in the planning of green spaces. For the first time, legislation stipulated mandatory urban land use planning and required municipalities to draw up preparatory land use plans and local development plans. These regulations did not stipulate open space plans for urban areas, even though a myriad of the utilization categories were directly related to open spaces, and consequently required landscape expertise. Grzimek already had experience on a similar scale from his citywide open space plan for Ulm, and he saw new opportunities for his practice. Many cities followed Darmstadt in seeking to engage Grzimek's expert services in contributing to the conceptual stage of the preparatory land use plan. He developed a new concept in Darmstadt, which much later became a mandatory and integral part of regular urban land use planning in Germany in the context of the federal nature conservation legislation of 1976.

Darmstadt's rapid growth made intervention necessary. Initially, a negative plan was prepared to identify areas that should not be built on; this in turn would produce a positive plan to show developable areas and help establish requirements for future green spaces. In his planning approach, Grzimek described the potential impact that landscape planning could have on town planning.

The statement "landscape planning by way of town planning" still causes friction with town planners today. Grzimek's concept for Darmstadt at that time arises from the realization that three factors in the postwar period had led to poor living conditions in cities. These were, as he wrote, motorization, urban flight, and the structural change of agriculture—phenomena of the 1960s that led to large transport problems in large cities, urban sprawl on the periphery by designating ever more development land, as well as industrial forms of agricultural production in cleared landscapes. Not until the late 1960s did professional circles and politicians begin voicing concern about the limitations of urban growth. With the formulation of the objectives of the German Federal Nature Conservation Act (1974), landscape planning became a tool for creating regulatory effects on these processes. As early as 1960, Grzimek believed that managing landscape ecology and maintaining an ecological balance should be fostered. By then he was already demanding that landscape planning become a major factor when planning housing developments:

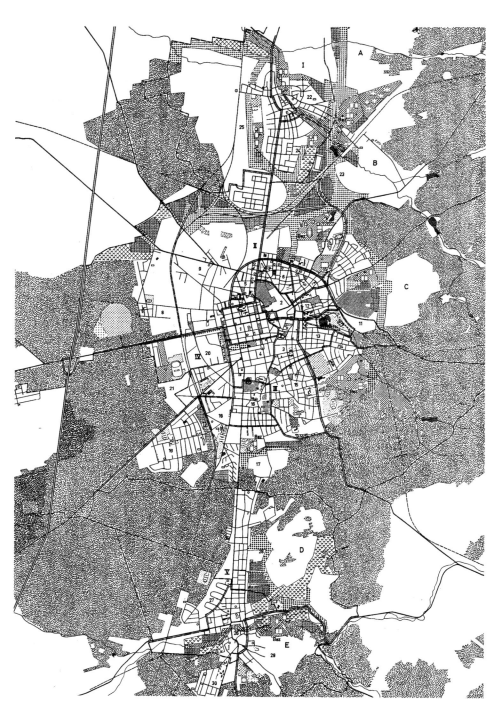

Green spaces planning for Darmstadt, green areas plan, 1963

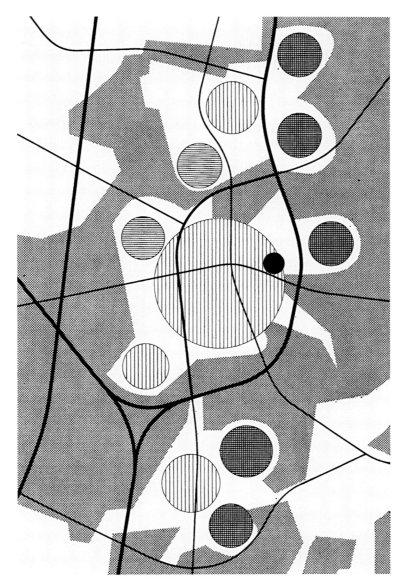

Green spaces planning for Darmstadt, structural concept, 1963

... not to protect the landscape, but to increase its social, ecological, and health effectiveness. It does not mean that landscape and urban civilization are incompatible, as was previously believed. A progressive landscape concept does not shy away from the risk of interpenetration.[1]
This is clearly aimed against the concept of garden cities, which were to form a complementary model for industrialization, or the goal of only protecting landscape from "large-scale land destruction," as was formulated by, among others, the landscape architect Walter Rossow at the Deutscher Werkbund in 1959.

Grzimek called for a new type of landscape and wrote, "Structured landscape planning, instead of evenly spread disorder, will attempt to create density in limited areas, and instead of a sprawling city, create local concentrations. This will free up open spaces for new functions to be allocated in between the single core areas."[2] Today the capacity of landscapes to provide ecological benefits is called ecosystem services.

In Darmstadt, Grzimek proposed new housing developments, which he called "woodland satellites," alongside the open spaces. They are developments in their own right, surrounded by open space and to be understood as a countermodel to cities whose edges develop concentrically outwards. Between 1965 and 1970, together with the urban planner and architect Ernst May, Grzimek worked on one of these developments at Kranichstein in the northeast of Darmstadt.

In considering the landscape needs of the entire city, several design projects ensued for Grzimek in Darmstadt: urban parks as at Treppenstrasse and Döngesborngasse, the so-called Wolfskehl'scher Garten, and Bahnhofsplatz.

Grzimek hoped for a wide audience when he published his ideas on giving landscape architecture a town planning focus. Therefore, he wrote an easily comprehensible introduction to his book. The chapters "Analytical Open Space Planning," "Urban Climate," and "Urban Health," as well as his ideas on vegetation types, were all intended to make the need for a well-considered network of green spaces in growing cities accessible to a general readership. His work was well received among town planners and architects, while the professional associations for landscape architects only adopted his pioneering concepts much later.

When explaining his concepts, Grzimek talks of vegetation types, describing them as "performance vegetation" (*Leistungsgrün*), a term coined by him and which he had developed from his experiences in Ulm. He had initially devised this concept for a potential research proposal he wanted to submit to the Technical University of Munich in 1960. In *Grünplanung Darmstadt*, he published the text in an easily intelligible form. With the term "performance vegetation," he attempts to evaluate the benefits of vegetation types used in landscape construction, agriculture, and forestry, in terms of their recreational value and with a view to their impact on urban health. In the city, he differentiates between green spaces for recreation, play, sports, transport, schools, ornamental value, and work. These areas should deliver the optimum ecological and functional benefits—in other words, they should be green spaces that perform. He critiques cities whose open spaces generally have low usability, inadequate space for vegetation, and underused opportunities for visual separating areas with vegetation, and whose maintenance costs are too high. His study begins by looking at vegetation in social housing areas, and he points out that there were no scientifically substantiated numeric values for quantifying the open space requirements in cities.

In a preliminary study in 1965, he wrote:
In its ideal form, vegetation in social housing guarantees physical exercise in terms of play and movement (seating, sandboxes, footpaths), it provides the largest possible mass of vegetation (oxygen, humidity, noise filter) to have health and therapeutic effects, it creates visual isolation between apartments.… It should be possible to achieve these benefits at a low cost—especially in maintenance.

Grzimek developed what he called "greening scores":
Garden – 5
Open-air swimming pools – 3
Park – 2
Ornamental planting – 1

As well as characteristic values for the assessment of surfaces:
Lawn – 1
Meadow – 3
Shrubs – 3
Trees, shrubs, groundcover – 5

His goal was to provide characteristic values that would serve as a tool for planners and decision makers to help achieve the previously described requirements of high effectiveness and low maintenance. Based on this hypothesis, Grzimek developed analysis plans which, furnished with the aforementioned characteristic values, would provide an illustration of the open space score. For example, in one balance sheet he applied his system to the vegetation in existing social housing areas, and wrote:

Using the above scores one must conclude that the vegetation in current social housing areas represents exactly the opposite of what would be needed according to its quantifying.… Performance vegetation seeks to expand usability to the largest possible area of the total green space.… The vegetation surface can be increased by several hundred percent, provided good light levels in the vegetation layers have been considered and despite consideration of the housing frontages. In order to achieve this, itwill be advisable to plant in three layers: herb layer, shrub layer, tree layer. We can speak of three vegetation levels.

Material inspection, experience, and collaboration with experts enable the selection of plants and plant groups with the goal of finding an assessment scale. Assessment is made according to the following qualities:

Botanic qualities—ecological competition, self-fertilizing plants, light requirements, resilience, vigor, lifespan, etc.

Social qualities—noise filter, dust filter, oxygen production, evaporation, hazard, maintenance costs.

In his ideas about performance vegetation, Grzimek had anticipated as early as 1965 what we are currently practicing in climate action plans and Biotope Area Factors (BAF). So far, the BAF system has only been adopted in Berlin, while it has not yet been implemented in Munich, for example.

In this respect, too, Grzimek is a pioneer in describing the ecological and social framework conditions that urban vegetation can deliver.

1 Günther Grzimek, *Grünplanung Darmstadt* (Darmstadt: Eduard Roether Verlag, 1965), 19f.
2 Grzimek, *Grünplanung Darmstadt*, 21.

Green spaces planning for Darmstadt,
"performance green" design, 1963

			Grünmasse Sommer	Grünmasse Winter	Grünmasse insgesamt	Einfluß Kleinklima	Sauerstoffproduktion	Staubfilter	Lärmschutz	optische Isolierung	**Gesamtleistung**
Rasen		kurz geschnitten immergrün hohe Pflegekosten	1	1	1	1	1	1	0	0	**0,7**
Wiese		2–3mal im Jahr geschnitten immergrün	3	1	2	3	3	3	1	0	**2,0**
Gemüse		Boden intensiv bearbeitet keine geschlossene Fläche im Winter offen	2	0	1	2	2	2	1	1	**1,4**
Getreide		nur im Anwuchs grün	1	0	0,5	1	1	3	2	2	**1,3**
Büsche		in Vegetationszeit intensives Grün geringer Pflegeaufwand	6	2	4	6	4	6	5	6	**4,9**
Hecke geschnitten		Verdichtung der Gesamtstruktur hoher Pflegeaufwand	4	2	3	5	3	6	4	4	**4,0**
Park		getrennter Wuchs in Bodendecke-, Busch- und Baumzone hoher Pflegeaufwand	13	3	8	12	8	10	8	6	**8,5**
Nadelwald		immergrün geringe Bodendecke kein Zwischenwuchs	12	8	10	10	10	8	16	16	**11,2**
Laubwald		Sommergrün im Frühjahr Unterwuchs	18	6	12	16	12	14	14	14	**13,2**
Leistungsgrün		intensiver Wuchs in drei Zonen	20	12	16	18	16	20	20	20	**17,7**

New Botanical Garden Marburg

New Botanical Garden in Marburg, greenhouses, 2017, photo: Gesa Coordes

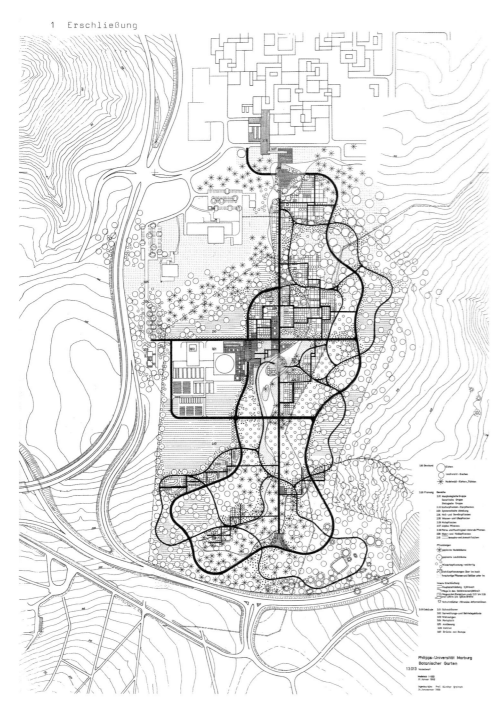

New Botanical Garden in Marburg, preliminary plan development, 1966

In 1961, the Hesse government decided to relocate the natural sciences department of the Philipps University—which was undergoing expansion—from the center of the city to the woodlands of the Lahnberge hills to the north.[1] The old Botanical Garden had been situated in the middle of Marburg since 1527, and plans for a new botanical garden in 1966 called for the relocation of the Institute of Systematic Botany to this new site; the move, however, did not take place until 1977.[2] The new Botanical Garden, about ten hectares in size, was to be laid out on a twenty-hectare site south of the new buildings. Since the garden was to be located around three kilometers from the town center, it was clear to Grzimek that it had to be designed for scientific and educational purposes and not for general visitors.

Grzimek found a stand of spruce with scattered birch, ash, and oak in the existing Lahnberge woodland. A stand of oak trees, some of them mature, contained beautiful single specimens that he wanted to retain. In the south, a woodland of mature beech trees was waiting to be felled. The site has a north–south aspect extending over a length of about 750 meters. Its width varies from 110 to 420 meters. It contains a one-hectare area of Celtic burial mounds that had to be integrated and made accessible by footpath only.

Grzimek was able to influence the siting of the administration buildings, the greenhouses, and the plant nursery. He chose a central position to avoid long distances in the future operation of the site. The proposed greenhouses were also to benefit from this position as a central "station" within the site, as Grzimek described it.

Grzimek was solely responsible for this project and was free to act on his design approach. His program proposed integrating the design into the local site conditions, retaining about 50 percent of the existing woodland, which amounted to around ten hectares. The classical teaching program used by institutes of natural sciences served as a starting point for developing a concept. This included the presentation of the botanical system, morphology, plant genetics, and pharmacognosy (medicinal herbs). However, Grzimek did not follow conventional approaches as to how systematic gardens should be laid out, and his rational, functionalist way helped with this. In addition to the botanical-scientific program that needed to be established, the garden could provide a learning and recreational space for the institute's staff and students, a social benefit that ranked highly in Grzimek's concepts, which were always user-oriented. He thought it important not to deliver prestigious green spaces, but to develop the design brief into new and very specific aesthetics. In 1967, he wrote in an explanatory text for his preliminary design:

The need to meet scientific and educational demands ruled out creating a plant and flower show along traditional values. In fact, a site that follows its scientific purpose can even lead to

top: New Botanical Garden in Marburg, perennial beds at the Botanical Institute, 1969/70

bottom: New Botanical Garden in Marburg, view to the Botanical Institute, 1969/70

New Botanical Garden in Marburg, forest edge with azaleas, 2022, photo: Alexander Ruppel

New Botanical Garden in Marburg, forest scene with perennial plantings, 1969/70

New Botanical Garden in Marburg, perennial plantings at the Botanical Institute, 1969/70

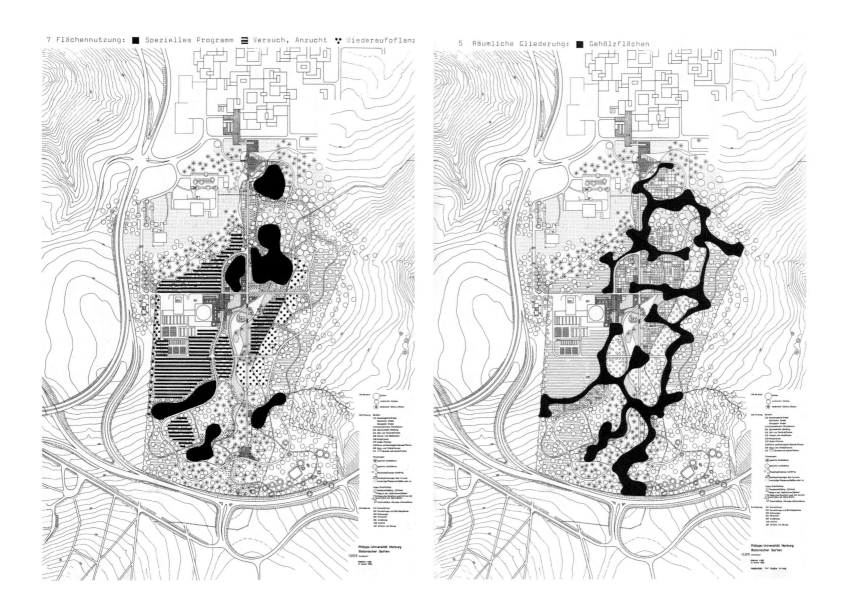

left: New Botanical Garden in Marburg, preliminary plan of land use program, 1966

right: New Botanical Garden in Marburg, preliminary plan of spatial arrangement, wood areas, 1966

innovative design criteria. These include the design and boundary treatment of characteristic green spaces and a correspondence in scale of space and access.

Using extensive site analyses, Grzimek developed his design ideas based on existing soil qualities and moisture gradients. Insufficient sunlight on the site required extensive ground modeling to create areas that would be exposed to the sun for planting. The required soils could be taken from the site itself. Earthworks within the site did not require long transport routes. Additional fill material was taken from the excavation at a neighboring institute's construction site, a resource-saving method that also ensures a favorable ecological footprint. Grzimek wanted to integrate the garden into the surroundings by means of visual links. In the north, these are views of the valley landscape at Amöneburg; in the south, a view of the wooded hilltops.

Grzimek categorized the site of the Botanical Garden according to three vegetation groups: botanical groups, woody plants, and woodlands. The far south of the grounds was suitable for the alpine garden. In the southeast, he placed the fern ravine in an existing erosion gully, and the heather and acid-loving plants were established in the pine woodland according to appropriate site conditions. Another of the design's features is a pond located near the greenhouses with viewing terraces and heated pools.

Water

Grzimek emphasized the significance of the aquatic components in the botanical program. A watercourse and a pond were given special importance. A stream was to traverse the site from north to south. The pond was sited in a central location near the greenhouses and the terraces.

Plants

The botanical program of herbaceous plants was to be established in small areas. The theme of woody plants was to extend through the whole garden in a self-contained system. The division of woody plants into groups followed systematic and ecological criteria. The third theme, forest area, was established in the existing woodland, which extended into the landscape beyond the site boundary.

Paths

Access and circulation within the site were laid out around the buildings: the institute building in the north, the administration and nursery in the west. The access concept corresponds to the three vegetation areas and follows a strict system of coordinates. Grzimek based this on the structural grid of 7.2 x 7.2 meters used for the new institute building; that is the design dimension of the prefabricated reinforced concrete supports. A 3.6-meter-wide and 750-meter-long spine runs along the center. It forms a main axis starting at the institute building in the north. The aim of the clear and functional layout was easy orientation and its potential to serve as an information axis between applied and theoretical botany. The botanical classification system is given a guiding direction here. Orthogonal to the main axis is a secondary network of paths whose widths range from 1.8 to 0.3 meters. The botanical groups are systematically mapped against this grid. Additionally, an organic, park-like network of paths mainly provides access to the peripheral areas.

Construction costs

At the preliminary design stage in 1967, Grzimek estimated the Botanical Garden, comprising ten hectares requiring high maintenance and ten hectares requiring low maintenance, would cost 5,915,000 Deutschmarks. After a preliminary cost assessment by the building control authority, Grzimek had to issue a statement and reduce the project to 4.8 million Deutschmarks. The stringent path axis was met with criticism. While the building control authority did not appreciate the gesture, the Botanical Institute's representative, Professor Wilhelm Nultsch, considered the systematic axis to be indispensable. The concept of the axis was finally retained, but Grzimek had to make some amendments. The files at the archive show the painstaking process Grzimek had to go through to achieve the required cost reductions. Cuts were made in the project right up until the end. The total number of paths was reduced, and work on soil cultivation was carried out by the nursery staff, among other measures. Even during the final stage of the project, savings had to be made, for example by reducing the width of paths from 1.8 to 1.5 meters. This still seems to be the procedure today.

Wonderful plans have been preserved in the archive that once again illustrate the clarity of the design and the systematic nature of the concept. The Botanical Garden in Magdeburg, designed in a collaboration between the landscape practice Günther Grzimek and Lore Kellinghaus, deserves to be rediscovered.

1 Christian Reichard, *Kurze Übersicht über die Entwicklung des Fachs Chemie an der Universität Marburg von 1609 bis zur Gegenwart* (Marburg: Philipps–Universität Marburg, 2020), https://www.uni-marburg.de/de/fb15/fachbereich/dekanat/chemie.pdf, 12.
2 Reichard, *Kurze Übersicht*.

New Botanical Garden in Marburg, alpen garden, 2022, photo: Alexander Ruppel

View of the Olympic Park, 2021,
photo: The Pk. Odessa Co / Markus Lanz

Olympic Park Munich

Olympic Park Competition, first prize,
Behnisch & Partners, Stuttgart, 1968

Olympic Park Competition, second prize,
Nickels, Orth, Marg, Hamburg, 1968

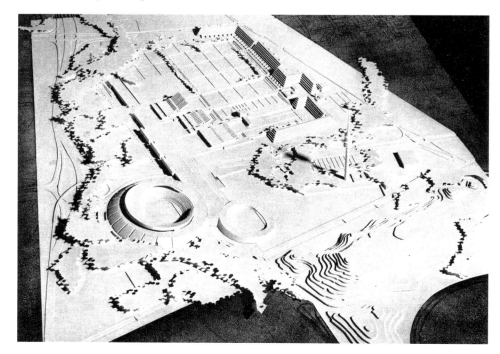

The design of the Munich Olympic Park is a milestone in modern landscape architecture. The park and its buildings are world-renowned for their architectural significance, and since 1998 they have been listed individually as monuments by the Bavarian State Office for the Preservation of Historical Monuments. A bid by the City of Munich to make the Olympic Park a UNESCO World Heritage Site has been ongoing since 2021. The occasion of the park's fiftieth anniversary in 2022 offers an ideal moment to review the history of the Olympic Park's origins, its fundamental themes, and its future.

A look back at Munich's application phase in 1965 shows that favorable conditions already existed in the city for such a complex. A site for the Olympic Stadium had already been found: the Oberwiesenfeld, a wide flat area, a former military parade ground, and later Munich's first airport. At that time, the area, which was next to the BMW production plant, still lay on the outskirts of the city and seemed to offer sufficient land for development as a venue. A connection via the later "Middle Ring" (ring road) was already planned here and was integrated into future development ideas. A central sports facility had already been slated for the site as part of a general urban development concept in 1963, as well as a student dormitory since 1960. Another component of the future site development was the integration of the sixty-meter-high hill south of the Oberwiesenfeld; it had been heaped up from the rubble of the ruins of the Second World War. The telecommunications tower of the Federal Post Office, as well as the ice rink at its foot, were further elements ready to be integrated into the complex.

It worked in the plan's favor that the city had already envisioned constructing a large stadium here in the north of Munich. A competition was held in 1964, in which the architects Rüdiger Henschker and Wilhelm Deiss had won first and second prizes respectively; third prize went to Heinle Wischer; and fourth to Erwin Schleich and Günter Herbst.[1] Based on this result, within four weeks the building department drew up a concept for the remaining Olympic buildings on the Oberwiesenfeld. A large parking lot was planned for the area of today's Olympic Lake, and the stadium was initially foreseen on the location of today's university sports complex. These were the plans that Munich presented in 1965 as part of its bid for the Olympic Games.

In that same year, during the bidding phase, the designer Otl Aicher was appointed director of design for the Munich Games. From 1966, he built up the

Games' visual design department. Aicher had achieved great success with designs for the corporate identities of well-known companies such as Braun, Lufthansa, and BASF. Resistance to his appointment arose within the city because Aicher was not a Munich resident. The Bavarian chairman of the Deutscher Werkbund, Werner Wirsing, successfully campaigned for Aicher in two letters to Hans-Jochen Vogel. Aicher had demonstrated his "modern functionalism" design approach at the World's Fairs in Brussels and Montreal; his idea of a new aesthetic, developed at the Ulm School of Design among other places, fitted in with the basic idea of providing the 1972 Olympic Games with a modern and open appearance.

At their meeting in Rome in 1966, the International Olympic Committee awarded the 1972 Games to Munich, but not without criticism regarding the architectural concept. It was judged too car-friendly and was further criticized for sacrificing the most beautiful part of the landscape to a parking lot. The purely functionalist appearance also came in for critique. Voices were raised in architectural circles as well as in the media, with calls for an international competition. Rejecting the appeals of the building department, which advocated the time- and cost-saving plans submitted under its direction, the city council decided in favor of a national competition, to be held the following year. Finally, on February 1, 1967, a national urban planning ideas competition

Olympic Park Competition, fourth prize A, Ludwig, Raab, Wiegand, Zuleger, 1968

Olympic Park Competition, fourth prize B, Holstein, Frowein, 1968

Olympic Park Competition, third prize, Heinle, Wischer, Stuttgart, 1968

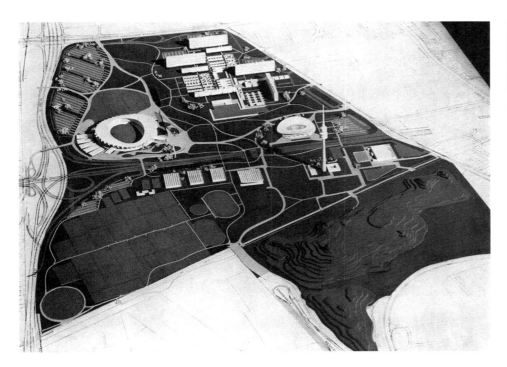

Olympic Park Competition, fourth prize C, Beier, Dahms, Grube, Harden, Laskowski, 1968

for the Oberwiesenfeld was announced, as well as a building competition for the individual Olympic Games buildings. Five months later, on July 3, 101 architects submitted their proposals. In order to display them for the jury, three exhibition halls with a total area of 10,000 square meters were needed. Then, from September 4 to 8, nineteen judges evaluated the competition entries, with the architect Egon Eiermann from Karlsruhe as chairman of the jury. The final jury meeting took place from October 11 to 13. The team Behnisch & Partners, with its legendary silk-stocking model of the bold tent roof construction, emerged victorious. This proposal had triggered heated discussion in the jury; nevertheless, it won seventeen of the nineteen votes. Eiermann wrote in his jury statement:

The jury does not see itself in a position to comment definitively on the usefulness of this proposal. Unfortunately, with the questionable nature of the proposed roofing, it must impose restrictions on this design, which is excellent in all respects, as regards the required durability and operational safety.[2]

Second prize went to the team Klaus Nickels, Timm Ohrt, and Anke Marg from Hamburg. Third prize was awarded to Erwin Heinle and Robert Wischer from Stuttgart. Three fourth prizes were given to Gordon Ludwig, Franz Raab, Gerd Wiegand, and Wolf Zuleger; the Stuttgart office Freie Architekten Eberhard Holstein and Car-Herbert Frowein; and the Brunswick group Baier, Dahms, Grube, Harden, Laskowski.[3]

The period that followed was marked by disputes about the feasibility of the tent roof construction, which had already been a subject of debate in the jury. Doubts about the feasibility of the structure, qualified as "utopian" by the jury members, remained persistent. The teams of architects who won first and third prizes were initially asked to revise their designs.

Günter Behnisch had recruited Frei Otto (1925–2015), an architect specializing in biomorphic constructions, to manage the technical aspects of the planned tent roofs. Together with Fritz Leonhardt

left: Carlo Weber, Olympic Park, trans-regional connections, sketch, undated

right: Carlo Weber, Olympic Park, initial situation, sketch, undated

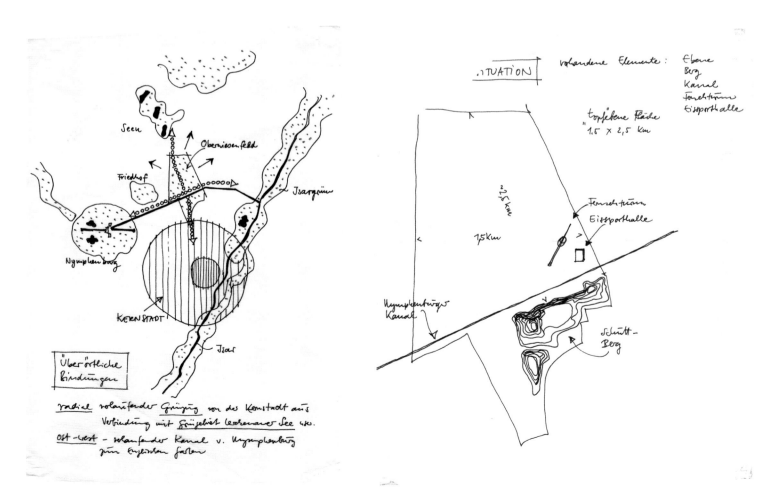

left: Carlo Weber, Olympic Park, buildings in the landscape, sketch, undated

right: Carlo Weber, Olympic Park, modeling of the terrain, sketch, undated

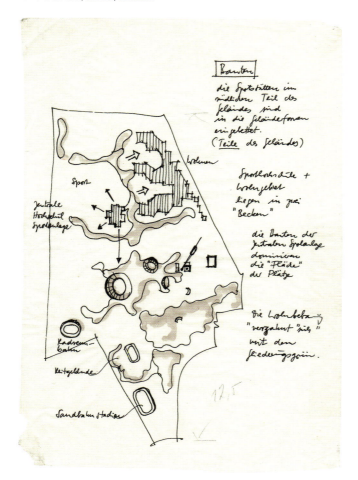 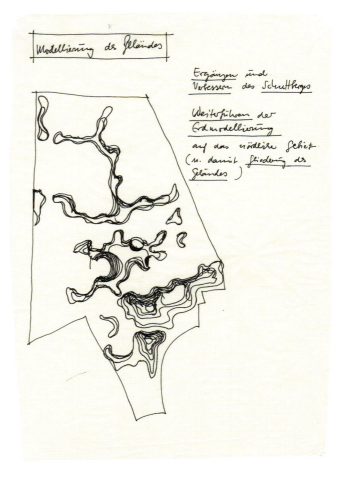

Carlo Weber

Carlo Weber (1934–2014) was born in Saarbrücken. He studied at the Technical University of Stuttgart and at the Ecole Nationale Supérieure des Beaux-Arts in Paris, graduating in Stuttgart in 1961. From 1960 to 1965 he was employed at Behnisch and Lambart in Stuttgart, becoming a partner at Behnisch & Partners in 1966. In 1980 he founded his own office with Fritz Auer. From 1980 to 1990 he lectured at the University of Stuttgart and from 1992 to 1999 was professor for Building Design and Planning at the Technical University in Dresden. In 1996 he became a member of the Saxon Academy of Arts.

and Wolfhart Andrä, he was responsible for the calculations and realization of this bold idea. Frei Otto, together with Rolf Gutbrod, had already proven that he could master such tasks with the German Pavilion in Montreal in 1967. A "roof without shadows" was envisioned.

Doubts remained, however, because the pavilion in Montreal was much smaller and the production was not considered comparable. Two expert opinions by professors at the Technical University of Munich subsequently declared the structure to be unfeasible. The engineers working with Frei Otto were nevertheless able to convince the authorities, and so the team of Behnisch & Partners prevailed and, against all odds, received the commission in 1968 to implement their architectural ideas.

In addition to the design, there was also intense discussion about the construction budget, which was judged insufficient on account of the proposed roof construction of the first prize. The recently founded Olympic Building Society had to commission new

Fritz Auer

Born in Tübingen in 1933, Fritz Auer studied at the Technical University of Stuttgart and at the Cranbrook Academy of Arts in Bloomfield Hills, Michigan, in the United States, returning to Stuttgart to earn his diploma in 1962. Like Carlo Weber, he worked for Behnisch and Lambart in Stuttgart in 1965 and in the same year became a partner of Behnisch & Partners. In 1980 he started his own office with Carlo Weber. From 1985 to 1992 he was professor for Building Construction and Planning at the Technical University of Munich, from 1993 to 2001 professor for Planning at the State Academy of Fine Arts in Stuttgart. He has been a member of the Academy of Arts in Berlin since 1993.

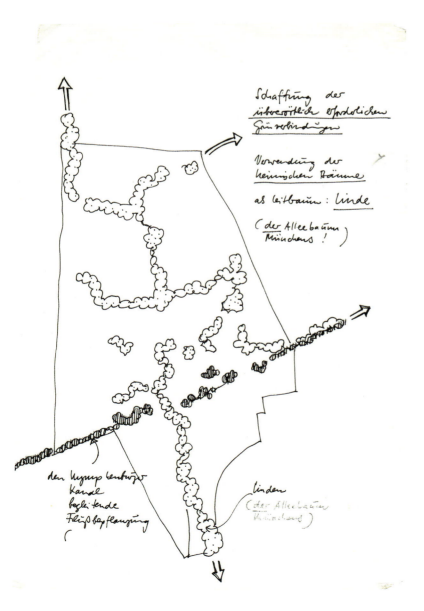

Carlo Weber, Olympic Park, supra-local green connections, sketch, undated

estimates, which then led to the decisive approvals from the supervisory board in 1968 and 1969 for construction. Friction also arose in the technical and commercial management, which could only be resolved by replacing those in executive positions. The issue of finances dogged the project throughout, not only due to changes in design and technical conditions, but also because of enormous increases in construction prices. From 1965 to 1972, the national average construction cost index rose from 114.6 to 166.2 percent. The initial cost estimate of 47.7 million Deutschmarks ultimately swelled to a sum of 170 million.

After decisions regarding the commission were finalized in 1968, the prize-winners—whose team included Günter Behnisch, Fritz Auer, Werner Büxel, Eberhard Tränkner, Carlo Weber, Jürgen Joedicke, Heinz Isler, und Ulrich Hundsdörfer—were able to assemble the final team of planners, and this brought landscape architect Günther Grzimek into the picture. Behnisch and Grzimek had known each other since 1963 from their successful collaboration designing the School of Engineering in Ulm (1959–1963). The new collaboration in Munich sought to create a symbiosis of architecture and landscape. Grzimek was brought into the team to help realize the goal of *Spiele im Grünen* (Games in a Green Space). Other team members included Otl Aicher for the visual appearance and the engineers around Frei Otto—Fritz Leonhardt, Wolfhart Andrä, and Jörg Schlaich—for the tent roof construction. The team of architects expanded to include numerous employees assigned to subsections of the sports buildings.

Given the 280-hectare size of the Oberwiesenfeld, a division of tasks was necessary from the outset. The competition, moreover, had only given secondary consideration to the Olympic Village, which had yet to be specified in planning terms. After some back and forth, the northern part of the Olympic area, with the residential buildings for the athletes, was awarded to the third-prize winners of the competition, Heinle, Wischer and Partners. Another competition was originally planned for the Olympic Village; however, the board of the organizing committee favored the direct award, with the stipulation that the Village be incorporated into the overall landscape design of the first-prize winners. In addition, plans for a student residence by the architects Werner Wirsing and Günther L. Eckert, which had existed since 1960, were to be incorporated into the Olympic Village concept.

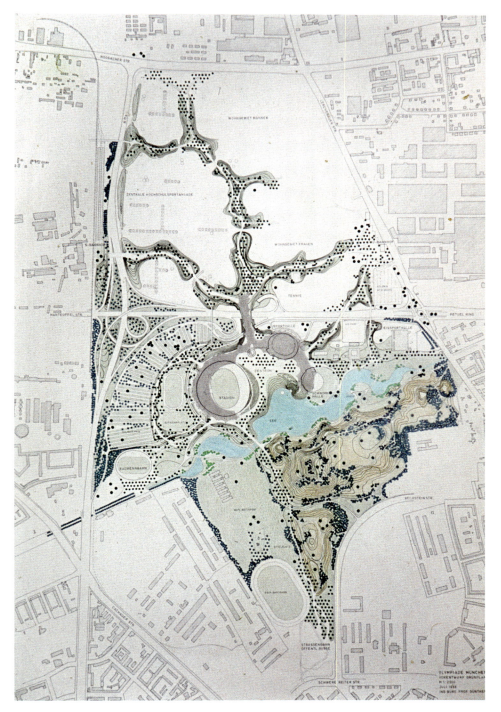

Olympic Park, preliminary design, 1968

The entire commissioning process was hounded by massive criticism from the architectural community, which attacked it as autocratic. That the second prize winner was not considered for the Olympic Village was also criticized. On this point, even jury chairman Egon Eiermann appealed to the National Olympic Committee president, but to no avail. The decision in favor of Heinle, Wischer and Partners remained. There was also censure from the architects' associations that no Munich architects were selected, only Stuttgart architects. As a consequence, Heinle, Wischer and Partners employed the architects of the fourth prize, Gordon Ludwig, Franz Raab, Gerd Wiegand, and Wolf Zuleger. The outdoor facilities of the Olympic Village and the university sports facilities were commissioned from the Stuttgart landscape architects Wolfgang Miller and Hans Luz.

Beginning in 1968, Grzimek and his team—for which he, together with the architects and engineers, established a planning office on the Olympic site for four years—focused on the development of the Olympic landscape. It was crucial for the design of the modeled topography, which was to provide a fluid transition to the tent roof construction of the stadiums, to deal intensively with the local conditions and the determining factors of the architectural proposal of the competition design. This design envisaged sunken stadiums integrated to a large extent in the terrain of a modeled landscape. The light and transparent tent roof structures "floated" above, and the hilly landscape flowed under them. Carlo Weber, who had created the wonderful explanatory sketches for the spatial disposition and design of the site, had specified the overall composition with these. He was also responsible for the overall planning and coordination with those involved in the planning. Grzimek was intensively involved in landscape research prior to his plans, looking in particular for the connection between landscape form and recreational value. Looking back on the project, he wrote that "three central categories emerge: relief energy, edge effect, and manifoldness."[4] What did he mean by this? For him, relief energy represented the variety of topographic modeling possibilities, such as surface, peak, slope, and trough. The edge effect was based on the psychological moment of liminal experience, that is, the perception of contiguous landscape phenomena such as lake and shore or forest and forest edge. Finally, manifoldness included, in addition to relief energy and edge effect, fauna and flora, climate, and the range of possible uses.

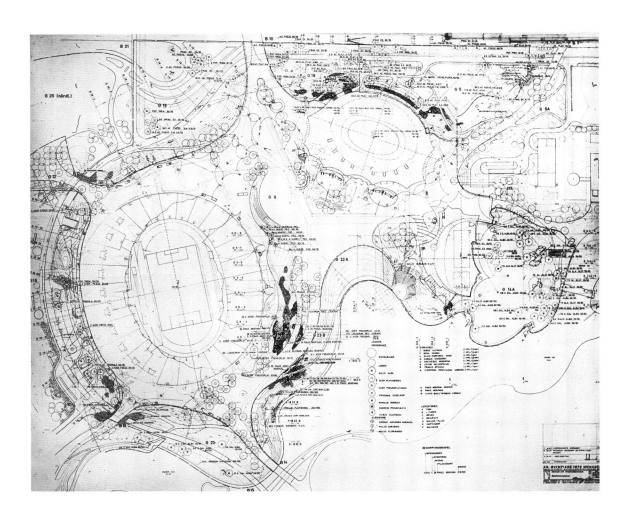

Olympic Park, planting plan stadium area, 1968

For the Oberwiesenfeld, a continuous dialectical juxtaposition and opposition of significant basic elements was developed as a guiding concept, whose formal polarity corresponds to that of "privacy" and "communication." Openness and closedness, grouping and isolation, movement and tranquility are relationships readable from the landscape, which enable or even provoke corresponding social behavior. In our definition, landscape is both: a topographical and a sociological phenomenon.[5]

This gesture was more than just an architectural experiment. Rather, the Olympic landscape and its buildings were explicitly intended to contrast visually with the "stony" 1936 Games in Nazi Berlin. When the bid for Munich was accepted in 1966, it was clear that the decision to hold the 1972 Olympic Games in Munich—which Hitler had called the "capital of the movement" in recognition of the city's importance to the Nazi party's growth—was naturally overshadowed by Germany's past. In contrast to the 1936 Olympic Games in Berlin, which stood for National Socialist power, the concept in Munich was to step out of the dark shadow of the past.

In terms of world politics, the decision was not only a statement and an opportunity, it also demanded an architecture that took a clear position vis-à-vis the past. The architects and designers were well aware of this responsibility. The guiding ideas of an "Olympics in a green space, Olympics of short distances, Olympics of sport and the muses" were intended to set this counterpoint. The Olympic Park

strove to represent a different Germany, a tolerant, free country. The "Olympics in a Green Space"… aimed to leave behind a large urban recreation area, an Olympic landscape that, unlike the city itself, allowed and tolerated the freedom of improvised user behavior.[6] The mosaic-like juxtaposition of quiet niches and lively open spaces with a variety of offerings, including those calling for users to become independent or encouraging engaged observation, was characteristic of the Olympic Park.[7]

Program

The idea of an "Olympics in a green space" was translated by Grzimek into distinctive landscape qualities. One must remember that at the beginning of construction in 1968 there was not a single tree or shrub on the site, only a few trees along the Nymphenburg Canal. With only four years until the opening, it was necessary to plant 3,000 trees of a stately size, with a trunk circumference of up to two meters. Another 100,000 smaller trees and shrubs were added to produce a completed park by 1972.

top: Olympic Park, stadium construction site, July 1970, photo: Peter Prinz

bottom: "Big Boss," September 1969, photo: Peter Prinz

Grzimek chose a real-world model, the Allgäu foothills of the Alps, for the overarching landscape motif. In doing so, he had in mind the image of an idealized landscape. However, unlike the ideal of the romantic landscapes of the eighteenth and nineteenth centuries and the idea of the English garden, he labored to create a new Olympic landscape as an urban artifact.

The emphasis on the urban ... might be alienating. If there is something like a paradox perceptible in it, let it remain unresolved for the time being. This seems all the more necessary, because a social romantic element of urban flight still resonates, at least for many ears, in the concept of garden and landscape architecture—even more so in the slogan "Olympics in a green space." In contrast, the design of the Oberwiesenfeld was based on a consciously artificial, a manipulative attitude if you will. Landscape was understood as viable, as a manufacturable artifact, and even more profanely, as a commodity. In other words, nature is the major player in green planning, and ultimately the actual creative agent. But it would be odd not to mention that it is a domesticated nature. Here as everywhere. What we call landscape is nature that is entirely manipulated, or cultivated, by humans. Untamed nature, as for example in the jungle or the high mountains, is something we hardly experience anymore.[8]

Elements and materials

The implementation of such a conception of landscape meant for Grzimek designing with clear means. He decided to use simple landscape architectural elements and methods: tree, path, meadow, lawn, mountain, lake, and modeling. These elements were to harmonize with each other as a matter of course and in their arrangement, depending on the lay of the terrain and the planting, and to encourage people to linger or play.

An essential factor ... besides the elementary and cheap materials (gravel, stones, lawn, trees, bushes) was the program. Large areas of the hilly landscape—such as the steep mountain sides—were formed as flower meadows on poor soil. The soil was worked exclusively with machines. The gravelly soil proved to be highly resilient for our uses.[9]

In order to understand this approach, it is useful to look in detail at the elements mentioned. The following sections are devoted to the elements and facilities that constitute the site: hill, paths, trees, meadows, lake, art, and play.

top: Modeled Olympic Hill

bottom: Winter at Olympic Hill, undated, photo: Christian Kandzia

Hill

For the planning on the Oberwiesenfeld in the north of Munich, Grzimek found a very flat, tertiary gravel landscape, only significantly punctuated by the sixty-meter-high Schuttberg (rubble hill). This hill had already been landscaped in the past by the Munich city parks director Josef Höllerer (1903–1987).[10] Today it is known as the Olympic Hill and is an important destination for many visitors. From here, one can see the city in a beguiling 360-degree panorama. The original conception for the large hill, which Grzimek always referred to in his documents as the "Schuttberg," was to give it flanks with different types of vegetation. The north side of the hill, facing the stadium and lake, was designed as a mountain meadow, enriched with hollows and knolls and so-called "swallows' nests" that provided wind protection. Here one could retreat and take in the view. The preexisting planting of poplars was removed, as Grzimek believed these ruined the proportion of the hill. Instead, the flanks were planted with smaller, stoutly growing mountain pines, which were intended to create the right scale in the terrain and thus purposefully make the hill appear larger. The south side of the hill was fashioned as a quotation of an alpine torrent. From the top to the base of the valley, at what is now the Ackermannbogen, a dry river landscape was installed with large stones and boulders as well as deadwood logs. This artificial flank was primarily intended to provide an area for children, as natural materials encouraged unstructured play. Black pines populate this hillside to this day. The river landscape has disappeared, now overgrown by tall shrubs. The stones, hidden under scrub, are still there. On an intermediate meadow on the hill is the so-called Alm (mountain pasture). This was already included in the 1968 planning and featured a cave, with camping and play areas situated in front of it. This plan was not pursued further. The Alm, as a resting place offering food and drink services, continues to exist and is a popular destination for excursions, after successfully climbing the hill.

Paths

The idea of having park paths was copied from the grazing paths of shepherds in the mountains. Grzimek always led the course of the paths laterally past the modeled hilltops, just as paths in the mountains do. This is already visible in the sketches by Carlo Weber. The paths in the park are clearly hierarchized, but without this being obvious. Where large streams of

Olympic Park landscape, 1972,
photo: Karsten de Riese

top: Dry river landscape at Olympic Hill, undated, photo: Peter Prinz

bottom left: Gravel landscape with dead wood, undated, photo: Peter Prinz

bottom right: Hill made of rubble, water stairs, June 1972, photo: Peter Prinz

top: Path on the hill, undated, photo: Christian Kandzia

bottom left: Production of "Olympiamastix," November 1971, photo: Peter Prinz

bottom right: Production of "Olympiamastix," November 1971, photo: Peter Prinz

top: Carlo Weber, resolving of the pedestrian areas, sketch, undated

bottom: Modeling on the hill, undated, photo: Walter Sack

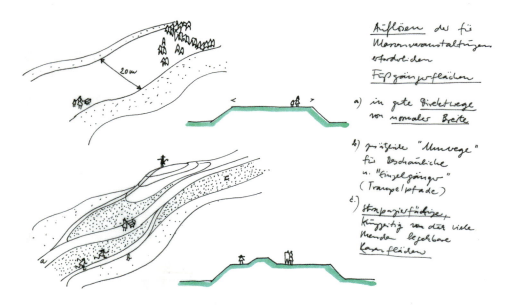

visitors were expected, the paths were expansively wide and ample. Grzimek deliberately inserted large curves and frequent branchings that adhere to the natural patterns of human movement. In this way, he aimed to ensure that visitors would have an impression of short distances, in keeping with the Games' motto. Moreover, the variety of access routes to the sports facilities was meant to prevent what Grzimek called huge axes of deployment, as was common for events with large crowds. Use of the paths, moreover, should be pleasant. Despite the great differences in altitude in the terrain, there were no stairs in the park, only inclined paths and ramps. Visitors should not walk on concrete, and so the paths were paved with the so-called "Olympiamastix," a bituminous surface developed especially for the site, which gave the impression of a simple gravel path due to its scattering of stone chippings. Away from the major paths, the trails were smaller and paved on the hillsides with "grass paving," that is, large granite paving stones with joints through which the grass can grow. The lawns were also designed to be walked on.

Trees

As previously mentioned, a large number of fully grown trees were planted. Wooden fermentation barrels had been obtained from large breweries for this purpose; these barrels, cut in half, served as temporary tubs for the large trees. They had to be watered regularly in this temporary nursery of barrels, since a large tree absorbs up to 2,000 liters per day. Occasionally the fire department had to assist in keeping the valuable greenery sufficiently watered. In addition, fabrics were used to reduce the trees' transpiration, and awnings were set up. The trunks were wrapped with canvas to protect them from too much sunlight. Tree surgeons treated any injuries that appeared. The planting concept included mainly native tree species that were optimally adapted to the site conditions and climate. The mountain pines on the hillside, for example, have already been mentioned. Down by the lake, silver willows lined the shore. Individual trees such as oaks and pines served to emphasize visual relationships in the terrain. In order to mediate between landscape and architecture through more than just modeling, Grzimek selected a primary tree species in order to introduce a design constant in the vegetation. He chose the linden tree, which was planted in a grid of 7.5 x 7.5 meters. The overall plan from 1968 makes evident this design constant in the park.

Olympic Park and city, 2021, photo: The Pk. Odessa Co / Markus Lanz

top left: Watering the trees, May 1969, photo: Walter Sack

top right: Planting a large tree, May 1969, photo: Walter Sack

bottom: Trees in grid, with open tree discs, undated

top left: Fire department watering trees, undated

top right: Fire department watering trees, undated

bottom: Trees in halved fermentation barrels, undated, photo: Peter Prinz

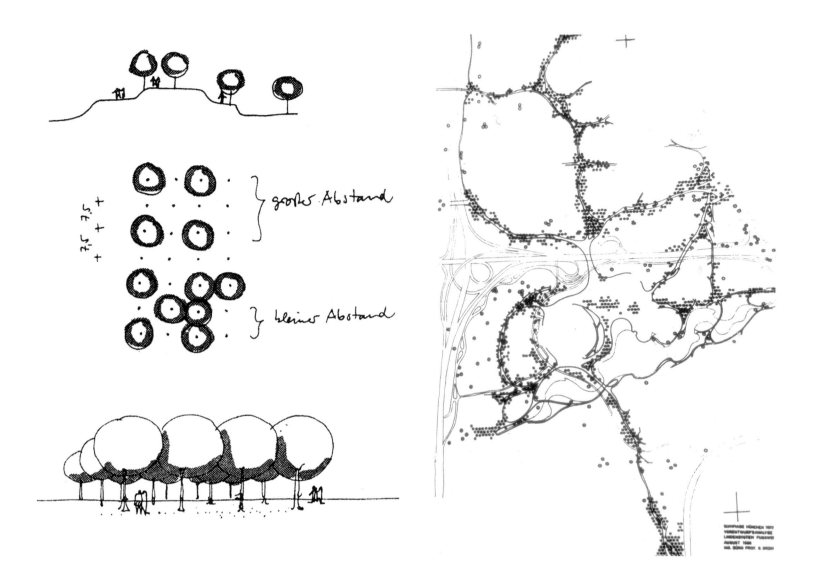

left: Carlo Weber, tree grid, sketch, undated

right: Olympic Park site plan, leading tree species in grid, August 1968

The position of the trees based on the large grid can be recognized in the north, associated with the meandering but orthogonal construction. This grid disappears in the south, replaced by loose groupings of trees.

The woody plants lend character to their respective sites; here the mountain pine, dog rose, wild pear, blackthorn, and dwarf rose are complemented by individual oaks and a selection of single flowering apple and cherry trees. The plants hold their own against the many visitors.[11]

As for the shrub plantings, Grzimek selected varieties that yield edible fruit. Cornelian cherries, sloes, and hawthorns line many areas to this day and provide an important stepping stone for the park's wildlife within the fabric of urban green spaces.

Meadows

The annual blooming of flowers in the Olympia Park's meadow remains a spectacular event to this day. The original sowing of the meadow with a variety of flower species has endured, delighting visitors throughout the summer months.

The flowering meadows replaced the magnificent perennials in the Olympic Park, which would have required more intensive care and superior soil. Following an aesthetics of the self-evident, a varied distribution of sage, woundwort, yarrow, and daisies now grow in spontaneous vegetation. These "cheap" flowers could even be picked, which corresponded to the aim of avoiding prohibitions.[12]

The seeding of the flower meadows, which do not tolerate too much use, was carried out only

Layout of paths in the park, 2021,
photo: The Pk. Odessa Co / Sebastian Schels

Meadow and mountain pine planting,
undated, photo: Walter Sack

Daisies in front of the Olympic Village, undated

on the slopes that were difficult to reach. More level slope areas and flats were seeded with tread-tolerant landscape grass that could and should be mowed and walked on regularly. The goal was to offer residents of the city a type of landscape that seemed to have disappeared from the urban fabric. Thus, Grzimek early on adopted an attitude that we are rediscovering today with the creation of flowering meadows, especially as nourishment for insects. Grzimek always spoke out against purely decorative greenery that did not make ecological sense. His plantings in the park were forward-looking.

Lake

The Olympic Lake was created by damming the historic Nymphenburg-Biedersteiner Canal, which flows into the lake from the west; the lake covers a total area of nine hectares, then empties again into the canal, which today flows along the Petuelpark. The banks of the lake are partially terraced in the transition between the stadiums and the lake: on the north side of the lake, the so-called "Theatron" with a stage is inserted into the steep slope. The lake varies in depth from 0.8 to 1 meter, and is sealed with asphalt concrete to make the bottom passable for clearing—a measure that continues to influence the lake's ecological balance. Large areas of the banks were once covered with bulrushes and marsh iris,

top left: Olympic lake under construction, May 1970, photo: Peter Prinz

top right: Olympic lake, undated, photo: Peter Prinz

bottom: Section of plan of Lake Olympia, undated

top: Olympic lake in winter, undated, photo: Peter Prinz

bottom: Heinz Mack, *The Water Cloud*, 1972

taken in large quantities from their natural setting and planted in pots under water. Over time, park maintenance has reduced the number of these plants, eliminating their purifying effects. The lake's banks are planted with silver willows, which Grzimek introduced as a contrast to the hill: "The silver-gray foliage of the willows will contrast clearly with the olive green of the mountain pines that populate the flank of the hill in the same field of vision."[13]

A section of the lake shore was once enclosed by a concrete wall bordering the ice stadium and artfully designed by Bernd Maecker. Various parts of the so-called "Maecker Wall" later fell victim to the construction of the aquarium, amounting to a substantial intervention in the topography.

Otto Piene, *Sky Art Project*, closing ceremony of the Olympic Games, 1972, photo: Karsten de Riese

Art in the Park

A competition held specifically to solicit artwork for the park resulted in thirty submissions. The jury seemed to have a hard time with the idea of adding art to the already strong impact of architecture and landscape. Many of the submitted designs did not survive the discussion stage and remained concepts, such as the Olympic Mountain Project, popularly known as the "Earth Nail," by Walter de Maria. The plan was for "conceptual earth art," as de Maria himself called it: a 2.8 meter wide shaft with a borehole to a depth of 122 meters. The shaft on the hilltop covering was to be sealed by a bronze plate with a diameter of 3.65 meters. This would have been the only visible part of the artwork. The installation was rejected by the Munich City Council in 1971.

Mathias Goeritz's work for the city's freeway entrances, which was intended to enhance them decoratively and artistically, met a similar fate. It was considered too large-scale for Munich standards.

Heinz Mack's project, on the other hand, won over the authorities. *Die Wasserwolke* (The Water Cloud) was created for the Olympic Lake: finely sprayed water created a delicate cloud of mist over the surface of the water. The technology, which had long been inoperable, was ultimately dismantled in 2009. A light sculpture by Otto Piene was installed in the central university sports facility.

In the Olympic Village, Hans Hollein's idea of a colored tubular steel construction, the so-called "Medialine," was accepted. Tubes measuring 40 centimeters in diameter meandered through the village at a height of 4 meters. Through their color scheme and interactive use, they provided orientation in the individual quarters. The system contained light elements and, at certain spots, water, taking shape as a waterfall. It still exists today.

The works of the artist Roland Martin in the Olympic Village marked entrance areas by a rotating aluminum sculpture. A plexiglass sculpture by Josef Gollwitzer was created for the Olympic catering areas, today the Alte Mensa.

Added to the park later was Rudolf Belling's *Schuttblume* (Debris Flower), a memorial dedicated to civilian air war victims, donated by the Munich city government and the German Trade Union Confederation. The sculpture *Olympia Triumphans* by Martin Mayer, play objects such as the spatial mill game by Peer Claasen, and a large chess set in the courtyards of the university sports complex by Carl Auböck, complemented the artworks in the park.

Donkey rides in the park, 1971

top: Olympic Park Children's Festival, July 1971, photo: Horst-Jörg Schliep

bottom left: Olympic Park Punch and Judy show, July 1971, photo: Horst-Jörg Schliep

bottom right: Olympic Park Children's Festival, July 1971, photo: Horst-Jörg Schliep

Olympic Park, Campfire at one of the hill festivals, 1971, photo: Horst-Jörg Schliep

Also worthy of mention is the Carillon am Coubertinplatz, a set of bells installed at Coubertinplatz in 1972 and since then stored at the Stadtwerke (regional energy supplier). Proposals in the city council to rebuild it were rejected because of noise levels. Today, the square is home to a beer garden. A large part of Coubertinplatz was renamed Hans-Jochen-Vogel-Platz in 2021.

Activities

The combination of sports and leisure was an essential factor for the designers, meant also to distinguish the park in its post-Olympic era. After 1972, therefore, an educational program promoted options for playing and games offered in the park. For cost reasons, it was soon discontinued by the city.

It was a vital part of the park's conception not to offer demarcated play areas with the usual equipment. Grzimek encouraged a "free improvisation" of behavior, which was to be encouraged by the terrain modeling, among other things. Since his involvement with the topic of how children play, beginning in Ulm with the Sand Flea Campaign, Grzimek had been closely engaged with the idea of freely motivated play and had always been interested in this topic. Among other things, he was a member of the International Council for Children's Play, an organization founded in Ulm in 1959, and of the Swiss foundation Pro Juventute, which was concerned with research into children's play and had set up the first so-called "Robinson playgrounds" in Switzerland. Inspired by these ideas, he chose stimuli in the form of play sculptures, a dice field, and a "bald head" to encourage activity. To this was added the idea of organized celebrations, children's parties, pony rides, skiing, tobogganing, and ball games—all were meant to make use of the area in the most diverse ways.

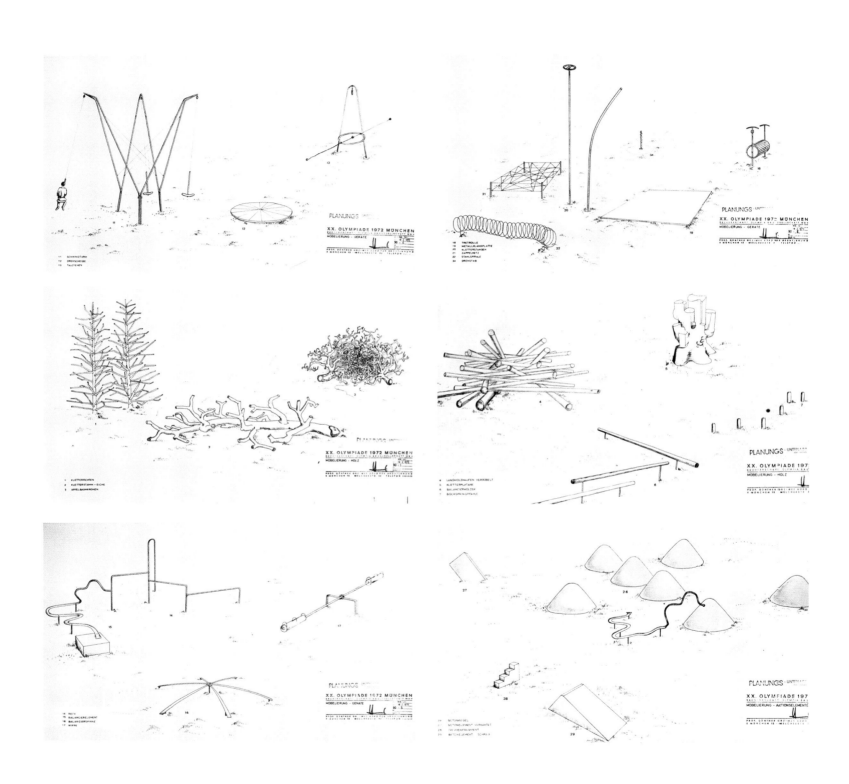

Playground structures, six plans, February 1970

At the same time, the space was to be inviting and open to all. Grzimek called it a "landscape that should be nature-like and at the same time durable, like a good utility object."[14]

Playing in the Olympic Village and the "Play Street"

The KEKS group (KEKS stands for *Kunst, Erziehung, Kybernetik, Soziologie*: art, education, cybernetics, and sociology), responsible for the concept of "play" in the Olympic Village, was represented by Friedhelm Klein, Hans Mayrhofer, Henning Wiesinger, and Wolfgang Zacharias. It was based on the pedagogical principle of providing different learning experiences in an open space. Play objects, such as a walk-on globe, water play areas with colorful communicating tubes, and movable objects that could be modified again and again, were all part of the concept, as was the so-called "Red City": an area of half-height brick walls that represented an unfinished small city, intended to encourage finishing construction. Many of these areas and objects still exist today. Parent initiatives in the Olympic Village are currently working to revive the ideas. Support from the relevant sponsoring units was discontinued two years after the Olympic Games for financial reasons.

Game objects à la Grzimek

A special feature were the concrete models for game sculptures, which were designed but not executed. Grzimek wrote:

> The ... game elements have no function in the sense of a certain rational sequence. They only generate stimuli, the manipulation of playful activity is eliminated here. In this way, traditional behavior patterns can lead to an increased possibility of communication. This program includes cubes, cones, craters, cuboids, slopes ... The material is wood, earth, concrete—but no plastic and no color treatment, because a signal effect in terms of intrinsic value should be avoided.[15]

Playable wooden sculptures by the artist Kastner were also installed in the area. The whereabouts of the sculptures are unknown. Presumably they were made only for the time of the Olympic Games and were not further maintained.

Concrete models of playground structures, February 1970

Design

The park seemed to "function" automatically, not least thanks to the excellent orientation system created by the designer Otl Aicher. The question of design will not be handled here, as it was brilliantly documented in the design handbook of the 1972 Olympic Games, reissued in 2015.[16]

User-determined park

After the Olympic Games, the park's conception withstood the enormous influx of visitors that has continued to this day. At the same time, the Olympic Park forms an increasingly important open space resource in an ever-denser city.

No one walking through Munich's Olympic Park today would ask themselves whether this park is used or not. In terms of its variety of uses, the park is anything but outdated. At any time of year, countless visitors pursue activities there such as tobogganing and cycling, walking and skating, playing and doing sports. Almost everything is allowed there. Uses that would immediately be punished as gross violations of the park rules in the Nymphenburg Palace Park are completely normal here. On a summer afternoon, one encounters kite fans and runners as well as bikini wearers and beer garden fans. Everything is possible in this expressively modeled landscape, which functions excellently as a "user-determined park." It is still occupied fifty years later just as it was in 1972 when the idea of the appropriation of public open space was not yet self-evident. "Do Not Walk on the Grass" signs were the norm in urban green spaces in the 1960s, most of which were nothing more than meticulously mowed lawns in public spaces. When Günther Grzimek curated the exhibition *The Appropriation of the Lawn* in 1983, the Olympic Park had already been in use for ten years. As the main planner of the Olympic Park landscape, Grzimek was driven by the realization that open spaces in the city had to be usable places of unfettered development for citizens—places that called for appropriation, as he called it.

Today, the concept still seems relevant, and the park is more popular than ever. But maintenance of the landmarked Olympic landscape, along with its structures, requires constant attention. The stadium has been repeatedly repaired and renovated. The park, in its dynamism and metamorphoses, requires just as much care, but also further development. Many areas have changed significantly over the years, something unnoticed by many. Natural areas for playing, which were meant to invite occupation and appropriation, have disappeared, as has the former planting of bullrushes and irises along the lakeshore. Park maintenance has replaced mountain pines with newer varieties that are not as vigorous, and in some places wood species have been planted that no longer follow the principle of the original planting scheme. One success, after years of efforts by the city to care for the park, was the commissioning of an area-wide survey of the park's visual appearance and the reissue by Professor Kilian Stauss of the design manual based on historical principles.[17] In addition, the city now has a park maintenance manual.[18]

Density

The districts adjacent to the park—Milbertshofen, Schwabing, and Neuhausen—have become more densely settled with time. New developments, such as the residential settlement on the former Schweren-Reiter barracks site, now Am Ackermannbogen, can only achieve such a level of urban density because the nearby Olympic Park offers a refuge of open space. For the park, this has meant a further increase in users. Other planned developments on Dachauer Strasse, such as the Kreativ-Quartier and in Schwabing, are only possible if good multifunctional open spaces

Olympic Park, visitors in the park, undated, photo: Peter Prinz

Olympic Park, design of the flags in the park, undated

are available or can be created. The housing pressure on Munich, the capital city of Bavaria, is enormous. Isolated, open spaces with minimal dimensions, created as part of new construction projects, are of little use to residents of dense multistory housing. Consequently, the need for a good "user park" is more relevant than ever, giving renewed importance to the Olympic Park.

The green planning office of the city's planning department is countering this growing density with, among other things, the idea of keeping the western flank of the Olympic Park free of construction over the long term. This area includes the so-called Tollwood Grounds, where an annual summer festival with tents, art, and cultural events takes place from the end of June to the end of July. A significant expansion of the park is planned here in the coming years. Ideas for this are to be debated in a competition. From the point of view of monument protection and urban space, it is vital that the basic democratic principle of this important park is not lost, despite all the pressure for development.

In his concepts, Günther Grzimek always placed the user at the center of his functional and design considerations—a maxim that should still apply to today's park concepts. His designs were robust yet highly aesthetic. He shared this gift with other landscape designers like Sckell and Lenné, whose works still fascinate us today. Good green spaces take time and care. Just like good democracy.

1. "Stadium Competition for Munich," in *Baumeister* 5, vol. 62, 1965.
2. From the jury's assessment of the Olympic facilities: saai/Werkarchiv Egon Eiermann/Preisgerichterätigkeit, Olympische Spiele, 1967.
3. Paul Löwenhauser and Werner Göhner, "Die olympischen Pläne und ihre Verwirklichung," in *Münchner Leben* 13 (1968): 22–36.
4. Günther Grzimek, *Spiel und Sport in der Stadtlandschaft. Erfahrungen und Beispiele für morgen*, Schriftenreihe der Deutschen Gesellschaft für Gartenkunst und Landschaftspflege, vol. 9 (Munich: Callwey, 1972) 11.
5. Grzimek, *Spiel und Sport*, 12.
6. Günther Grzimek and Rainer Stephan, *Die Besitzergreifung des Rasens. Folgerungen aus dem Modell Süd-Iscr*, Grünplanung heute (Munich: Callwey, 1983), 109.
7. Grzimek, *Spiel und Sport*, 12.
8. Grzimek, *Spiel und Sport*, 10.
9. Günther Grzimek, "Olympische Park-Ideen," *Garten + Landschaft* 103 (1993): 30–35.
10. Joseph Höllerer, "Der Schuttberg auf dem Olympia-Gelände," *Garten + Landschaft* 5 (1968): 148–49.
11. Grzimek, "Olympische Park-Ideen."
12. Grzimek, "Olympische Park-Ideen."
13. Grzimek, *Spiel und Sport*, 19.
14. Grzimek, *Spiel und Sport*, 13.
15. Grzimek, *Spiel und Sport*, 15.
16. Kilian Stauss, Fritz Auer, and Carlo Weber, *Olympiapark München. Gestaltungshandbuch 2015* (Munich: Landeshauptstadt München, 2015).
17. Stauss and Auer, *Olympiapark München*.
18. Schulze/TOPOS, *Parkpflegewerk Olympiapark. Amtsinternes Konzept* (Munich, 2012).

Olympic Park, reflection, 2020, photo: Regine Keller

The engineering office of Günther Grzimek worked on the park with its employees Peter Prinz, Gerd Linder, Horst-Jürgen Schliep, Günter Hänsler, Bert Maecker, and Zdenek Zvolsky; consultants: Professor Richard Hansen, Professor Ludwig Roemer, and Dr. Werner Skirde.
The construction team included a large number of architects, engineers, and designers. Günter Behnisch was assisted by Fritz Auer, Erhard Tränkner, Carlo Weber, and Jürgen Joedicke. Godfried Haberer, Cord Wehrse, Rudolf Lettner, Heinz Isler, and Ulrich Hundsdörfer were involved in the competition.
Carlo Weber was in charge of the overall coordination of the concept. Christian Kandzia was responsible for public relations.
Frei Otto, Leonhardt + Andrä were responsible for the roofing, with Jörg Schlaich as lead engineer.
Günther Domenig and Eilfried Huth worked on the restaurant, while the registers and kiosks were designed by Jochem Jourdan. The pavilion in the aquatics center was designed by Günther Domenig and Eilfried Huth.
Otl Aicher was responsible for the visual appearance.
Art objects: Heinz Mack's *Wasserwolke* (Water Cloud) and Adolf Luther's spherical objects.
Karla Kowalski was involved in the outdoor areas of the stadium.
Bert Maecker was responsible for the concrete wall at the lake.

Lake, aquatics center, tower, 2022
photo: The Pk. Odessa Co / Markus Lanz

Flower picking allowed, 2022,
photo: The Pk. Odessa Co / Sebastian Schels

Meadow flank, 2022,
photo: The Pk. Odessa Co / Markus Lanz

Alpine pasture, 2022,
photo: The Pk. Odessa Co / Markus Lanz

User-determined park, 2021, photo:
The Pk. Odessa Co / Sebastian Schels

Surface, peak, slope, hollow, 2021,
photo: The Pk. Odessa Co / Markus Lanz

Olympic Hill, 2021,
photo: The Pk. Odessa Co / Markus Lanz

Hill and lake, 2021,
photo: The Pk. Odessa Co / Markus Lanz

M of Munich Airport: Elements of the Corporate Design, 1992, © Pierre Mendell Design GmbH

Munich Airport

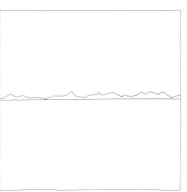
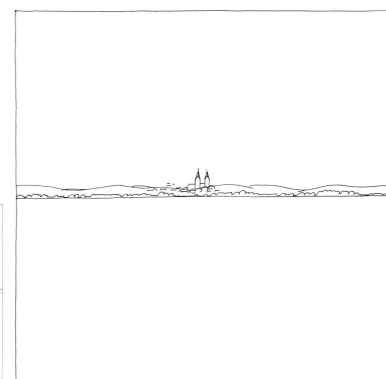

Components of the landscape in Erdinger Moos, three drawings

The new airport, named after the former Minister-President of Bavaria Franz-Josef Strauss, is located just thirty kilometers from Munich in the district of Erding. Following the location of the first Munich airport at Oberwiesenfeld, then the airport in Riem, the site in Erding, which included extensive moorland, was selected in order to meet higher demands for safety and an increased number of flights. It had become clear that a new site for Munich's airport was necessary, far away from the dense urban fabric, especially after a plane crashed in downtown Munich on December 17, 1960, killing fifty-two people. As a result, discussions were held about possible new sites and a "Commission on the Location of a Large Airport for Munich" was formed in 1964, which went on to evaluate a good twenty possible sites. Many of them, including Erding, where an air base had been located since 1935, were rejected for various reasons. The closure of flight operations at the Erding air base brought the site back into consideration, and in 1969 land to the northwest was designated as the planning area for an approximately 1,500-hectare site. At the same time, an operating company was founded, Flughafen München GmbH, and a permit was issued in 1974, despite great resistance from the surrounding communities. The expected noise pollution was the main reason for complaints, but these objections were being rejected as early as 1973. The communities challenged the ruling in several appeals, but were ultimately unsuccessful. Lawsuits continued to be filed—as many as 5,724 of them— even during the planning approval process. The Munich Administrative Court reduced the total _ number to forty so-called "representative sample lawsuits," a procedure that the conservationist association BUND filed a complaint against, but again without success. The vehement demands from the public at least caused a reduction from the originally planned three runways to two. A second planning approval procedure became necessary in 1981. It was not until 1986 that the last appeals were dismissed. In 1992, the airport began operations.

In 1987, the architect Hans-Busso von Busse, together with the landscape architects Gottfried and Anton Hansjakob, won the competition for the first phase, Terminal 1. The competition for Terminal 2 was won and realized by Norbert Koch + Partners in 1997. As early as 1975, Günther Grzimek was commissioned to draw up a so-called "framework and program planning of the open spaces" for Munich Airport's new site in Erding.

As in all his planning projects, Grzimek intensively studied the landscape, including functional, ecological, and social conditions, in an analysis phase

Drawing, landscape elements

Drawing, components of landscape

Four drawings, components landscape

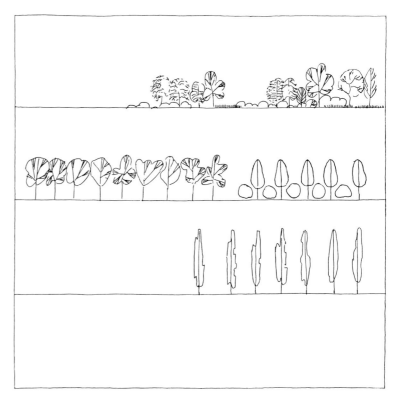

Two drawings, structures in the landscape

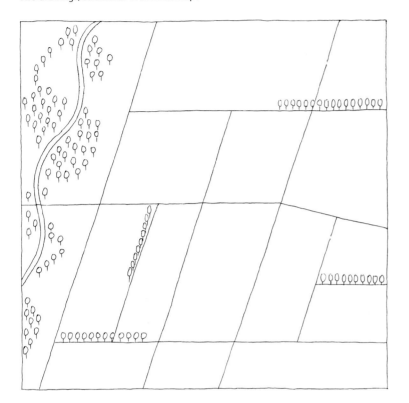
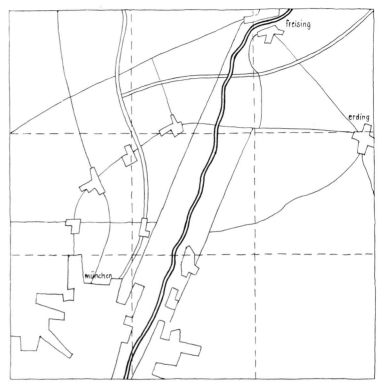

before formulating his concept. His planning proposals responded to previously prepared studies by consultants, for example on the lowering of the groundwater levels (Dorsch Consult) in the Erdinger Moos moorland and its possible ecological consequences (Heinz Ellenberg). The operation of the airport itself and its impact, especially on flora and fauna, were likewise the subject of preliminary studies incorporated into Grzimek's planning. Finally, he was also concerned with the airport's impact on the landscape of the Erdinger Moos and with working out how to make the area more attractive for recreational use.

The principles guiding the development of the airport's appearance were, as he phrased them:
—*An airport in the landscape;*
—*A green airport;*
—*An airport for excursions;*
—*An open airport.*

To this end, he formulated design theses that were to be realized as follows:
—*Airport landscape: through landscape and architectural, geometric design;*
—*Coordination with the Erdinger Moos environment: through analogous elements and structures;*
—*Visible conflicts: through characteristic, large-scale forms that stand for themselves in the airport area, with the various operational areas, and through the visitor program;*
—*An individual image: through information transmitters, horizontal and vertical vegetation structures, and the visitor program.*

He initially saw the airport layout as a "functional break between the technical and rural landscape, an ecological conflict between the airport and the site, and a visual break between the monotonous magnitude of the airport and the countryside of small fields." The aim of his submitted design was to minimize these conflicts through the following means: "Concentration and a closed ordering principle in the architecture as a contrast to the flatness; structuring of the area by rows of trees and avenues on the airport grounds and on the expansion areas; rows of trees and avenues in the street area."

In addition to a precise treatment of all functional areas and their description in terms of soil cultivation, vegetation, and maintenance expenses, the development system of the streets and parking lots and their greening were precisely detailed. In addition, there was the idea of a visitor park, which was to be equipped with a viewing hill, recreational facilities

Four drawings, structure of the airport landscape

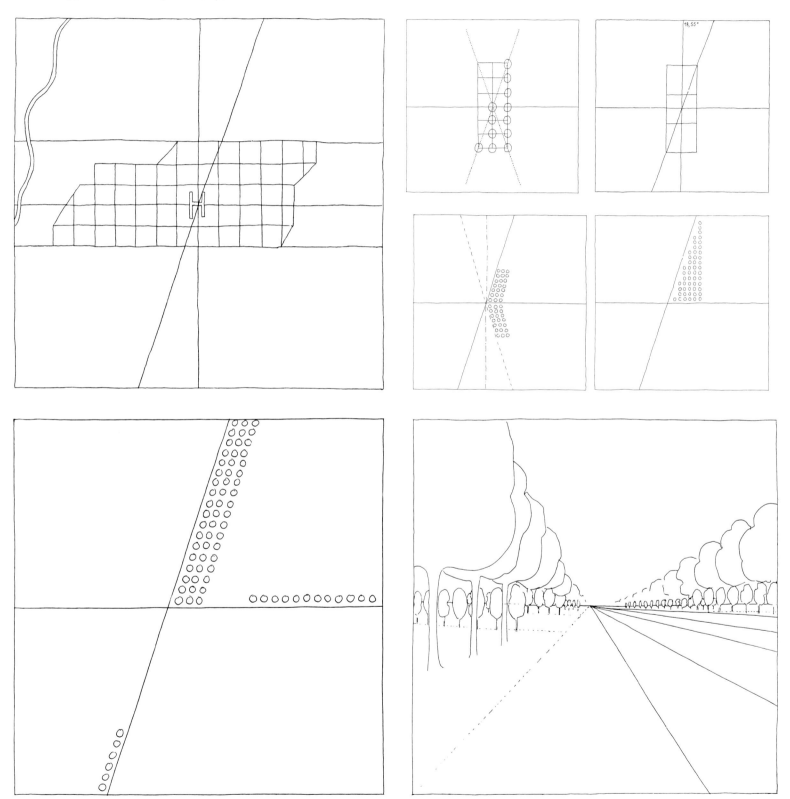

for sports and amusement, a restaurant, and an open-air exhibition area. Another concept envisaged agricultural and semi-agricultural use of the large open spaces necessary for the area. It was understood that any agriculture which attracts birds through arable farming, for example by growing grain crops, must be avoided; the dreaded hazard of bird strike and the ensuing danger for flight operations would thus be avoided. Another limiting factor for agricultural use was wind erosion, as well as the lack of knowledge at the time about the effects of emissions. It is clear from the study that economically profitable use of the green areas was not expected. Arable farming, with the limitations mentioned, appeared more lucrative at the time. These statements referred primarily to the reserve area of about 500 hectares to the north, which was included in the airport area for possible further expansion.

A Theory for the Site's Appearance

Grzimek discussed in detail the local population's attitude towards the planned project. In doing so, he clearly distinguished between those on the one hand who disliked the airport because of its size, disruption, and landscape exclusivity, and those on the other hand who would have a heightened interest in the site given the airport's potential employees, passengers, and visitors. He was motivated by the idea of turning the negative image attached to Munich's airport in Riem into a positive image for the new airport. Here is what Grzimek himself had to say:

The airport's appearance is essentially determined by the landscape of the Erdinger Moos agricultural land and the forests of the Isarauen. Both will be comprehensively opened up and brought closer to the population by the establishment of the airport. A technical operating unit that can no longer be grasped in terms of its surface dimensions and infrastructural equipment is installed in a landscape and experienced via landscape. Landscape becomes the medium for the experience of the airport.
Airport in the landscape.

The formula of landscape-and-technology regulates the visual balance of forces between the land and the structures built upon it. The formal pattern of the façade is not primarily derived from the construction of the building, but rather from the uses, structures, and visual rules of the landscape in which the building is placed. The landscape concept, with its diverse structures and vegetation forms, shapes the architecture of the site.
A green airport.

All technologies that are developed towards connection and exchange—that is, towards communication—are of the highest interest to the population. The desire and idea of moving freely, overcoming borders, searching for places, leaving paths behind, is fulfilled by technology in various ways: cars, ships, airplanes. The self-evident effort, the knowledge of how it works, the experience associated with it, create a fascination with technology. This is the root of the attraction that ports have exerted on people—and today, airports in particular. This is clearly demonstrated by the increasing number of visitors to all international airports. If an airport wants to be visitor-friendly, it must offer additional facilities to the visitor.
An airport for excursions.

The airport offers services and public functions. This results in free accessibility, under the responsible and inventive, but not bureaucratic, consideration of safety risks. Every visitor, employee, and passenger should be able to experience the facility in its entirety for himself, as far as it is in his interest, and learn to understand and use it. Through the principle of the open door, environmental understanding can be generated.
An open airport.

In 1981, Flughafen München GmbH published the first design principles based on Grzimek's planning proposals. Booklet 1 describes the external buildings.

Team members:
Eberhard Krauss, Lore Kellinghaus, Winfrid Jerney, Andreas Burkhardt, and Marja Turakainen, in cooperation with Otl Aicher and Eberhard Stauss

Drawings:
Eberhard Stauss and Winfrid Jerney

Four drawings, planting structures, framework plan for Munich Airport II, AGG

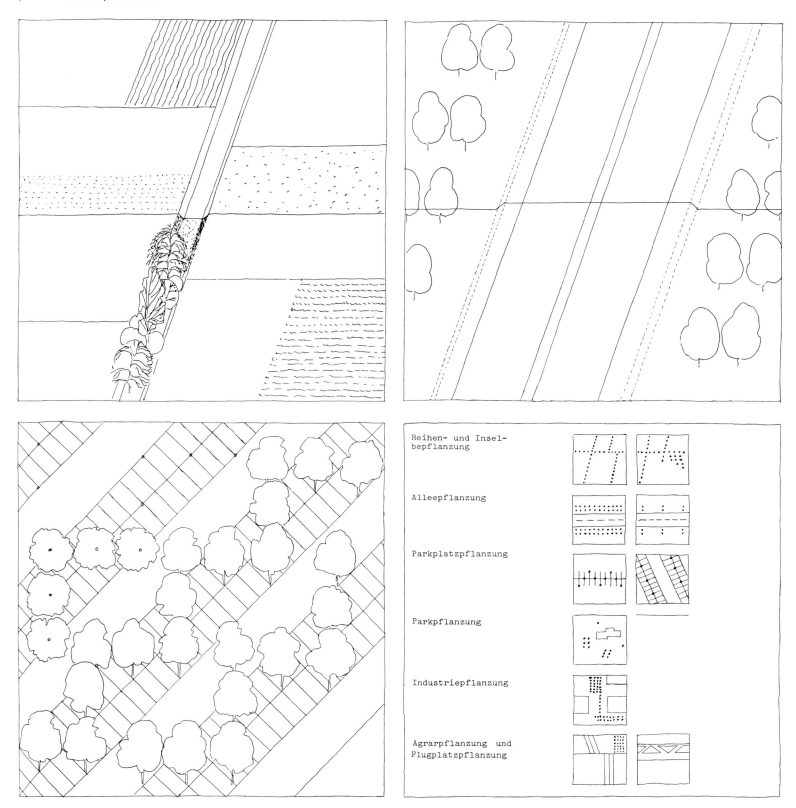

Otl Aicher, *The Appropriation of the Lawn*, book cover, 1983

Die Besitzergreifung des Rasens

Folgerungen aus dem
Modell Süd-Isar
Grünplanung heute

Ausstellungsreihe
der Bayerischen Rück
»Erkundungen«

Callwey

South Isar Model

Ten years after his 1973 exhibition *Democratic Green Space* at the Bavarian Academy of Fine Arts in Munich, Grzimek published *The Appropriation of the Lawn*. It served as the catalog to an exhibition of the same name, part of the "Explorations" series held at the Bayerische Rückversicherung (Bavarian Reinsurance) in Munich. True to its name, the exhibition addressed nothing less than the possibility of participation, the appropriation of recreational space in the city, something what was by no means a matter of course in the 1970s and 1980s. More often it was the janitor on his riding lawn mower, rather than the residents, who determined who was allowed on the lawn and who was not. The observations that Grzimek made on the South Isar River in Munich with his students and colleagues from the university opened up a new perspective for him on urban landscapes and their appropriation for recreational uses. The exhibition was designed together with Otl Aicher and his Rotis studio, and it featured wonderful black-and-white photographs by Karsten de Riese. It focused on thoroughly investigating the needs of urban inhabitants and building on those results to plan contemporary green spaces. The author Carl Amery gave a talk at the opening, drawing on the initial theses from the earlier 1973 exhibition for his thoughts on the democratization of the lawn. The later exhibition, however, went even further and called for a "design from below" and the rejection of ostentatious plantings. Pursuant to Grzimek's ideas, this would allow for spontaneous vegetation on open spaces, and likewise avoided planning of green spaces that was reduced to an exclusively artistic intention.

He put seven theses (see p. 177) up on the walls in the exhibition. Neither his professional colleagues nor the municipal green administrations escaped unscathed. As expected, the uproar triggered by the exhibition was thunderous, especially within the profession. Grzimek was accused of fouling his own nest, since the exhibition was held in the same year as the grand International Garden Show in Munich.

If the Olympic Park was presented in the exhibition as an example of a successful user-determined park, the Westpark—site of the International Garden Show—conversely must be regarded as a mannered show of ostentation. Disputes among colleagues raged and were argued about publicly in specialist journals. It was the beginning of a long-lasting hostility.

But what was actually at stake?

Grzimek demanded nothing less than a paradigm shift away from the sovereignty of municipal planning, and thus from municipal administrations: away from "administered recreation" and towards user-oriented and thus participatory models, promoting the individual appropriation of open spaces: "It is not the administration that has ... to formulate demands, but the users themselves *that* formulate them by behaving according to their own needs."

This emancipatory approach was not entirely new in 1983. It was based on Grzimek's many years of experience as an administrator, planner, and trained, meticulous analyst. In 1978, the landscape architect Werner Nohl completed his doctorate on the subject of *Open Space Architecture and Emancipation* and relayed his findings to Grzimek while a research assistant at the Technical University of Munich. Urban open space, in its significance as a place for the reproduction of labor, has been a historically known fact since the age of industrialization at the latest, implemented by urban planners and landscape architects such as Martin Wagner (1915) and Leberecht Migge. Whereas the goal of *Volksparks* (public recreational parks) was to improve the population's health and to respond to the hygienic and housing situation of the urban population with so-called "sanitary green space," the situation after the Second World War in the precipitately growing cities was completely different. Rapid urban growth and a severely bureaucratized parks administration no longer met the needs of the population for open spaces. In addition, the attitude of urban inhabitants had changed, and they too wanted to participate in planning. In the 1980s, however, the tools of civic participation were neither sufficient nor applicable. Consequently, the occupation of public space became a means of participation. In this context, it is interesting to note how history repeats itself, for example in the "Occupy" movement of the 2000s.

Günther Grzimek in the Olympic Park,
undated, photo: Karsten de Riese

Günther Grzimek

Seven Theses from the Exhibition
The Appropriation of the Lawn

Thesis 1: Park as representation
Today's green space planning has its roots in the ostentatious gardens of past rulers. This is still apparent in green space planning today. The green spaces of the past were understood as works of art, as designed nature, as green open-air scenery for the edification and ethical elevation of the ruler's subjects. Urban green planning provides designs for the recreation of the inhabitants of cities. A large part of the land is consumed for a merely decorative design of paths and plantings.

Thesis 2: Administered recreation
The planning of urban open and green spaces is subject to sovereignty of municipal planning. The utility value of public green space is determined by the authorities as well. A green space freely used by inhabitants or groups of inhabitants does away with the anonymous power of paternalism and regulation by authorities. Authorities tend to claim overarching design control when they assume responsibility for equipping and maintaining green spaces. This does not have to remain so.

Thesis 3: The lawn is to be stepped on
Since the beginning of the 1970s, there has been a progressive appropriation of the park. The lawns, for so long forbidden to walk on, are now used in many ways. Residents have discovered the green areas as an open space for whatever activities they choose. The open space of public green areas has thus acquired a new meaning. First understood as merely a space free of built structures, it is now interpreted as a space free from planning constraints, from disciplining, and as site for individual development. The profoundly democratic concepts of personal responsibility and self-help can also be applied to inhabitants' behavior toward public green space.

Thesis 4: Better green for less money
Usable green spaces are cheaper than decorative plantings. In conventional parks, the annual maintenance costs are one tenth of the plant costs: in ten years, the price doubles. By comparison, the maintenance costs of user-determined parks are almost zero.

Thesis 5: South Isar
Munich's South Isar has become an exemplary model of a metropolitan user-determined park—not in spite of, but because of the fact that garden planners were only occasionally active here. Planning from above is complemented by design from below. The user determines the contents and forms; the administration assumes the role of a learning, guiding companion. Dictated planning turns into guiding care. A user-determined park such as the South Isar in Munich does not have to be understood as a purely green landscape. Technical structures for flood control or energy production reinforce the character of the users' green space more than they disturb it.

Thesis 6: Spontaneous vegetation
Even plants growing uncontrolledly can be thought about in a controlled way. Functional green space planning in particular cannot abstain from the inclusion of spontaneous vegetation. The plant forms of the South Isar make many green forms of the traditional park seem outdated. The era of flower borders, hedge architecture, and prefabricated squares is over. Vegetation in the user-determined park is not overbred and arranged nature: it remains spontaneous. It is characterized by self-regulation even where there is intervention.

Thesis 7: The aesthetics of the self-evident
The aesthetics of the green space should not be determined by the ideals of planners, which are characterized by artistic expression, but by the demands of users. It is not the administration that has to formulate these demands, but the users themselves by behaving according to their own needs. The user-determined park creates a new kind of aesthetics, which does not serve ostentation, but demonstrates content, conveys use value, and incorporates the active human being as part of its appearance: an aesthetics from below.

(Text from Günther Grzimek and Rainer Stephan, *Die Besitzergreifung des Rasens. Folgerungen aus dem Modell Süd-Isar*, Grünplanung heute [Munich: Callwey, 1983], 14–15.)

Competitions

In his notes for this book, Günther Grzimek highlighted five competitions in particular, which will be briefly described below. Unfortunately, he did not make any further written comments on them.

Even before Grzimek left the Ulm municipal administration in 1960, he increasingly devoted himself to his freelance practice, in part by participating in numerous competitions. One of his first achievements was the cemetery in the Stuttgart district of Weilimdorf, where he received a purchase in 1956. In retrospect, this place would hold special importance for him, though his plans for it were never developed.

In 1967, together with the architect Harald Deilmann, he won the competition for the All-Weather Zoo in Münster. It was then built between 1968 and 1971, in parallel to the Landesbank in Münster, by the same team. The zoo was moved to another location in the city in exchange for its property, which was given to the Landesbank (see "Kassel," p. 35).

Furthermore, he made note of his winning the competition for the Office for Land Reallocation in Munich in 1987. The site continues to offer a salient example of Grzimek's approach to design in the 1980s: the sidewalk on the corner of Loth and Lazarettstrasse is strikingly different. It is unusual for Munich, at least, because it is not the usual slab of mousy gray concrete measuring 30 x 30 centimeters, but instead porphyry paving in a wild, looping ornamentation. The pavement curves around the corner and even raises three-dimensional waves, like furrows. The perennial plantings along the façade testify to a good knowledge of the site conditions—semi-shade to full sun. Here, barrenwort, geranium, daylily, and hosta flourish. In 1985, Grzimek's office won the competition for the exterior design of the Office for Land Consolidation, which was eventually finished in 1987. This office implemented land consolidation procedures, which were anchored in Germany by the 1953 Land Consolidation Act, to improve working and production conditions for agriculture and forestry.

In 1987, together with the architects Werz, Ottow, Bachmann, and Marx, he won first prize in the urban planning ideas competition for the Erlangen University Hospital and the building competition for the first construction phase of the care center there.

In the same year, Grzimek participated in the international competition for the "Biozentrum" at the University of Frankfurt in a joint venture with the office of Behnisch & Partners.

Finally, in 1992, Grzimek and his collaborator Winfrid Jerney won third prize for the Neue Messe (new convention center) in the Munich suburb of Riem in collaboration with the architects Groethuysen, Mauerer, Otzmann, and Wirsing.

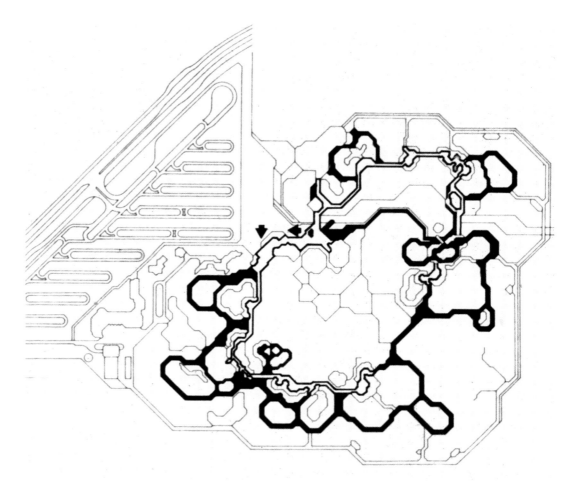

Competition plan for the zoo in Münster

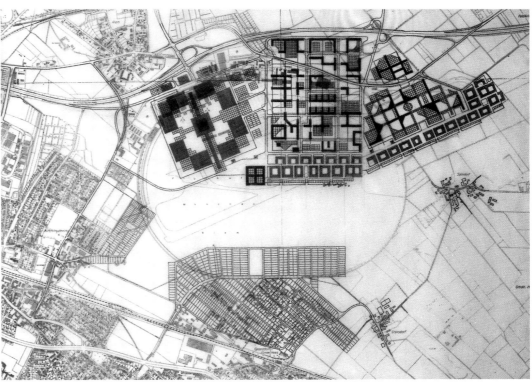

Competition plan for Munich-Riem

Teaching

Günther Grzimek began teaching early on, in 1948, when he became involved with adult education at the community college (*Volkshochschule*) in Ulm. In 1954, Grzimek attempted to gain a foothold at the Technical University of Munich in Weihenstephan, and then at the Technical University of Berlin. As he was in contact with other university teachers at the time, it was not long before he was invited to give lectures. It was mainly urban planners such as Gerd Albers or Erich Kühn who were interested in exchanging opinions at a practical planning and academic level, since Grzimek was head of the parks department in Ulm and later ran his own studio there. From early in his career, Grzimek entertained the idea of working as a university lecturer, but it was only Hermann Mattern's recommendation to bring him to Kassel in 1965 that actually resulted in a professorship.

Grzimek began his university teaching career at a time when students were increasingly dissatisfied with the university system. The criticism that reforms had not been implemented at universities in the postwar period eventually led to the student protest movement of the years around 1968. "Under the gowns – the mold of a 1,000 years" was a slogan spread by student committee representatives at the University of Hamburg in 1967, alluding to Nazism and its ambition of a thousand-year Reich. Numerous university lecturers had returned to their positions directly after the Nazi era and taught according to their old ways. Grzimek had also been exposed to the ideological superstructure of the Nazi era during his own studies with Heinrich Wiepking-Jürgensmann in Berlin. The ideas in Ulm were entirely different, especially when he was involved in shaping the new School of Design. The school's division into classes, the design-theoretical approaches, and the pedagogical-didactic teaching methods there vitally inspired him to reform teaching methods at the University of Fine Arts in Kassel. He was certainly helped by the fact that the structure of the art academy was a better starting point for reform than a science- and technology-oriented course of studies. Nevertheless, it was important to him to establish links to the life sciences, such as biology and ecology, at an early stage. In addition, he was alone responsible for setting up new subjects such as "Open Space and Construction" with Tassilo Sittmann and sociology with Manfred Troll. Didactically, he sought to transform seminars into interdisciplinary projects and to base them on real planning goals. Students were to gain learning experience in real projects, in direct dialogue with instructors. These teaching forms and formats also corresponded to the demands by students, who called for a democratization of the universities and a voice in their operation. In 1968, Grzimek formulated a "Mission Statement for Studies at the Chair of Landscape Culture at the University of Fine Arts in Kassel."

It is also interesting to draw parallels between the activities of individual protagonists of documenta 4 and Grzimek's ideas on teaching during the same period in Kassel. In 1968, the artist Bazon Brock created the "Visitors' School" for those interested in art. Here Brock attempted to didactically complement the reception of art. To this end, he wrote:

The visitors' school—as I understand my task—has to do more than the usual guided tours of the exhibition, which can rightly only provide data and other information about the most diverse objects in the exhibition. The visitor school has to demonstrate to the audience how to see and appropriate the multitude of objects of an exhibition from a unified point of view, in a propositional context. Yes, the prerequisite for any appropriation is precisely that it becomes possible to form a propositional context. One could also say that appropriation has succeeded when the visitor succeeds in forming such a propositional context regarding the multitude of objects.

The question of how well artifacts can be appropriated also appears in many of Grzimek's reflections. He designed the Olympic Park like a good utility object, and in 1983, in the exhibition *The Appropriation of the Lawn*, the occupation of open spaces once again explicitly supplied the heading for his statements.

It was clear, therefore, that spaces and designs needed to be made available for appropriation. In Kassel, he expressed his structural reforms and demands for teaching reform by titling the course of studies "Environmental Design." In this context, urban planning, architecture, and landscape architecture were disciplines that acted together, in constant mutual exchange, without clearly delimited boundaries. By changing the name of the chair from "Landscape Culture" to "Landscape Architecture," he also tried to free the subject from the problematic term that was associated with Paul Schultze-Naumburg's "cultural works," at the same time incorporating the active aspect of architectural thinking.

Grzimek did not abandon this attitude after he became professor at the Technical University of

Offprint from the Chair for Landscape Culture, Kassel, 1968

Hochschule für Bildende Künste Kassel, Lehrstuhl für Landschaftskultur 1968

Munich in 1972. Here, too, there was a need for reform, but he could no longer make decisions on his own. He also found different structures there. The "Landscape Management" course of studies was housed in a branch of the Technical University that until then had been primarily focused on agriculture. From the beginning, however, he saw this as an opportunity to align his structural ideas from Kassel with a more holistic concept of landscape, in Alexander von Humboldt's sense. Grzimek was interested in understanding landscape not only as an aesthetic or geographic phenomenon, but also as what we would today call an ecosystemic entity, which should therefore be studied from a transdisciplinary approach. When attempting to define the term "landscape," many authors, including Grzimek, refer to Humboldt's description of landscape, which he terms a "region" in his *Views of Nature*:

> That which the painter designates by the expressions "Swiss scenery" or "Italian sky" is based on a vague feeling of the local natural character. The azure of the sky, the effects of light and shade, the haze floating on the distant horizon, the forms of animals, the succulence of plants, the bright glossy surface of the leaves, the outlines of mountains, all combine to produce the elements on which depends the impression of any one region.

Grzimek envisioned the disciplines of landscape architecture, ecology, forestry, agriculture, and horticulture as an antipodean model to urban planning and what he called "housing settlement planning." He was unable, however, to realize this ambitious academic vision at the Technical University of Munich. Nevertheless, he concentrated on the further development of the course of studies and achieved a good mixture of course contents by engaging an interdisciplinary group of lecturers. Augmenting the number of professors in the field of landscape architecture took many years and was repeatedly postponed. A second professorship was only approved in 1980 and occupied by the landscape architect and urban planner Christoph Valentien. Grzimek retired as professor emeritus in 1981. He was succeeded by the landscape architect Peter Latz, who had taught in Kassel until then.

As of 2022, two more professorships in the field of landscape architecture have been created at the Technical University of Munich. Nevertheless, the improvement of teaching capacities and the expansion of this enormously sought-after and successful course of studies still remains difficult.

Günther Grzimek

The Profession of Landscape Architect

The profession of landscape architect has its roots in the late stages of feudalism. At that time, the ruling monarchs would have acted as patrons, while today, in most cases, their place has been taken by the individual clients of democratic society. However, the profession still struggles to recognize this development and shed the constraints of the feudal tradition. Whereas architects work with associations, public authorities, and other organizations when designing and constructing factories, social projects, and technical structures, landscape architects have long been focused on their clients—the only difference being that the monarch has been replaced by members of the upper-middle class. In the course of this development, the significance of landscape architecture has also taken on a secondary role compared to that of architecture, downgrading the garden itself to what is essentially a virtuoso-designed adjunct to the building.

In short: the profession has lagged behind its social conditions. This explains its unusually strong affiliation with conservative ideals—a handicap that is particularly noticeable in the egotistical designs of supposedly "modern" garden artists.

This topic may invite dispute; but what is more important is to incorporate the approaches of contemporary discussions around landscape architecture—as we are attempting to demonstrate with the example of the South Isar—into a programmatic review that also considers current developments in the profession. A consideration of new objectives must allow for a critical analysis of the trends, projects, and practices of how open green space has previously been planned. The brief overview provided below is intended to offer some key reference points in this context.

Gardening as a profession is probably as old as the principle of division of labor. Relatively early, a distinction was drawn between the practical aspects of the gardener's craft and the aesthetic focus of landscape architecture.

In this part of the world, the term "art and pleasure gardener" first appeared in the sixteenth and seventeenth centuries; it was mostly master builders or simple gardeners whose sense for effective plant associations had been noticed and fostered by courtly patrons. The most famous member of the trade is André Le Nôtre (1613–1700): he was commissioned by Louis XIV to design the gardens at Versailles.

In Germany, this development emerged around 1680, after the country had recovered from the Thirty Years' War. It followed a similar course to that of France: Baroque gardens were often laid out around the monarch's summer residence, as at Nymphenburg, where Joseph Effner (1687–1745), a gardener's son from Dachau, designed the park.

The Baroque park was followed by the English landscape garden—and it was not until the late eighteenth and nineteenth centuries that the landscape architect became a profession founded in theory and developed in practice.

At the Wildpark in Potsdam, Peter Joseph Lenné (1789–1866), creator of the English garden at Sanssouci, founded the first training school in 1824. Its students graduated as *Gartenbauingenieure* (horticultural engineers)—a title that shows that the profession's technical aspects prevailed against its artistic ones.

Apart from that, the title of the profession has itself been an indicator of uncertainty for a long time: even after the Second World War, the terms "garden architect," "garden designer," and (under the influence of Wiepking-Jürgensmann) "landscape designer" coexisted. A university degree for *Diplom-Gärtner* (qualified gardeners) and the respective course of study was established in 1929 in Berlin. Appropriately, a mandatory gardening apprenticeship preceded the course of study.

While the development of the landscape and its management was then part of the course of study, the connection between city and landscape was not really considered. Landscape architects applied their skills here and there, with their attention mainly focused on individual projects.

At that time, the specific objectives of town planning were hardly ever considered, and town planning became exclusively the task of architects and engineers—but they often lacked a comprehensive understanding of landscape matters. A council for urban development and construction still does not exist; despite the economic problems facing urban development, such a council could have based its efforts on the landscape and the inherent landscape potential. Only after the war does the university qualification become *Diplomingenieur* (graduate engineer). At least on the face of it, this put members of the profession on an equal footing with architects and transport engineers; yet during the 1950s and 1960s, landscape architects still failed to attract the attention of the political public sphere.

Only during the profession's most recent phase of development, beginning in around 1965–70, has there been a significant diversification of the traditional areas of responsibility; it is a phase that we remain in to this day. The situation at the University of Kassel is typical, also in terms of the expansion of study programs: after a common preliminary course, graduates can decide whether they want to specialize in the subjects of landscape architecture, architecture, or urban planning, and then qualify in one of these specializations. This kind of preliminary education should finally enable landscape architects to do more than take over the administration of a city's parks department; it should also qualify them for leading municipal planning and building. By retaining a status closely associated with architects—scientifically, intellectually, and culturally—they could reciprocally incorporate the landscape and its inherent potential and development opportunities into the current problems facing the design of cities and the landscape.

In this context, human ecology should eventually be established as a part of urban ecology. Designers should understand that their work is not limited to allocating areas for lifeless materials and amassing waste products of civilization, but that they are also accountable for mitigating the destruction of green infrastructure in the context of responsible development.

Reorienting landscape architecture in this way would go along with overcoming the aesthetic factors that in many places still continue to have an impact on the profession's self-image. As difficult as it may be for landscape architects to realize, the claim inherited from the fathers of the English garden—to value their work in artistic terms—is hardly a yardstick for landscape projects, which need to accommodate the technical and economic constraints within our urban culture.

Centuries of experience amalgamated in cottage gardens, for example, were generally unaffected and oblivious of the trends and practices in official "garden art." Cottage gardens impress mainly by their practicality. Their recurring principle relies on the well-considered and simple arrangement of fruit trees, berries, shrubs, herbs, and vegetables, as well as summer flowers and perennials. A rectangular system of paths provides access while making the gardens manageable.

This type of geometric structure cannot be transferred at will. The aesthetic design principles of all landscape proposals should be derived from the _ site's natural conditions, as well as the actual purpose of each project. This demand could be taken as a matter of course—however, to this day it is still not accepted by all. The exemplary interplay between practical value and form makes unspectacular sites like cottage gardens important models for precisely this reason.

(Text from Günther Grzimek and Rainer Stephan, *Die Besitzergreifung des Rasens. Folgerungen aus dem Modell Süd-Isar*, Grünplanung heute [Munich: Callwey, 1983], 130–31.)

Günther Grzimek

Thoughts on Urban and Landscape Architecture since Friedrich Ludwig von Sckell

Lecture at the Bavarian Academy of Fine Arts on the occasion of the award of the Friedrich Ludwig von Sckell Ring of Honor to the author on June 19, 1973, in connection with the opening of the exhibition *Demokratisches Grün—vom Schlossgarten, zum Volkspark, zur Erholungslandschaft* (Democratic Green Space—From Palace Garden, to Public Park, to Recreational Landscape).

The following text is a reprint of a publication with the above title in a series by the Bavarian Academy of Fine Arts, published by Callwey Verlag in Munich in 1973. Günther Grzimek presents his views on landscape architecture, open space planning, and landscape planning in detail and places his designs for the Olympic Park in a professional context. This essay is one of the central sources for how Grzimek is viewed by academics and critics, as is demonstrated in the contributions to this book.

The exhibition at the Bavarian Academy of Fine Arts in the city of Munich, on the occasion of the 150th anniversary of Friedrich Ludwig von Sckell's death, is dedicated to the topic of "Democratic Green Space." The title, as I hope to demonstrate, has historic origins and refers to demands that we still experience in the present day. In particular, we wish to honor Sckell by covering a broad range of history, while assigning ourselves the task of evaluating history from a contemporary perspective.

In the era of feudalism, and especially in the era of absolutism of the seventeenth and eighteenth centuries, the large gardens in towns were reserved for the nobility. They were exclusive. The uprising of the bourgeoisie against the ruling clergy and nobility in the French Revolution marks the onset of public green spaces. At the turn of the eighteenth to the nineteenth century, the people's park replaced the princely gardens of the Baroque period. Since secularization, many parks have been completely or partially opened to the public. The first public park on the European continent was built in Munich following Sckell's designs. What was probably Germany's first town planning competition was held in Munich in 1808. Sckell played a decisive role. The first plans for public green space were drawn up and the first social infrastructure facilities linked to green spaces were implemented.

I shall describe how these objectives, which are still relevant today, have degenerated in the course of the nineteenth and twentieth centuries. And how we may once again look to Sckell, even while pursuing entirely different planning goals.

In the exhibition, we have tried to highlight the alarming observation of an international team of scientists, who, in the so-called "Club of Rome," researched the limits to growth and incorporated a situation analysis of the development of our urban civilization and landscape. We wish to express that it is no longer enough to develop urban green spaces and protect landscapes. Some single resolutions may succeed—we could save trees and make lakesides accessible, possibly even establish mixed continuous-cover woodland—yet global developments could make a catastrophe inevitable, rendering all individual efforts nothing but a pipe dream. We are talking about excess demands on limited resources, threatening life on earth. If my thoughts on landscape design are still based on Sckell's work, it is because our environment is also threatened by grave dangers from a Gestalt psychology point of view. These dangers are being neglected, or at least fewer programmatic statements are being made about them. The transformation at the beginning of the nineteenth century is interesting in terms of the difficulties facing our time. Any attempt to evaluate the past can only be done in a very brief form.

Sckell became the city of Munich's first director of gardens, as we might call it today. This means that the landscape architect was involved in all of the city's major design interventions and further development, as well as overseeing their implementation and maintenance.

Moreover, Sckell, who came from a family of gardeners and was educated in garden design as well as languages and painting in Schwetzingen, Versailles, and England, was also director of royal gardens until his death in 1823, a position overseeing all large and small parks in Bavaria. These mostly extensive palace gardens and parks, like Nymphenburg and Schleissheim, were often located in the periphery of towns; and, given the still relatively small area of these towns, they were placed in a spatial context by means of a green framework, including visual axes with woodlands, or avenues.

Sckell had given consideration to the topic of "city and landscape." He planned and arranged, as for example in the city of Aschaffenburg on the river Main, according to principles that would still befit a landscape architect today. He created a green framework that connected the major natural landscape types: the Spessart, the banks of the river Main and its floodplain. This radial network of green spaces comprised local sites, including the pheasantry, the enclosed and open Schöntal, and the renowned Schönbusch Park.

A few years ago, I had the particularly important and satisfying task of drawing up a green infrastructure plan on behalf of the city of Aschaffenburg in conjunction with a preparatory land use plan, which Max Guther was working on.

It makes sense that Sckell won the town planning competition held in Munich, the seat of royal power, and that, together with the chief architect for the Bavarian court, Karl von Fischer, he drew up an urban land use plan which served as a framework for the extension of Maxvorstadt. The rigid town boundaries were broken through, and, following their defortification, cities opened up to the landscape. Whereas the medieval fortified town had been a monolithic element in the landscape—usually skillfully placed in the topography, and often in a dominating position—the end of the eighteenth century saw the onset of a development that in our day finally dissolved the city into the landscape, brutally destroying large parts of it.

Sckell designed a magnificent plan for Mannheim that would transform the fortifications into a peripheral green belt. Even though these and other plans were not, or only partly, implemented, Sckell's work in Munich was a lasting success. Green urban squares were created in Maxvorstadt; Sckell sought to connect the Hofgarten at the palace across the current Finanzgarten with the Englischer Garten. Since private properties obstructed his endeavors, he pursued these plans for several years. Sckell wanted to transform the larger grounds—the Englischer Garten with the Maximiliansanlagen and the upper Isarau—into a continuous green belt, enclosing the entire eastern part of the city.

Equally modern were his ideas on planting in streets and squares. He supported a transition from an architectural towards a nature-embracing townscape. He created the botanical gardens at Maxvorstadt and, in the heart of Ludwigsvorstadt, two social institutions: a hospital garden and a cemetery. One of his greatest achievements in garden design, apart from the Englischer Garten, is the development of the Baroque Nymphenburg. In a compelling simplification, he successfully retained all essential large-scale elements of the Baroque period and thus accomplished a synthesis of the original Baroque form with the lateral, significant sections of the overall park, fashioned in the style of an English landscape garden.

Seen from our perspective, Sckell held a singular position, and it fully absorbed him. Charles Theodore, Elector of Bavaria, his royal partner and patron, had already promoted him in his youth when he had him travel to England to learn about the new English landscape garden. Sckell had a client who not only devised the program but also represented the cultural standards, and who finally also approved the funds. Such conditions no longer exist today.

Sckell is at the brink of a new age of open space planning, a category of town planning that emerged much later. He was garden artist, town planner, and landscape designer.

Let us now turn to the English landscape garden in more detail: the English landscape garden was established in a phase of intellectual and political emancipation, which seems topical to us especially in these times, though in new conditions. At the turn from the eighteenth to the nineteenth century, the English landscape garden replaced the princely garden of the Baroque period on the European continent. It is significant that the construction of the first English garden—which was conceived, planned, and implemented in Munich—began in 1789, the year of the French Revolution. According to the will of the Elector of Bavaria, Charles Theodore, and his advisor Count Rumford, it was to be a "people's park." The significance of this decision cannot be overestimated. Initially, Sckell only took the role of advisor as he was still employed at Schwetzingen. However, after taking up service in Munich in 1804, he fully applied himself to the project. The final version is largely his work.

In his study *Der Landschaftsgarten* (The Landscape Garden), published published in 1928 [*sic*, 1927], Hallbaum writes:

In his memorandum, which reflected the requirements of aesthetics and the pleasure of the people to a rare degree, von Sckell assumes a social humanitarian viewpoint and links it with several fundamental considerations about the typification of garden design. A people's garden, like the Englischer Garten, should be halfway between a royal state garden and a park. Its purpose is exercise and recovery from work, socializing and the convergence of all strata of society. It is to have a moral disciplining effect and is a part of the most necessary educational art institutions of a humane and wise government.

That is the quote.

The reasons for the renunciation of the strictly stylized Baroque garden of absolutism, with its courtly etiquette demanding depersonalization, and the turning to the landscape garden, corresponded to the notion of self-discovery in [the German Romantic movement] Sturm und Drang and Classicism. In his call to turn to nature, Rousseau paves the way to a pantheist stance in society.

Baroque gardens were also sharply criticized by literary figures and philosophers. In the home country of the English landscape garden, Sckell became acquainted with a form of government that allowed greater freedom for individuals. Shakespeare, as a performer of the unusual and original, set new standards.

While up to that point the king was the highest authority and instrument of divine will, nature in a pantheist sense is now brought into interconnection with the people.

This liberation and partly rapturous devotion to nature and the landscape will uphold the appreciation of the garden as a work of art of the highest standards. In part, this is only theoretically substantiated today.

The classical style of the English landscape garden alludes to an idealized landscape. The sequence of spaces is conceived in sculptural green scenery with predetermined enclosures. The buildings, including classical temples or small palace-like structures, are architectural references juxtaposed with these spaces; views into the landscape to distant villages or part of a town's silhouette are carefully chosen and well composed. Landscape painting, by Ruysdael for example, influenced such landscapes. The transformation from the Baroque garden to the English landscape garden can be traced back to its intellectual roots.

First, it was the dissolution of the French type of absolutism by turning to English democracy in the aftermath of the French Revolution. It was the philosophy of Rousseau that replaced Descartes's rationalism. Individualism emerges in society, abhorring the conventions and etiquette of courtly feudalism. In religion, pantheism emerges as a progression from state religion and ruler by the grace of God. The Baroque garden is ultimately condemned as an unnatural mutilation of nature, while the English landscape garden is celebrated as a liberation from political oppression and as a work of art in harmony with nature.

In the mid-nineteenth century, the city of Munich also saw the dissolution of its well-considered and designed urban development. In most comparable cities, the breach of their green ramparts in the early nineteenth century was the beginning of sprawling development in the surrounding landscape. Industrialization determined growth according to its own laws. The maximization of profits began to have an impact on land use.

Energy for urban development dwindles. Architectural assets become dilapidated. The social programs for municipal green spaces are often passed to private initiatives. This leads to a kind of social reformist self-help.

And so the German allotment or community garden movement emerged in cities, inspired by the Leipzig physician [Moritz] Schreber. It came about as a result of hazardous factory work, child labor, and unhealthy rental housing. The gymnastics movement of the "father of gymnastics" [Friedrich Ludwig] Jahn followed, and beautification associations were set up everywhere. The *Wandervogelbewegung* (wandering bird movement) was the first movement for escaping the city. At the end of the century, cities "horticulturalized" their parks and ornamental squares.

The bourgeoisie rose during industrialization, but did not find its own form of urban green space. Those who achieved affluence copied feudal examples in the gardens of their villas. It was the era of historicism.

Dr. [Willy Hugo] Hellpach in Heidelberg studied urban ecology and behavior patterns of citizens early on. He held that people fled the sunlight seventy years ago. Ladies wore large-brimmed hats, parasols, and gloves. They shaded their living rooms with thick curtains and built their houses with northerly aspects, often surrounded by dense dark conifers. Polite society had a pale complexion—this distinguished the lady in the city from the peasant woman.

A survey of typical urban green spaces shows that the significant open spaces within the urban fabric are mostly parks from the era of feudalism. Often they are on sites that were difficult to build on, for example, land threatened by floods. "Postage stamp" greens is how we describe these isolated urban green spaces laid out in the nineteenth and early twentieth centuries. They are single sports grounds, allotments, ornamental squares, and cemeteries. They have no impact on structure. Their distribution is generally incidental and the city has simply developed around them.

It would be two hundred years before Munich gained another public park whose size and significance is comparable to the Englischer Garten. From 1968 to 1972, the Olympic site was developed on the Oberwiesenfeld, covering an area the size of Munich's city center and situated only a few minutes away by subway. Of its 280 hectares, 160 hectares are public green space.

In line with the exhibition's didactic objective, the differences between the Englischer Garten and this landscape, officially known as "Olympiapark," are examined in order to bring to light concepts that, in my opinion, can take the discussion further.

I would like to point out a successful example of cooperation between a client and the team of architects. The Elector and Count Rumford had been Sckell's partners in the concept, program, and cultural standard, and the favorable conditions at the Olympic site matched this: Willi Daume and the Olympic Committee formulated the program, the concept for the contents of the plans, and the architects Behnisch and Partners met the objective of delivering the *Olympiade im Grünen* (Olympics in the Park) and *Olympiade der Musen und des Sports* (Olympics of the Muses and Sport) in their magnificent scheme, which placed the landscape above the architecture, making it a kind of intra-architecture. Mr. Behnisch asked me to take on the most important part of the scheme, the landscape.

We worked as a team, keeping up a mutual exchange of proposals and approval. And so we succeeded in building an innovative green public open space—a landscape—in the center of the city. [Günter] Behnisch, [Fritz] Auer, [Werner] Büxel, [Erhard] Tränkner, [Carlo] Weber, and I have demonstratively included one another in the honors, even if they were meant for us individually. And this is what I wish to do with the award of the Sckell Ring.

The objectives of the Munich Olympic Park of 1972 stand in contrast to the spirit and architecture of the Olympic site built for the 1936 Olympic Games in the era of Hitler. It was to represent a different Germany, a tolerant and liberal country.

Similar to the Englischer Garten, it sought to offer city dwellers a space for recreation and pleasure. Indeed, this objective has become its main theme. The versatility of its functions and the site's stimulating character have evolved.

The effectiveness of the Olympic Park was derived from a landscape analysis, which was carried out to establish general behavioral patterns of people seeking recreation in the landscape. This led to categorizing different landscape elements: mountain, lake, entrances, and parking lot were each given characteristic key plants.

Some paths can be modified. They are often created by the users themselves. Elements like these reappear in the variability of the vegetation, particularly the grasses and perennials in the meadows. The transplanting of a marshy meadow from Lake Starnberg into the Olympic landscape, along with bringing in gravel, rocks, and logs, demonstrates that the built landscape also strives for greater freedom for people and vegetation. Everyone can pick the meadow flowers as they were sown in a huge mass.

Oberwiesenfeld was to integrate the city visually by opening up the site towards its urban surroundings, be they industrial, residential, or roads. Visitors find themselves within an autonomous green complex while they experience the city and remain in the city. They are aware of where they are, within a robust composition of green elements: mountain, lake, tree and grove, meadow and wetland, riverbank and trail are the components of a landscape that is both natural and durable like a good everyday object.

This urban landscape not only differs from traditional parks in terms of its program and vegetation, it determines and tolerates the integration of the city. It provokes an urban awareness of life and lends itself to free use without risking its survival. It is, in a way, built for this purpose from its foundations up.

The landscape is sculptural in character: plane, crest, vale, swale, and slope form visual connections and spatial boundaries. This principle lends itself to different functions like resting, or gathering for play, which is easily anticipated.

While the Englischer Garten is designed for predetermined uses such as sitting, observing, walking on predetermined paths, squares and benches with predetermined views and in well-proportioned green spaces, the Olympic Park is laid out for uses that visitors largely determine themselves.

The extensive visual communication achieves a certain humanizing effect as regards to technical civilization by keeping roads, cars, and technical structures at a great distance. The city and recreation within the city enter a process of mutual participation.

The objective of the scheme was to do away with the constraints in the city—and move towards free improvisation. The design of green open spaces in the city and the landscape, as always, places aesthetic issues alongside, and often before, functional reasoning and rational considerations: gardens, parks, and landscapes are essentially applied vegetation. Thus, landscape is makeable, a conceivable artifact—or more crudely, an everyday object. Nature is the landscape architect's greatest ally—the true creative player, when you come to think of it. We are dealing with domesticated nature. What we call landscape is without exception nature cultivated by humans.

Gardens, and eventually the Garden City, lead to a number of attempts to integrate green spaces into the city, and particularly into housing areas. The Athens Charter was finally drawn up. The ideal city emerged as an "urban landscape."

However, the attempt to bring the landscape into the city resulted in the city sprawling across the landscape. In order to avert the negative impact of this development, it is necessary to mutually recalibrate the terms "city" and "landscape."

Let us start with some analytical observations.

Research on the behavior of urbanites in cities and in the landscape led to two fundamental findings. It became clear, firstly, that more than 70 percent of free time is spent in or immediately around the home; and secondly, that people want to withdraw from excessive social demands, meaning individualism and privacy, while also wanting a social life in the form of communication, social contacts, and taking an active interest. These two expectations are at a ratio of 20 to 80 percent of available time.

Studies that examine the connection between landscape design and recreational value can be particularly helpful.

Three central categories emerge: relief intensity, margin effect, and diversity.

Relief intensity results from the relationship and arrangement of horizontal and vertical axes in the landscape. It increases with the diversity of the topography, the wealth of topographical elements, including plane, crest, slope, and swale, etc. The margin effect is based on the psychological phenomenon of threshold experience. Limit situations of any kind, even relating to landscape, and you intensify self-experience. River and lakeside, woodland edge, all places where two landscape areas meet—like the lines between plane and slope—result in an increase in sensitivity. The diversity of a landscape is the sum of relief and margin effects as well as the general diversity of the vegetation, fauna, climate zones, and—essential for artificial landscapes—the range of uses offered.

In landscape architecture, a continuous dialectical juxtaposition and contrast of significant topographical elements needs to be found, utilized, strengthened, or newly created. Their formal polarity corresponds to the content-related contradiction of privacy and communication, openness and enclosure, grouping and isolation, movement and repose, which become distinct connections in the landscape and enable or even provoke simultaneous social behavior.

In another complex analytical consideration, we must look at the field of the garden designer, who only began aspiring to become a "landscape architect" in recent years. Municipal open space planning was limited to the maintenance of existing parks, its focused ambition being the design of ornamental parks in prestigious urban locations.

Garden designers created gardens for citizens who had come into money. The ornamental horticulture industry cultivated flowers, perennials, ornamental shrubs, and trees. Until well into the twentieth century, gardens and garden exhibitions were the domain and demonstration grounds for the skill of garden designers.

With increasing technical and industrial interventions in the landscape, such as highways, power plants, canals, and refineries, individual garden designers became committed to integrating these structures into the landscape. There are approaches for a comprehensive concept—in terms of new aesthetics as well.

However, garden designers could not provide new blueprints for town planning, or even influence it: garden cities and the Athens Charter contained well-meaning intentions for green open spaces in cities and for the landscape that had almost exclusively been drafted by architects.

Moreover, garden designers missed the period of functionalism. Functional reasoning would have been particularly important for urban, green, public open spaces. Thus, it was only recently that methodically founded open space planning was applied in land use planning.

A criticism of the usual development of green spaces in social housing led me to the following analysis in a model study in 1959: all areas designed for ornamental effect were unusable and of little therapeutic value because of their insufficient green infrastructure. They failed to exploit the visual separation opportunities that vegetation can provide in the third dimension, from window to window, and their maintenance was far too expensive.

"Performance vegetation" [*Leistungsgrün*] is the working title for a type of vegetation that enhances the potential quality of green spaces. This has two important outcomes: large trees and groves were once again planted in housing estates, and lawns were only laid where they could be used.

It is quite conceivable that public green spaces in cities could have a considerably greater effect on the urban climate than they currently have, indeed with the aim of disrupting the persistent tendency of the harmful urban climate. It is high time that theoretical open space planning should take facts and figures on the performance of vegetation types out of isolation and bring them together in a conceptual approach.

For landscape architects the questions arises: what do agricultural vegetation types—like meadows, grain fields, turnip and potato fields—do for cities? What are their recreational value and their function in terms of structuring and public health? One criterion is limited access for the city dwellers' recreation, another is the relatively low therapeutic impact on health in the urban climate.

This becomes evident when we apply this effect to a unit area and compare it to other vegetation types, such as woodland. It seems obvious that a one-hectare rye field has only a fraction of the ecological cleansing effect on the urban climate than one hectare of woodland of mature trees. The same applies to its usability.

The usability of green open spaces can often be increased manifold in terms of its functions (work, play, sports, walking, resting, sunbathing, sitting). This allows its therapeutic qualities (ground contact, air, light, tranquility) to be exploited to their best possible effect. Once these values have been compiled, conclusions can be drawn as to which open spaces could be used most effectively and to what quantity of the total system they should be allocated.

The vegetation area can be increased by several hundred percent with good lighting within the vegetation layers. Planting should take place in three zones: herb layer, shrub layer, and tree layer. Apart from the horticultural qualities, which are necessary for their performance, we are interested in the plants' characteristics in terms of health, such as noise filter, dust filter, oxygen production, and evaporation.

The three growth zones of vegetation layers can achieve a strong barrier effect with the vegetation. Layering and different heights make it possible for sunlight to penetrate where it is needed. The right species of trees and shrubs can be found at all conceivable heights.

Maintenance costs can be significantly reduced by simplifying the maintenance visits. The design methods we are currently using are not economical. The fact that the maintenance costs within five to ten years will be the same as the construction costs is not a consideration during the design process. In contrast to, for example, industrial production, landscape architecture is encumbered with aesthetic concepts that make the practical application of scientific findings difficult. Individuals' and the schools' views are still paramount.

When greening our cities, it is necessary to consider our limited land resources as well as the health and therapeutic demands made on green spaces, and to place maximization principles in the foreground. It is high time to develop methods that achieve the optimum physical and psychological effects for the urban social fabric on relatively small areas, and at low cost. It can be said with some certainty that the aesthetic impact of these green spaces, based on rational thinking, is no less than that of green spaces that are laid out with unnecessarily high maintenance costs.

More generally, new vegetation types can be defined according to functional requirements. This also includes a program for horticultural cultivation that must be geared to new social objectives.

Functionalism is accused of having been responsible for monostructural developments and uses. Plants make it easier for us than industrial products. All plants are basically made up of similar components, but they are all different. A linden tree has thousands of leaves, all are linden leaves, but no single one is exactly like another—just similar. It is claimed that this principle of the plant eliminates monotony, even if used in large numbers.

The theory that designers must work on the premise of a trend for city and countryside to merge into one overarching structure, making the land use and configuration of both landscape zones and threshold areas of the utmost interest, shall be explained by describing the type and effect of processes. Essentially they are:

1. The growth of building developments, and hence the coalescence of urban elements and landscape elements. Neither city nor landscape result in this process.

2. A vast increase in mobility makes the landscape available for after work and weekend recreation, which in turn prompts service provisions in the landscape. Tranquility is sought while communication is expected.

3. The necessary elimination of the disadvantage of the rural population through specialization and mechanization of farms. Farms and villages cease to have a function. Farms resemble industrial enterprises and exclude recreational use—but also the right to public subsidies.

If landscape planning is now understood to be the equivalent of landscape architecture in cities, this would mean that the plan must contain programs with site allocations and area delineations that were not previously within the purview of landscape architects.

The existing legal instruments are based on false premises: legislature generally presumes that the order of the landscape is a given and "only needs to be protected from inappropriate interventions."

This is simply wrong. We need laws that make the drafting of land use plans mandatory, and these plans must be binding. Landscape and regional planning in cities and industrial agglomerations have been in the focus for some time. The terms local and regional planning have supplemented—if not superseded in an overriding sense—the terms urban development and town planning. A number of examples of large developments attempt to put the diverse needs of civilization in a context of ever-decreasing space and the opportunities afforded by nature. The trend is towards the landscape becoming a reproduction zone for predominantly urban spaces. Thus, the programming, development, operation, and maintenance of the landscape are not only left up to the perspective of a team of planners but fall within the responsibility of policies and legislation.

The latter issue in particular causes difficulties. It is still largely thanks to the initiative of some local politicians, farsighted administrative staff, and planners if the local plans and landscape plans do not stop at the administrative boundaries of a municipality, but consider the wider area that is characterized by landscape criteria. The German Constitution [*Grundgesetz*] and Federal Building Act [*Bundesbaugesetz*, today: *Baugesetzbuch*] concede that the municipalities have complete planning powers. It is inevitable that urban and regional planning must be reorganized from a landscape point of view, as land use plans [*Flächennutzungsplan*] must address the future uses of the entire municipal area, including the landscape as well. Only rarely do political boundaries coincide with the boundaries between different landscape character areas. However, the different land uses are often determined by landscape zones.

At about the time of the enactment of the Federal Building Act in 1960, comprehensive landscape plans were drawn up in municipalities to embrace all green open spaces in an overall network for the first time since the masterplans for Baroque towns, or later garden cities.

It was recognized that isolated projects often lacked context, and so at many levels did not promote the necessary complexity of all parts in similar facilities. The goal was to use green space to connect different types of playgrounds, play areas, sports grounds, swimming pools, gardens, and recreation centers with various programs, which would have a structuring function within the urban fabric, and to draw them together in an overall context. This green space structure is conceived like a network of connected areas linking up to the smallest capillary-like branches, ranging from landscape character areas to the front door and could be compared to a similarly differentiated transport network. If such planning concepts have been implemented at all, their objectives still hold as guiding principles for urban open space planning.

What has been neglected for the past two hundred years during the rapid growth of mid-sized cities into large cities, or even cities with over a million inhabitants, is structuring the expanding city by expediently allocating open spaces for built-up areas, green space networks for transport networks, which should now be done at the regional planning level. We must think about a new and positive approach to determine what respective functions building developments and landscapes should have in order to form a practical system. The landscape areas in between the town centers must be actively developed, in the same way as building projects are developed.

Hundreds and thousands of people from metropolitan areas flock to the countryside on a fine weekend. Camping and summer homes have brought many city dwellers in closer contact with the countryside and made the most remote corners accessible. "This has an impact on the spatial development of the countryside: concern for agricultural production is replaced by multiform development policies for the countryside."

In Holland, for example, unprofitable farms and forests are bought by the state and used for recreation. The state also pays compensation to landowners who provide public access to their properties. The appeal of variousness is part of the plan. Access and development are subject to the law of maximization of "spatial yield," that is, the greatest possible intensification of recreational potential. This concept aimed to retain as many specific types of natural areas as possible. The most important natural habitats were carefully surveyed and categorized.

The new landscape to be developed is no longer a purely agricultural landscape, but takes on the equally important task of providing opportunities to satisfy city dwellers' demands to connect with a predominantly "natural" environment for their necessary recreation, which cannot be done in cities.

However, this assertion conveys only one part of the matter. Regional landscapes increasingly adopt the quality of reproduction areas in contrast to areas used for production. Woodlands also serve as "timber factories," and farmers produce basic foodstuffs, but on the whole, the supply of clean water, clean air, the provision of habitats for a diverse flora and fauna, as well as the integration of city dwellers in their spare time into this biotically determined space, has become so important that the land's main emphasis has shifted to production.

This defines the political task for both agriculture and forestry, giving it a perspective that had previously been considered a side issue. Town and country enter into a completely new frame of reference. Introducing aspirations that are essentially urban in character into the existing rural hinterland, combined with the results of transformations on the land in agricultural cultivation, creates severe problems, particularly from an environmental point of view, and could lead to dangerous developments. These must be seen in the context of production-maximization processes in agriculture and forestry, which increasingly resemble industrial production and could lead to a denaturalization of the affected landscape areas. They must also be seen in the context of the farmers' work, which is changing with a trend towards agricultural engineering. However, it is feasible to produce high quality foodstuffs using intensive agricultural cultivation.

Agriculture, and to some extent forestry, has been subsidized by structural improvements with the aim of increasing production per unit area and worker. In the case of any resulting overproduction, these subsidies should at least be questioned. This may free funds that could be used for the maintenance of the landscape.

Agriculture cannot be made to provide services without reward, as it is required to do, for example, in maintaining woodland commons that need to be retained solely for their social value and the public good. The same applies to the management of woodland valleys, whose special climate and large margin effects support a great variety of plant and animal habitats. There is another aspect that is not covered by function alone and cannot be maximized: the spatial distribution of the existing cultivated landscape has a characteristic quality from a Gestalt psychology point of view, which is lost once even the smallest woodland common or woodland meadow falls into disuse. Some encouraging approaches in legislature, such as the Bavarian Agriculture Act of 1970, seek to end these processes. However, an overall concept is lacking and no clear sociopolitical objectives have been formulated for marginal agricultural land.

If, as previously held, the landscapes should be considered a diverse network of green spaces within a region, whose function is to act as a regeneration area that balances construction and transport areas within settlements, this claim needs further explanation. The cultivation of land since the Middle Ages had established an equilibrium, which justifies the claim that the landscape was a regeneration area for settlements, even if it was used primarily for the production of timber and foodstuffs. Fertilizers and chemical pesticides were rarely used and posed no threat to the artificial balance maintained on cultivated land. The waste products of civilization in the settlements brought about the pollution of, for example, rivers, which were able to recover through self-purification.

Danger looms as the increasing yields of agricultural production, to which farmers are now encouraged, cause almost more hazardous environmental pollution than cities, because it is uncontrollable.

Directives need to be found that are based on the fact that modern agriculture has a two-fold function: producing high-quality foodstuffs and delivering services related to enhancing and maintaining our natural resources.

Active landscape planning needs to focus on subdividing the landscape within the plan area into defined zones that allocate functional priorities. A rather coarse grid will provide information on suitable areas for the expansion of settlements, areas for forestry and agriculture, and areas that should not be used for the production of economically viable products.

The latter areas should receive a new function. However, the other land use priorities must, besides fulfilling their allocated uses, take on functions that arise from the necessity to develop the land in an environmentally responsible way, ultimately meaning to develop it to a standard that is fit for human beings. This must be seen in the context of people who, aside from their intellectuality, are natural creatures and dependent on general biological regularities, as is indicated by just two basic factors: their nutrition and their reproduction.

Professor [Heinz] Ellenberg designed the botanical garden in Göttingen where, by observing the plant communities he had transplanted there to see how they would respond to a specific increase of moisture, drought, or higher light levels, and how they would respond to heat or lowered temperatures, it becomes clear how easy it is to manipulate vegetation. So far, we have been cultivating plants to increase food crops. Or we have enhanced the aesthetic effect of garden plants by turning filaments into petals. This is apart from the fact that we have neglected to cultivate plants that tolerate urban site conditions: plants that grow on rooftops and thrive on roadsides without requiring special care.

Alexander von Humboldt defined landscape as the appearance of a geographically relevant part of the geosphere, whose total character can be understood as one unit. He does not distinguish between nature and cultivated areas, between urban and rural. Contemporary ecology defines landscape not only as an aesthetically classified, physical appearance, but also as the ecological structure made up of its individual landscape factors. Such landscapes are not rigid, static systems, but are in continuous transformation—a dynamic system or interplay of natural landscape factors and the landscape factor of human society ([Konrad] Buchwald).

How we perceive nature or landscape is largely dependent on the cultural perception of social development. Evaluations are colored by convention ([Renate] Krysmanski).

Traditional landscape planning still considers rural farming landscapes to be the ideal—that is, the landscapes of a preindustrial technological standard.

The aesthetics of the rural landscape are founded in history. The landscape has developed since the Bronze Age and was preserved in its former condition, thus corresponding to the configuration of medieval cities.

The medieval landscape, which is as valued as Rothenburg ob der Tauber, a town that is preserved as a historical monument, cannot by any means be saved by conservation alone, which would cost a lot of money.

Landscape ecologists hold that the old rural landscape was in harmony with natural resources.

Giving up old cultivated areas threatens to destroy the spatial structure of entire landscapes. They are typically characterized by alternating open areas and woodland areas.

In these areas of low crop yields lies an opportunity relevant to the general problem of our development.

It is estimated that 30 percent of our current agricultural land will become marginal land in order to maximize profits, as its cultivation will be of no interest in the future. The reason is that more will be produced on a smaller area.

Cultivated land, which is taken out of agricultural production and thus removed from private enterprise interests, should not be left to the free play of forces. These large landscape areas must be placed at public or even cooperative disposal; for example, they could become new common land.

One possible objective would be: areas that are no longer privately cultivated should be developed to become highly effective in terms of human ecology. This does not preclude new programs that allocate extensive and varied uses. Parts of the landscape could be privately maintained, as is already done in some fisheries.

These kinds of demands may not seem practical at first sight. That may be because we lack imagination about how such demands can be made at an economically feasible scale.

I believe that the findings of landscape ecology can help their practical application. Presumably, processes occurring in natural succession can be controlled to create a large amount of ecotopes, and eventually ecosystems, some of which are then left to themselves. On the other hand, interventions in these processes are to be devised, which must be sensible and economical.

In this context, the question arises of how we can best establish a natural balance. In some areas, natural resources can develop and be preserved. They include the extensive or unutilized landscape elements, such as protective forests, mountain ranges, heaths, and bodies of water.

We have neglected problems related to the regeneration of natural potentials by overusing them, and we have done nothing to set processes in motion that are able to create new biomass, that is, the sum of all life processes.

It would be wise if each depletion or each consumption of biomass would be balanced by not only a natural production of biomass, but also by an artificial production that is manipulated. This would mean that the over-exploitation of the landscape would be brought under control.

An ecosystem does not exist from the beginning. It is established through gradual development—and it does this for a reason. In this development, production of biomass varies in intensity as the process unfolds. It is certainly possible to regulate production. This requires knowledge about the processes and interventions that need to be devised under the heading of "maintenance."

Ecology that functions in the sense of a cybernetic control circuit can deliver a kind of code for each program and sub-program. Measures in the landscape are able to establish their control from this ode—provided that such a control system is developed. A diverse palette of new opportunities is derived, latently contained within the natural potential.

We manage our vegetation to become meadows, pasture, vineyards, fields, and woodlands; all are areas of controlled vegetation. The same is true for urban parks, gardens, or flowerbeds.

Vegetation is determinable; it is processual in that it changes as long as its changing is not hampered, for example, by cutting a hedge, or prevented by mowing a lawn, or terminated by harvesting a grain field.

Predictable ecosystems are established under similar naturally or artificially manipulated conditions: marshes, woodlands, ponds. They can be planned and thus are implementable. They could become integral parts of current urban land use plans.

This means, for example, we can accumulate a great diversity of flora and fauna in a landscape by controlling the availability of water. We create a species-rich meadow through interventions—open and layered woodland—while retaining single characterful trees. We can create lakes and ponds—possibly only to set off the process of their silting up. This is how it could be achieved: a stream is dammed in a valley; a former meadow is turned into a body of water; the extent of the water area can be controlled, or in other words, the depth of water in different places of the lake or pond. This makes it possible to predict how and where riparian vegetation, or vegetation in shallow or deep water, will establish. It can be estimated how great the diversity of flora and fauna will be and how the necessary process of silting up will generally develop.

I can now decide whether certain parts should silt up with the aim of creating inaccessible areas in the long term, which could become essential nesting sites for birds, for example.

Or I can keep the water surface open with the goal of using it for water sports, and ice sports in winter. I can combine both goals, that is I can anticipate or allow the development of a differentiated system of areas of diverse water depths, ranging from zones that silt up to higher dry zones, and control the processes by managing them.

This type of "second-hand nature" is still unfamiliar among town and regional planners. Landscape design in cities is something else, something stylized, despite the fact that the city and the landscape are more closely connected than ever before.

The architectural coordination of urban and rural green spaces has not been accomplished. In the landscape at Oberwiesenfeld in Munich, we replaced the herbaceous border, and its delphiniums that always flower in the same spot, with meadows transferred there from the landscape; trails along desire lines are an integral part of the concept. These are initial approaches—again, for a new aesthetic concept.

But are there any cities and urban regions where woodlands and lakes, wetlands and heathland are earmarked in land use plans? At best, they are left where they happen to be.

The design of the landscape, as it emerges after its agricultural use has been abandoned, is an unprecedented challenge for our culture. We must retain the diversity of ecosystems in a mosaic-like transformation, or allow them to grow.

A variety of possible uses should be provided for people. They will find this landscape developed on natural principles beautiful, and its new wealth makes it interesting.

It is possible to create areas specifically encouraging recreational activities that alternate between communication and areas for tranquility, observation and retreat.

Heathland, like the Lüneburg Heath, and steppe heaths in the mountains, are examples for such a concept. They have been created through cultivation and turned into conservation areas that are managed by maintenance measures to retain them as they are. Although made by humans and ecologically unstable, they are attractive.

The landscape of a new type will have pristine and natural characteristics. The cultivated countryside that dominates the appearance of areas in intensive agricultural production will be contrasted by a structure consisting of a varied change between pools, ponds, lakes, wetlands, heathland, dunes, open woodlands, clumps of trees, groves, pioneer plant communities, and stable climax ecosystems, such as ancient woodlands.

We also have to reassess forests and woodlands. Forestry mostly defends the position that it can reconcile maximum yields of timber with the social effects of woodlands. Their social effects are generally recognized. However, it is no more than a nice side issue of forestry objectives.

Forests planted for a maximum yield of timber cannot simultaneously deliver a maximum of ecological quality ([Wolfgang] Haber).

The fact that woodlands cover another third of West Germany's total area is hard to accept. Where are the policy objectives that integrate overarching social criteria into the management of forests?

The succinct statement in the agricultural policy report for West Germany in 1969, "marginal agricultural land shall be reforested," does not attest to a deep understanding of a problem that cannot be solved by experts alone. These areas are almost exclusively planted with spruce monocultures. Our proposal for a landscape that is of a high socioeconomic quality must contain a multilayered continuous-cover forest. Woodlands grow slowly, so decisions are urgent here as well.

It will be down to developing an economically feasible concept that is able to deliver the maximum ecological and social functions. This proposal will require designs that address all three zones: agricultural land, woodlands, and a third new zone that is specifically set aside for ecological regeneration and recreation.

It can lead to the creation of a landscape that is primarily recreational while being able to accomplish an ecological balance between settlement and landscape. An ecological balance must now be found. The focus is on the concepts of "design" and "development."

When Humboldt in his definition of the landscape talks of the "total character of an earth region," the current situation will hold that this total character must determine the guiding principle to reset the balance between anthropogenic impacts on a landscape, including settlements and the natural conditions. Total character does not mean departmental thinking or specialized planning, which town planning is, but integrated overall planning. The objective is to create democratic green spaces for a mobile industrial society.

From a sociopolitical point of view, objectives arise that result in a new understanding of landscape for everyone through its higher degree of social and biological development.

The design for a new landscape remains a task for us: the concept for a feasible, meaningful landscape, because it is a necessary landscape, derived from measures that achieve a designed and thus aesthetic environment. And all this in an untraditional form of development. Utilization and maintenance is not just utopian, it is a realistic objective.

Biographies

Friedrich Ludwig von Sckell, by anonymous artist

Hermann Prince von Pückler-Muskau, 1837, copper engraving: Auguste Hüssener

Peter Joseph Lenné, 1854, lithograph: Friedrich Jentzen, after a drawing by Franz Krüger

The biographies, originally compiled by Günther Grzimek for the book *The Appropriation of the Lawn,* have been revised by the editor and supplemented by colleagues who were to be mentioned according to Grzimek's book concept.

Friedrich Ludwig von Sckell (1750–1823) moved with the Bavarian Elector Karl Theodor from Schwetzingen to Munich, where he was commissioned to design the Englischer Garten. Drawing on the ideas of Count Rumford, he created one of the first public gardens in Germany. Previously, he had made trips to England to learn about the new, enlightened style of garden architecture. In 1804 Sckell was appointed Royal Garden Superintendent and from then on was responsible for the Bavarian palaces, lakes, and gardens. In 1808, Sckell won a competition of ideas for the expansion of the royal residence beyond the old bastions, and in 1810 he was commissioned with the "General Plan for the Extension of the City at the Maxtor." The resulting designs had a significant influence on the formal urban development of Munich. His designs, such as those for Nymphenburg Park, were characterized by great circumspection. For example, he preserved the central Baroque section of the palace park and altered the surrounding area in the new style. In his honor, the Bavarian Academy of Arts awards the Friedrich Ludwig von Sckell Ring of Honor to recognize achievement in landscape architecture.

Hermann Prince von Pückler-Muskau (1785–1871) was a gardening enthusiast who first traveled to England in 1812, and it was there he discovered his passion for gardening. He soon began to redesign his estates according to the ideas of the English landscape garden. The immense amount of earthmoving and construction he had done caused him financial difficulties. He sold his property in Muskau in order to continue—as a true "parkomaniac"—remodeling his Branitz Palace estate in the same way. In addition to his love of gardening, he was also a well-traveled man of letters whose publications were widely read. After his death he was buried in Branitz under a pyramid made of earth. The "green prince" also wrote a book on gardening entitled *Andeutungen über Landschaftsgärtnerei* (Indications on Landscape Gardening). His parks are now protected as UNESCO World Heritage Sites.

Peter Josef Lenné (1789–1866) began his true career in 1816 as a "journeyman gardener" at Sanssouci Palace near Potsdam. In 1824 he was appointed Royal Prussian Garden Director and in 1854 General Director of all Royal Gardens. In 1842 he became a member of the newly founded Agricultural Economy Committee and in 1853 an honorary member of the Prussian Academy of Arts. In 1861, the University of Breslau (Wrocław) awarded him an honorary doctorate. Among other projects, Lenné designed and built the Tiergarten and the Zoological Garden in Berlin. Characteristic of the breadth of his fields of activity, he not only worked on park designs but also urban planning, for instance the development plans for Berlin, the Köpenicker Feld, boulevards such as the one from the zoo to Hasenheide, designs for the Landwehr Canal, and landscape supervision of the first Prussian railroad line. In 1824, Lenné was appointed the first director of the royal gardening school at Potsdam.

Friedrich Ludwig Jahn, lithograph: Georg Ludwig Engelbach

Dr. Daniel Gottlob Moritz Schreber, 1883, woodcut: Adolf Neumann

Paul Schultze Naumburg, 1919

Leberecht Migge

Friedrich Ludwig Jahn (1778–1852) was a teacher in Berlin. His initiatives earned him the nickname "Turnvater" (father of gymnastics) Jahn. The gymnastics movement he initiated is closely linked to the early German nationalist movement. In 1810, he declared his support for the "inner renewal of Prussia" in the journal *Turnkunst*. That same year, he founded the German Confederation for the Liberation and Unification of Germany, from which Jews were excluded. The first "Turnplatz" for the public practice of gymnastics was established in 1811 with the founding of the Berlin Gymnastics Association. In 1813, Jahn was a member of Lützow's Freikorps troops in the wars against Napoleon. He was eventually imprisoned in 1819 for his radical stance, released in 1825, amnestied, and rehabilitated in 1840. In 1848, Jahn was elected as a deputy to the Frankfurt National Assembly. He was a lifelong advocate of gymnastics: the famous "Four F's," *frisch–fromm–fröhlich–frei* (brisk, devout, merry, and free), served as his motto. Grzimek was interested in Jahn's biography in regard to the importance of sports facilities in open urban space and the construction of sports facilities.

Daniel Gottlob Moritz Schreber (1808–1861) studied medicine in Leipzig. In his works, he was concerned with the health of children, especially in the increasingly industrialized cities. He promoted spending time in the countryside and is considered one of the creators of *Heilgymnastik* (healing gymnastics). He called for more exercise and the establishment of public playgrounds and gardens. However, the origin of the allotment or community garden movement that is named after him can be traced back to an idea for the promotion of general public health developed together with the anatomist Carl Ernst Bock, who, together with Schreber, was one of the founders of the Leipzig Gymnastics Club in 1845. The first "Schreber Club" was founded in 1864 by the school principal Ernst Innozenz Hauschild, named in Schreber's honor shortly after his death. Grzimek was long interested in the topic of children's play and the importance of allotment gardens, and he considered the allotment garden movement to be of vital importance.

Paul Schultze-Naumburg (1869–1949) initially studied painting. After participating as a draftsman in architectural competitions, he continued his education at art colleges and spent two semesters studying architecture in Karlsruhe. After graduating, he moved to Munich, where he tried to establish himself in 1894 with a painting and drawing academy. In 1901 he founded the Saalecker Werkstätten (Saaleck Workshops). With his so-called "Cultural Works," published as a series of books between 1901 and 1917, he propagated a return to traditional building forms. In two volumes he also dealt with the garden in its many aspects. He was a pioneer of the *Heimatschutz* (Homeland Protection) movement and, beginning in the 1920s, a renowned architect who was also influential among leading Nazis. He became director of the Weimar Art Academy (1930), saw himself as a champion against "cultural Bolshevism," and in the process advocated and promoted racial theories. Eventually he also became a member of the Nazi party. He was commissioned by Hitler to undertake renovations starting in 1935, but was not successful with his Heimatstil (traditional style), which did not appear monumental enough. In 1940 he was forced out of the university at the age of seventy-one. Hitler included him in his list of the twelve most important visual artists.

Leberecht Migge (1881–1935) was born in Danzig and began an apprenticeship in horticulture in Hamburg in 1898. In 1904 he became artistic director at the renowned Ochs horticultural company. A study trip through England followed in 1910, and in 1913 he published his *Garden Culture of the Twentieth Century*. In it he set his hopes for a "renewal" of garden culture. This was followed in 1918 by the publication of his green manifesto, *Everyone Self-Sufficient!* In it, Migge advocates, in view of the supply shortages after the First World War, the principle of self-sufficiency—that is, the growing of fruit, vegetables, and flowers. The garden city principle, which he had become acquainted with in England, was groundbreaking for him. He became an important representative of this movement and lived in the artists' colony of Worpswede beginning in 1920. He worked with the architects Hermann Muthesius, Richard Riemerschmid, and Martin Wagner on numerous practical projects.

Alwin Seifert

Heinrich Wiepking

Hermann Mattern, 1962, photo: Beate zur Nedden

Gunnar Martinsson, photo: Thilo Mechau

The architect Alwin Seifert (1890–1972) studied under Theodor Fischer at the Technical University of Munich, graduating in 1913. In 1934, Fritz Todt, the General Inspector for Roads, appointed him "advisor on all questions of landscape integration for German roads and motorways." In 1937 he became a member of the Nazi party. In 1938 he was personally given by Hitler the honorary title of "Professor." In 1940, on the occasion of his fiftieth birthday, Hitler named him *Reichslandschaftsanwalt* (Reich Landscape Advocate). He planned numerous gardens for "prominent protagonists" of the NSDAP. During the Nazi era, he was critically responsible for the design and integration of highways and hydroelectric power plants in the countryside. He also developed a concept for the "Germanization of the Eastern Territories" through planting. After the war, he resumed his activities as an independent garden designer and lecturer at the Technical University of Munich. In a questionnaire for the de-Nazification tribunal (August 22, 1946), Seifert stated that he had no employment relationship with the Todt Organization. He remained a professor at the Technical University of Munich until 1954. Seifert is not an isolated case with regard to his Nazi past, as Heinrich Wiepking's biography shows.

Heinrich Wiepking-Jürgensmann (1891–1973) completed a gardening apprenticeship in the municipal nursery of Hanover. In 1912 he began to study architecture at the Technical University of Hanover (today the Leibniz University Hanover) but did not complete the degree course. He served as an intern at the gardening firm of Ochs in Hamburg. Beginning in 1922 he worked in Berlin and Cologne as a "freelance architect for garden and urban design" in Berlin and Cologne. In 1934 he succeeded Erwin Barth at the Institute for Garden and Landscape Design at the Friedrich Wilhelm University in Berlin, and thus set himself against Gustav Allinger, who was also National Socialist in orientation. His mentor was the influential Professor Konrad Meyer. In 1936 he participated in the landscape design for the Olympic Games in Berlin. In 1940, he was appointed special commissioner for landscape design and maintenance at the Reich Commission for the Consolidation of the German People. Together with Meyer, he was tasked with developing a set of rules for landscaping the conquered and annexed eastern territories that would be "appropriate for the [German] race." Immediately after 1945, he tried to regain a foothold in Hanover, where he was responsible for landscape management, garden design, and landscape architecture.

Hermann Mattern (1902–1971) was born in Hofgeismar, Hesse, and completed an apprenticeship as a gardener. He studied in 1924 at the Teaching and Research Institute for Horticulture in the Dahlem district of Berlin. He worked with the social reformist landscape architect Leberecht Migge (*Der soziale Garten* [The Social Garden], *Das Grüne Manifest* [The Green Manifesto]). After graduation, he took over the planning department in Potsdam-Bornim with Karl Foerster and Herta Hammerbacher, whom he later married. From 1935 he ran the office jointly with Foerster, the famous breeder of perennials. In 1935 Alwin Seifert brought him into the *Reichsautobahn* project (Reich highway system) as a so-called "landscape advocate" (*Reichslandschaftsanwalt*) and member of the Nazi party; he worked there until 1945. Among other things, he planned the 1939 Reich Garden Show on Stuttgart's Killesberg, with the collaboration of landscape architect Otto Valentien. After World War II, he oversaw the reestablishment of Kassel's Werkakademie (School of Applied Arts, today part of the University of Kassel). As a member of Club 53 in Kassel, founded by Arnold Bode, he played an active part in preparing the way for Germany's most famous art exhibition, documenta. In 1961, Mattern accepted a professorship at the Technical University of Berlin and continued to teach in Kassel until 1965.

Gunnar Martinsson (1924–2012) was born in Sweden. He was educated in a horticultural school in Stockholm, and then completed an internship in Germany in the office of Otto Valentien. After returning to Stockholm, he worked in the office of Sven Hermelin. This was followed by studies at the local art academy. In 1963 Martinsson designed the Swedish pavilion for the International Garden Show in Hamburg, which established his reputation in Germany. When a new chair for Landscape and Garden was created at the University of Karlsruhe in 1965, Martinsson was chosen to fill it. He participated in numerous committees and competitions and achieved great renown there. In 1983 he was awarded the Friedrich von Sckell Ring of Honor by the Bavarian Academy of Arts. After his retirement in 1992, he returned to Sweden. However, he maintained active contact with his German colleagues, especially at the universities. He was succeeded at the University of Karlsruhe in 1993 by Dieter Kienast.

Dieter Kienast | Wolfgang Haber | Peter Latz | Donata and Christoph Valentien

Dieter Kienast (1945–1998) came from a family of gardeners in the canton of Zurich. His career began with an apprenticeship as a gardener and a first internship with Albert Zulauf. In 1970 he began studying at the Technical University of Munich, where he found his studies too rigid and switched to the University of Fine Arts in Kassel, where he studied with Günther Grzimek. There he received further inspiration in his postgraduate studies in urban planning from Lucius Burckhardt and Karl-Heinrich Hülbusch. From 1975 on he worked in his own landscaping office, which he founded with partners. In 1978 he earned a doctorate in plant sociology. From 1981 to 1985 he directed the botanical garden in Brüglingen. From 1980 to 1991 he was professor of Garden Design in Rapperswil, and in 1992 he succeeded Gunnar Martinsson at the University of Karlsruhe. In 1995 he founded an office in partnership with Günther Vogt. From 1997 to 1998 he was professor at the ETH Zurich University. His projects earned him international recognition, and he was much in demand as a landscape architect. Kienast's gardens displayed great originality and a sophisticated level of design, making him one of the key figures in modern Swiss landscape architecture.

Wolfgang Haber (b. 1925) studied botany, zoology, chemistry, and geography. In 1966 he became head of the newly founded Institute for Landscape Planning at the Weihenstephan campus of the Technical University of Munich. He subsequently headed the Chair of Landscape Ecology until his retirement. He participated in numerous phases of the evolution of the landscape architecture and landscape planning courses of studies. In 1972 he oversaw the hiring of Günther Grzimek to succeed Ludwig Schreiber as professor. Haber was highly regarded as a researcher and consulted the federal government in numerous advisory committees. He was regarded as a realist and a tireless campaigner on issues of environmental development. "The path to a sustainable future," Haber said, "can … only succeed if we reflect on reality and focus our attention on the key problems of the twenty-first century."

Peter Latz (b. 1939) is the oldest of eight siblings. He grew up in the Saarland and studied landscape architecture at the Technical University of Munich. He completed postgraduate studies in urban planning with Erich Kühn at the RWTH Aachen University. During his studies he met his future wife, Anneliese, with whom he founded an office first in Aachen and then in Saarbrücken in 1968. In 1973 he was appointed successor to Günther Grzimek at the Comprehensive University in Kassel, to where he moved his office. In 1983 he became professor at the Technical University of Munich, where he again succeeded Grzimek. Since 2001 he managed his office, Latz & Partners, with his wife in Kranzberg near Freising, until he was succeeded by his son Tilman in 2011. Peter Latz's plans for the Duisburg-Nord Landscape Park made him internationally famous. His ideas for post-industrial landscapes brought him international projects, widespread recognition, and awards. His work has been exhibited at the Museum of Modern Art in New York. After his retirement from the Technical University of Munich in 2009, he was succeeded by Udo Weilacher.

Christoph Valentien (b. 1939) and Donata Valentien (b. 1944) both studied landscape architecture after graduating from high school: Christoph at the Technical University of Munich and Donata Seifert first at the University of Applied Sciences in Munich and then at the Technical University of Berlin under Hermann Mattern. Christoph Valentien completed postgraduate studies in urban planning at the RWTH Aachen University. In 1967 he was appointed research assistant to Professor Walter Rossow. There he met his future wife, Donata. In 1971, they founded the Valentien + Valentien office in Stuttgart, located in Wessling since 1981. In 1980 Christoph Valentien was appointed to a newly created chair at the Technical University of Munich. The work of both stands out for its high-quality design, at both a large and small scale. In 2010 and as director of the Architecture section, Donata Valentien memorably addressed the issue of landscape destruction and climate change in the exhibition *The Return of the Landscape* at the Academy of Arts in Berlin. In 2014 she received the Federal Cross of Merit for her work in leading advisory committees. Christoph Valentien has held a professorship in China since 2001 and became emeritus professor in 2002 and was succeeded by Regine Keller. The office Valentien + Valentien was taken over by their daughter Dayana in 2018.

Epilogue

Do you too always read the epilogue first? It can spur one to read, if one hopes for a summary of the previous chapters. With this book, however, it is not that easy, because Günther Grzimek's oeuvre comprises such a rich treasure of works on the most diverse levels, so that only a first brief insight into the vast legacy of this landscape architect could be provided here. As the list of works shows, Grzimek worked in all dimensions. While his work was initially oriented around cemetery planning, his range of commissions expanded to urban and open space planning studies, studies that were groundbreaking for the landscape architecture profession in the early 1960s. His landscape architecture perspective on rapidly growing cities differed from that of traditional urban planners and developers. He recognized early on the benefits of green spaces, of open spaces as places of refuge and recreation, as a counterbalance to highly dense construction and as suppliers of fresh air with the potential of equalizing temperatures. His ideas for Ulm, Darmstadt, Aschaffenburg, and Ludwigsburg—to name just a few of his major citywide green planning projects—are still visible and effective in these cities today. They were also groundbreaking in how urban land use planning evolved in the 1960s. In this context, he may be considered a pioneer, since long before his colleagues recognized green issues in urban land use planning, he was already being consulted on them in many places. The professional association did pick up on this trend until the 1970s.

In the 1960s, Grzimek began to participate in numerous competitions in collaboration with architects, often being called in to collaborate after the architects had won the competition. This resulted in building planning, such as the zoo and the Landesbank in Münster with Harald Deilmann, the engineering schools in Ulm and in Aalen with Günter Behnisch, the botanical garden in Marburg, and, as one of his major achievements, the Olympic Park in Munich with Behnisch & Partners. In each of these projects, Grzimek created landscapes of great expressiveness and timeless beauty. His approach, with detailed landscape, soil, and vegetation analyses, his intensive concern with the site and its future use, have consistently proven successful. His clear function-based plans laid the foundation for the systems derived from them, such as access, planting systems, modeling, and furnishings. His concepts were always profoundly thought out and clearly reasoned. Despite his often strictly functionalist approach, Grzimek's plans for cemeteries, parks, campuses, and residential environments are surprisingly poetic. This was surely due to his adept handling of topography, soil, and plants. In many cases, he honed the plans with a qualified circle of experts, and so his collaborators—in addition to architects like Günter Behnisch and Carlo Weber—were vegetation specialists such as Richard Hansen and Heinz Ellenberg, designers such as Otl Aicher, and colleagues who, as sociologists, had relevant insights to contribute, such as Werner Nohl. Grzimek was interested not only in the landscape, but in society and its demands on the places he planned. Especially revealing was his discussion of the concerns of citizens in the framework planning for the new airport near Munich. The airport's supporters were just as important to him as its opponents, as is expressed in his texts for the framework plan. This sociopolitical motivation had already inspired him in his early Ulm years to become involved in the community college, in adult education, and in working groups together with Otl Aicher and Inge Scholl. During his time in Kassel, he was active on the documenta council with Arnold Bode, and in the universities in Kassel and Munich he advocated reforms for the courses of study in landscape architecture, even against the background of student turmoil in the 1960s. In the process, he repeatedly found himself confronted with entrenched conservative forces, whether in city or municipal governments, university leadership, or professional associations, who understood planning more as an act of administration than as the fostering of creatively usable open spaces. At the same time, it was clear to Grzimek early on that green spaces can be more than just decorative. His assessment of what he called "performance green" spaces came at a time when he was receiving professional acclaim for these research ideas, but in practice open spaces continued to be treated more as complementary to transport or as visual dividers than as ecologically valuable areas. Only with the success of ecosystem research has the perception of the function—and thus the importance—of urban green space changed.

But is it too late?

That is the question we are so frequently asked today. Although in Germany environmental protection has become a topic of our environmental design—socially since the 1960s and institutionally since the 1970s—positive effects on the environment have been marginal. The consequences of the climate catastrophe raise an unprecedented global challenge for us. Warnings such as Rachel Carson's

Silent Spring of 1962 or the Club of Rome's 1972 recommendations on *The Limits to Growth* seemed to fade away quickly. The latest statements from the Intergovernmental Panel on Climate Change (IPCC) confirm that the adaptation strategies for our environment have so far been ineffective. These strategies include ecologically effective green spaces that are climate and ecologically resilient, which would require forceful policy decisions as well as experts in landscape architecture and planning, ecology, biology, and Climate Engineering. Only when these disciplines are brought to bear upon urban planning will we be able to intervene effectively in global climatic trends. To continue building as we have always done is no longer an option.

Günther Grzimek actively worked, taught, and published on these issues throughout his creative career. It is necessary to rediscover him.

Appendix

Awards

Sckell Ring of Honor

Playground "Ulm Silberwald," 1960

Friedrich von Sckell Ring of Honor from the Bavarian Academy of Fine Arts, 1972

Greater BDA (Association of German Architects) Award (for the Olympic Park) with Behnisch & Partners, 1972

Architecture Award Munich (for the Olympic Park) with Behnisch & Partners, 1972

Fritz Schumacher Prize, 1987

Posthumous: "Classic Nike" from the BDA (for the Olympic Park) with Behnisch & Partners, 2013

List of Works

Green spaces planning in the form of draft development plans as a contribution to land use planning in cities (landscape planning in the context of land use planning)

1951–1954
Green spaces planning for Ulm; *Problems of a Growing City*
Green spaces planning as urban development plan and part of the land use plan
Collaboration: Dr. Heinz Ellenberg, University of Hohenheim (plant location mapping), Otl Aicher (design)

1960–1962
Green spaces planning for Darmstadt
Urban land use plan for the city of Darmstadt based on the existing situation, prerequisites, and long-term necessities
Green spaces planning as urban development plan and part of the land use plan
Supplementary planning: General plan for Darmstadt 1964 (office of Professor Schaechterle)
Urban structure study (Professor Boeseler)
Staff: Kellinghaus (clerk), Watter (employee), Pfeiffer (employee), Aicher (design), Mühlberger (draftswoman), Laubender (draftsman), Knauss (draftsman)

1962–1965
Green spaces planning for Biberach
Consulting report on the development of a green space system
Green spaces planning as part of the land use plan
Supplementary planning: General plan 1963 (Professor Schaechterle, government building officer Holdschuer), General transport plan Biberach 1965 (Professor Schaechterle)
Staff: Strube (clerk), Kellinghaus (employee), Wassmann (employee), Laubender (draftswoman), Hummel (draftswoman)

1962–1966
Green spaces planning Aschaffenburg
Consulting report on the development of a green space system
Green spaces planning as part of the land use plan
Supplementary planning: General transport plan 1964 (Professor Schaechterle)
Urban planning (Professor Guther)
Staff: Strube (clerk), Kellinghaus (employee), Walter (employee), Laubender (draftswoman)

1964–1966
Green spaces planning for Ludwigsburg
Consulting report on the development of a green space system
Green spaces planning as part of land use planning
Supplementary planning: Urban planning basics for the transport plan for Ludwigsburg 1965, overall transport plan for Ludwigsburg 1966 (Verkehrs- und Industrieplanung)
Staff: Nolte (clerk), Kellinghaus (employee), Czinki (employee), Laubender (draftswoman)

1964
Erenlauh housing settlement, Ulm

1964–1967
Green spaces planning for Meckenheim-Merl
Green spaces planning as part of land use planning
Client: Meckenheim-Merl Development Company mbH
Collaboration: Planning Group Meckenheim-Merl, Friedrich Spengelin, Erich Kühn (Urban planning), Gisela Dahmen (Biological report 1966)

1965
Lyngsberg Bad Godesberg
Urban planning: Tassilo Sittmann, Walter Schwagenscheidt

1966–1967
Darmstadt Kranichstein
Urban planning: Professor Ernst May

1966–1967
Frankfurt Kelsterbach
Urban planning: Tassilo Sittmann, Walter Schwagenscheidt

1967–1968
Wolfsburg-Westhagen, Wolfsburg
Working group with the Development Group Landscape Architecture EGL-Kassel

1968–1969
Am Berg Fidel, Münster
Urban planning: Tassilo Sittmann, Walther Schwagenscheidt

1973
Urban planning report Billwerder-Allermöhe, Hamburg
Collaboration with Max Guther (urban planning)
Urban development planning, landscape planning, and green space planning (according to today's understanding)

1973–1974
Green framework plan and landscape plan Menzenschwand
Project at the chair of Landscape Architecture
Collaboration: Speerplan (local and regional planning), Chair of Landscape Ecology Weihenstephan (Professor Haber), Grünplan GmbH

1974
Green framework plan for the Lehrer Tal, Ulm
Project at the Chair of Landscape Architecture
Collaboration: Institute for Agricultural Business Administration, Weihenstephan

1974
Preliminary planning for the land development of Sonnenalb, Baden-Württemberg
Interdisciplinary consulting report
Collaboration: Albrecht Laubis (local and regional planning), Professor Bischoff, Professor Weller (agriculture), Tassilo Sittmann (urban planning), Erhard Franke (regional planning)

1974–1978
Development concept and landscape development plan Thermal Baths, Birnbach
Project at the Chair of Landscape Architecture
Collaboration: Chair of Rural Construction, Munich (Professor Gebhard) coordinator: Jörg Barteis, Chair of Landscape Architecture, Weihenstephan

1974–1977
Landscape framework plan for local recreational facilities in the district of Neu-Ulm
Project at the Chair of Landscape Architecture
Coordinators: Jörg Barteis, H.G. Erhardt, Chair for Landscape Architecture, Weihenstephan

1976
Landscape Planning Report Munich Airport II
Part 1: Landscape architecture
Grünplan GmbH, Freising
Overall concept with: W. Jerney, L. Kellinghaus, E. Krauss, E. Stauss
Part 2: Ecology
Collaboration: Professor Haber, Dr. Fritz Duhme, Chair of Landscape Ecology, Weihenstephan

1976–1977
Landscape plan for the market town of Oberstaufen
in the Allgäu region of Germany
Project at the Chair and Institute of Landscape
Architecture
Project head: H. G. Erhardt, Chair of Landscape
Architecture, Weihenstephan
Collaborators: W. Jerney, A. Gründel, et al.

1980–1982
Main River embankment in Aschaffenburg
Green space plan for the Main River embankment
Client: City of Aschaffenburg
Working group Grzimek EGL Landshut and
EGL Kassel
Collaboration: Armin Koch, Kaczor, Klinke,
Juliana Grzimek

1984
Consulting report development planning for
Hohenbrunn, Munich district
Landscape plan and disposition of green spaces
Working group Grzimek EGL-Landshut
Consulting report development concept Kegelfelder,
Taufkirchen, Munich district
Collaboration with: Stahr, Thiele, Matthias Grzimek
(urban planning), Alfons Leitl, Brenzel (architecture),
Cornelia Feyer EGL Landshut (green spaces planning),
Eichenauer and Streichert (transport planning)

1992
Interdisciplinary development consulting report
Bad Birnbach
Collaboration with: Hans-Jörg Lang, Keller (transport
planning), Professor Gebhard, arc-Architekten,
Biesterfeld, Brennecke, Richter (local planning),
Reppel & Partners (spa and tourism)
Interdisciplinary development consulting report
Frauenau, Regen district
Collaboration with: Hans-Jörg Lang, Keller, Burghardt
(transport planning), arc-Architekten, Biesterfeld,
Brennecke, Richter (local planning)

Building designs

Children's playgrounds

1950 Blauinsel playground with industrial bridge,
 Ulm, planning and realization of the green areas
1952 Römer-Insel playground, Ulm
1956 Rieslingweg playground, Ulm
1958 Wooden pile playground, Ulm-Eselsberg
1959 Small children's playground Neue Strasse, Ulm

Permanent allotment garden

1953 Permanent allotment garden Am
 Kuhberg (Alpenblick)
1957–1958 Permanent allotment garden
 Am Panoramaweg, Ulm

*Cemeteries, memorials, and open
 spaces at churches*

1947 Staircase planning at the abbey church,
 Weingarten
1952 Cemetery extension, Weingarten,
 planting plan
1952–1955 War Victims Area, New Cemetery, Ulm
1953–1959 Cemetery extension, Blaubeuern
1955 Cemetery extension, Scheer
1956 Cemetery extension, Mengen
1956 Cemetery planning Dürmentingen, draft plan
1956 Tomb Karl Gagstätter, Senden
1956–1957 Cemetery extension, Wiblingen, Ulm
1957 Cemetery design, Creilsheim, inspection
 and consultation
1960 Cemetery planning, Brenz
1960 War Memorial Setzingen, planting plan
1960 Evangelical church Burtenbach, planting plan
1960 St. Maria, Ulm-Söflingen, planting plan
1960 War Victims Memorial, Saulgau, planting plan
1960–1962 Cemetery extension, Saulgau, consulting
 report and preliminary design before
 announcement of tender
1960–1964 New planning of the municipal
 cemetery Biberach, planning and realization
 of the first construction phase
 Competition preparation and prize jury for the
 cemetery buildings;
 Collaborators: L. Kellinghaus, cooperation with
 Werner Rothenbacher (architect)
1961 External facilities cemetery, Bessungen
1961 Cemetery extension, Ulm-Söflingen
1961–1964 New planning of Weingarten cemetery
 and cemetery chapel in cooperation with Hans
 Frieder Eychmüller (architect)
1962–1965 Weingarten monastery external facilities
1962–1965 Cemetery extension, Erbach, buildings in
 collaboration with Karl Glöckner (architect)
1981 Extension of Biberach town cemetery

Transportation green planning

1953 Redesign of Ringstrasse, Ulm, cooperation with Heinrich König (civil engineering office Ulm)
1958–1959 Pedestrian connection with green corridor to town center and shopping center through the glacis at the Unterer Eselsberg fort, Ulm-Eselsberg
1962–1963 Pedestrian connection in the Bürgerhaus, Döngesborngasse-Kirchgasse, Darmstadt
1963 Parking lot on Heinrichstrasse, Darmstadt
1963–1966 Underground parking garage city center, Darmstadt, design studies
1987–1989 Redesign of Uhlandgarten, inner courtyard of the Albstadt municipal library Overall design and realization planning, working group Grzimek, EGL Landshut

Open spaces at educational centers

1951–1955 Multscher School, Ulm, planting
1954 Jörg Syrlin School, Ulm, green spaces design
1954 Schubart Secondary School, Ulm, green spaces design
1956 Kepler Secondary School, Ulm, green spaces design
1959 Spitalhof School, Ulm, planting
1959 Sägefeld School, Ulm, planting
1959 Wiblinger Elementary School, Ulm, planting
1960 Pestalozzi School, Ulm, green spaces planning
1960–1963 State School of Engineering, Ulm, planning of paths and plants, architect: Behnisch & Lambart
1961 School on the Frauenstrasse, Ulm, overall planning of outdoor facilities
1962 Secondary School Schwenningen, architect: Behnisch & Partners
1962–1965 College of Education, Weingarten, overall planning of the outdoor facilities
1963 Student dormitory Weingarten, overall planning
1963–1965 Ecumenical Nurses Residence, Darmstadt, overall planning of the outdoor facilities
1965–1968 State School of Engineering, Aalen, architect: Behnisch & Partners
1968 Duderstadt School Center, architect: Jochen Brandi
1968 Secondary school and sports hall Schwenningen, planting plan and ground modeling, architect: Behnisch & Partners
1968 Middle School Rothenburg ob der Tauber, planting plan, architect: Behnisch & Partners
1970 Secondary school (to tenth grade) Lorch, outdoor facilities, architect: Behnisch & Partners
1974 Air Force Officers' School, Fürstenfeldbruck, outdoor facilities and roof greening, client: Munich II Finance Construction Office, project management: Kurt Ackermann & Partners Collaboration with: H. Köhlmann, E. Krauss, L. Kellinghaus (Grünplan GmbH), J. H. Johannsen
1976 Green structure plan for the University of Passau, coordinator: G.H. Erhardt (Grünplan GmbH)
1976 Green structure plan for the Technical University of Munich, Weihenstephan, coordinator: G.H. Erhardt (Grünplan GmbH)
1979 Inner courtyard of the Technical University of Munich, consulting report on open space for the inner courtyard design, working group G. Grzimek, R. and V. Detterling, and R. Wirtesohn
1979–1981 European School Neu-Perlach, Munich, outdoor facilities and roof greening, design and realization, client: Munich II Finance Construction Office, architects: Michael Eberl and Helmut Weippert, artist: Hans Rucker, collaboration: Gründel, Scharl, Grzimek, Klink (EGL Landshut)
1980 Secondary School (pupils aged 10 to 14) Lorch-Schäfersfeld, outdoor facilities, consulting, architect: Behnisch & Partners
1994–1996 Montessori school in Ingolstadt, design and execution of outdoor facilities, client: Förderkreis für Integrierte Erziehung in Kindergarten und Schule e.V., working group Grzimek EGL Kassel, architect: Behnisch & Partners
1994–1996 Catholic Minster kindergarten, Ingolstadt, design and execution of the outdoor facilities, architect: Behnisch & Partners

Open spaces at hospitals

1962 Wangen District Hospital, planting plan
1963–1965 Regional psychiatric hospital in Schussenried, outdoor facilities
1980–1986 County hospital, district hospital, and care center in Günzburg, outdoor facilities and roof greening, client: Region of Swabia / District of Günzburg, architect: Jauss & Gaupp, working group Grzimek EGL Landshut and EGL Kassel

Open spaces at business and government offices

1947 Entrance area of the Rohr nursery, Ravensburg
1951 Carl Goetz GmbH, Ulm, outdoor planting area
1962 Weingarten tax office, planting plan
1970 Westdeutsche Landesbank, Münster, outdoor planting, architect: Harald Deilmann

1979 Landscape concept for the federal district of Bonn, architect: Behnisch & Partners
1980 Federal buildings in Bonn, "Inner Federal District Bonn," architect: Behnisch & Partners
1982 Rischart's Bakery, Munich, inner courtyard landscaping, working group Grzimek EGL Landshut, architect: Kiessler & Partners
1985–1988 ERCO Leuchten GmbH, Lüdenscheid, outdoor facilities, parking lot, and roof landscaping, working group Grzimek EGL Landshut and EGL Kassel, architect: Kiessler & Partners
1986–1988 Jost + Co. press distribution, Munich, outdoor facilities and roof greening, working group EGL Landshut, architect: Kiessler & Partners
1988 Bayerische Rückversicherung, Munich, outdoor facilities, design and realization, architect: Kiessler & Partners
1989–1990 Druckhaus Maack KG, Lüdenscheid, parking lot, working group Grzimek EGL Landshut

Sport and leisure sites

1961 District sports facility Lichtwiesen "Youth sports field," Darmstadt, design plans
1961–1962 District sports facility in Eberstadt-Modau, Darmstadt
1961–1963 Donaubad, Ulm, overall planning
1964 Wieseckau Sports and Recreation Center, Giessen Steinbrücker Teich Recreation Park, Darmstadt
1964–1966 Sports park Ludwigsburg, design plans
1991–1993 Spa Hotel Bayerischer Hof, Bad Birnbach, outdoor facilities, overall concept, EGL Landshut, architect: Jungwirth & Unterberger

Parks and other green spaces

1949–1953 Old cemetery, Ulm, redesigning
1949–1960 Friedrichsau, Ulm, continuous expansion and development of the park area
1953 Ehinger Anlage, Ulm, redesigning
1961 Wolfskehl'scher Garten, Darmstadt, overall planning
1961–1965 Green areas at the Wilhelmsburg barracks, Ulm, design plans
1963 Outdoor facilities with courtyard at the Justus-von-Liebig community center, Darmstadt, overall planning
1963–1965 Grosser Woog pond, Darmstadt, design plans
1965–1966 Kleiner Woog pond, Darmstadt, design plans

1968–1972 Olympic Park in Munich, overall planning of the Olympic landscape and artistic supervision: Behnisch & Partners
Overall planning of the Olympic landscape and artistic supervision: engineering office of Professor Günther Grzimek, collaboration: Günther Hänsler (technical supervision), Gerd Linder, Bert Maecker, Peter Prinz, Horst-Jürgen Schliep
1972–1973 Consulting report for Castle Garden Erlangen, Erlangen University, in cooperation with the chair of Landscape Architecture
1985 School meadow, Pfeffenhausen, design: Grzimek, realization: working group Grzimek EGL Landshut
1985–1986 Ice skating rink in the Olympic Park in Munich, outdoor facilities and miniature golf course, overall planning, realization: working group Grzimek, Kowollik, architect: Ackermann & Partners
1987 Green area at the "Freiberger Anlage" Bachstrasse, Pfeffenhausen, working group Grzimek EGL Landshut
1989–1990 Extension of the ice rink and open spaces at the Olympic Park and parking lot, Munich, design: Grzimek, realization: working group Grzimek, W. Jerney, EGL Landshut, architect: Ackermann & Partners

House gardens

1956–1969 Kurt Aicham, Ulm
1957–1958 Professor Hösel, Munich-Grünwald
1957–1960 Dr. Gottfried Bergmann-Fischer, Pieve di Camaiore, Lucca, Italy
1959 Hans Werner Eychmüller, Ulm,
1959 Tax inspector Hahn, Ulm, advice on redesigning the house garden
1960 Zink, Radolfszell, planting plan
1960 Otto Prinz, design plan
1960 Gunst, Bad Wurzach, planting plan
1960 Peter Dreschler, Ulm, preliminary plan
1960 Ottmar Brenner, planting plan
1960 Dr. Böwing, planting plan
1961 Professor W. Runge
1961 Otto Kässbohrer, Ulm, draft plan
1961 Senator Eiselen, Ulm, herb garden
1961 Herbert Brenner, planting plan
1969 Behnisch house garden, Kemnat near Stuttgart, overall planning
1980 Dr. Gunzenhauser house garden, Holzhausen am Ammersee, collaboration: Cornelia Feyer, Michael Scharl (EGL Munich)

1986 Wackerbauer house garden, Pfeffenhausen, planting plan
1987 Rank house garden, Pfeffenhausen, design
1987 Huber house garden, Aiglsbach-Oberpindhart, planting plan
1988 Dr. Ziegler house garden, Weihenstephan, planning and execution

Botanical garden

1965–1970 Botanical Garden of the Philipps University, Marburg, overall planning, collaborator: L. Kellinghaus

Zoological sites

1959 Bear pen in Friedrichsau, Ulm, architect: Dörmann
1968–1971 All-Weather Zoo in Münster, Westphalia, concept and design, partial realization, architect: Harald Deilmann

Competitions and consulting reports

1956 Competition for the realization, cemetery Stuttgart, Weilimdorf, purchase
1958 Competition for children's playgrounds "Aid through Green" of the Central Association of German Gardening, Bonn, first prize
1959 Competition for the realization, park cemetery, Kassel
1960 Competition, cemetery Baienfurth with cour d'honneur design, Baienfurth, Ravensburg district, third prize
1961 Competition for ideas for the Federal Garden Show in Stuttgart
1964 Urban planning competition for a new district of Bad Godesberg-Lyngsberg, working group with Walter Schwagenscheidt and Tassilo Sittmann, first prize
1967 Urban planning competition for the new city district Schweinfurt-Deutschhof, working group with Tassilo Sittmann, third prize
1968 Competition for the realization of a zoo in Münster, working group with Harald Deilmann, first prize
1968 Competition for the realization of a comprehensive school in Duderstadt, working group with Jochen Brandi, first prize
1974 Urban planning competition for the extension of the State Parliament and State Gallery in Stuttgart, working group with Behnisch & Partners
1975 Urban planning competition for the Federal District of Bonn, working group with Behnisch & Partners
1980 Urban planning competition for St. Michael, Munich-Berg am Laim, working group with Werz, Ottow, Bachmann, Marx, Henze, and Jerney
1981 Urban planning ideas competition for the Schwabenau site in Freising, in collaboration with Hubert
1985 Urban planning competition for Spreebogen, working group with Baier, Heidenreich, and Schuster
1986 Sports area for the Olympic site in Istanbul, working group with Behnisch & Partners
1986 Competition Exhibition and Conference Center in Hannover, working group with Behnisch & Partners
1987 Consulting report on the Volksparkstadion stadium and surroundings, Hamburg, working group with Schweger & Partners, Binnewies, and Masuch & Olbrisch
1987 Competition for the realization of the Biozentrum at Frankfurt University, working group with Behnisch & Partners
1987 Consulting report on future use of the airport site in Munich-Riem, working group with Groethuysen, Maurer, Otzmann, and Wirsing
1987 Urban planning ideas competition for Erlangen University Hospital and building competition for ambulatory health care center, first construction phase, working group with Werz, Ottow, Bachmann, and Marx, first prize
1988 Cooperative competition Science City Ulm, working group with Behnisch & Partners
1989 Building competition EAM Energy Supply Company Kassel, working group with Jochen Brandi, third prize
1992 Invited competition for the Cologne–Bonn Airport, working group with Behnisch & Partners, fourth prize
1992 Idea competition for extension of the Maximilianeum palace, Munich, working group with Ackermann & Partners
1992 Competition for the realization of the New Munich Trade Fair Center in Riem, working group with architects: Groethuysen, Maurer, Otzmann, and Wirsing, landscape architect: W. Jerney, third prize

Participation in juries

1957 Competition for the open-air swimming pool complex Donaubad, Ulm/Neu-Ulm, client judge

1960–1961 Competition for the development of an inner-city green area, Mathildenhöhe, Darmstadt, competition preparation and technical judge

1962 Competition for the cemetery building of the Biberach municipal cemetery, competition preparation and juror

1965 Competition for the children's playgrounds, "Hilfe durch Grün" (Help through Green Space), technical judge

1969 Competition for ideas for the Nordbad swimming pool, including indoor and outdoor swimming pools, Darmstadt

1976–1977 Town planning ideas and realization competition for the Federal Garden Show in Kassel in 1981, competition preparation, technical judge, and chairman of the jury

1978 Competition for the State Garden Show in Ulm in 1980, competition preparation, technical judge, and chairman of the jury

1978 Competition sports facilities of the University of Stuttgart, judge

1978 Urban planning competition Friedrichsplatz, Kassel, judge

1978 Urban planning competition for pedestrians in the Duisburg city center, judge

1979 Urban planning ideas competition for the municipality of Kirchheim near Munich, technical judge

1979 Competition for the redesign of Bismarckplatz in Regensburg, judge

1979 Urban planning competition for Leonrodplatz, Munich, judge

1979 Landscape planning competition for Mollgelände, Munich, judge

1979 Urban planning ideas competition for Weserpark, Bremerhaven, technical judge

1980 Competition for design of open spaces and Neckar riverbank, Klinikum Mannheim

1981 Competition "Südliches Oberwiesenfeld," Munich, technical judge

1983 General traffic reduction Ingolstadt, deputy technical judge

1987 Artistic ideas and realization competition Wallberg, Pforzheim, technical judge

1989 Competition for ideas and realization for the design of streets, lanes, and squares in the old town of Passau (Old Town Competition Passau), technical judge

1992 Urban planning ideas and realization competition for the Funkerkaserne area, Esslingen am Neckar, technical judge

List of Exhibitions

1958 Touring exhibition *Hilfe durch Grün* (Help through Green Space), exhibits: individual plan for children's playgrounds, land use plan for Ulm; playgrounds and playground equipment from "Aktion Sandfloh"

1958 South German Horticultural Exhibition in Ulm, exhibits: plans and photos of work by the garden and cemetery office

1960 Founding exhibition of the International Council for Children's Play ICCP, Museum Ulm, exhibits: photos of children's playgrounds and play equipment

1960 Triennale Milan, exhibits: photos of children's playgrounds and playground equipment of "Aktion Sandfloh"

1961 Touring exhibition of the committee "Gutes Spielzeug e. V.," Zagreb, exhibits: photos of children's playgrounds and playground equipment of the "Aktion Sandfloh"

1964 Vienna International Garden Show (WIG 64), Vienna, exhibits: plans of green spaces planning for Darmstadt, cemetery in Wiblingen, transportation greenery in Ulm

1965 Green spaces planning – urban planning, Essen Federal Garden Show, exhibits: plans and photos

1965 Cemetery and tomb, Stuttgart, exhibits: plans

1966 IFLA exhibition, Stuttgart

1967 New landscape design and sculptures, Lake Constance Museum, Friedrichshafen, exhibition concept and exhibits: plans and photos as selected examples of previous work

1969 German Building Exhibition (DEUBAU 69), urban and green spaces planning, Essen, exhibits: plans and photos

1973 *Democratic Green Space: From Palace Garden, to Public Park, to Recreational Landscape*, Munich, Bavarian Academy of Fine Arts, exhibition concept and foreword in the catalog

1983 *The Appropriation of the Lawn*, conclusions from the South Isar Model. *Green Spaces Planning Today*, the "Explorations" exhibition series from the Bavarian Reinsurance Company, exhibition and catalog concept, texts with Rainer Stephan

Bibliography

Aicher, Otl. *Innenseiten des Kriegs*. Frankfurt am Main: S. Fischer Verlag, 1985.

Behnisch & Partners / Christian Kandzia. *Bauten für Olympia 1972, München Kiel Augsburg*. Munich: Harbecke Verlag München.

Bode, Arnold. *Ars porcellana. Rosenthal Relief Reihe*. Exh. cat. Rosenthal Relief Reihe. Kassel, 1967.

Brecht, Bertolt and the Münchner Kammerspiele, https://mkammerspiele.wordpress.com/2015/05/20/bertolt-brecht-und-die-munchner-kammerspiele/.

Brock, Bazon. "Action Teaching, Kleine Besucherschule zur documenta 4." https://bazonbrock.de/werke/detail/kleine_besucherschule_zur_docume-655.html.

Bundesministerium der Justiz. "Gesetz zum Schutz des Olympischen Friedens, 48, 31.05.1972 C.F.R. (1972)." *Bundesgesetzblatt*, no. 48 (June 3, 1972).

Diem, Liselott. "Warum so viel Diskussion über den Spielplatz?" in *Die Aktion "Sandfloh" der Stadt Ulm/Donau*. Munich: Callwey Verlag, 1957.

Documenta-Rat. *Art* 11 (1989). 90.

Dümpelmann, Sonja. *Flights of Imagination. Aviation, Landscape, Design*. Charlottsville: University of Virginia Press, 2014.

Düwel, Jörn and Niels Gutschow. Ordnung und Gestalt. *Geschichte und Theorie des Städtebaus in Deutschland 1922 bis 1975*. Berlin: DOM publishers, 2019.

Egger, Simone. *"München wird moderner." Stadt und Atmosphäre in den langen 1960er Jahren*. Bielefeld: Transcript-Verlag, 2013.

Freytag, Anette. *Dieter Kienast. Stadt und Landschaft lesbar machen*. Zurich: gta Verlag, 2016.

Georgdorf, Heiner. *Arnold Bode: Schriften und Gespräche*. Berlin: Siebenhaar Verlag, 2007.

Gnahm, Andreas. *Giebel oder Traufe. Die Wiederaufbaukontroverse in Ulm nach dem Zweiten Weltkrieg*. Kleine Reihe des Stadtarchivs Ulm, vol. 5. Ulm: Haus der Stadtgeschichte - Stadtarchiv Ulm, 2008.

Go Jeong-Hi. *Herta Hammerbacher (1900-1985). Virtuosin der neuen Landschaftlichkeit. Der Garten als Paradigma*. Berlin: Universitätsverlag der Technischen Universität Berlin, 2006.

Göderitz, Johannes, Roland Rainer, and Hubert Hoffmann. *Die gegliederte und aufgelockerte Stadt*. Tübingen: Wasmuth, 1957.

Grillmeier et al. S. Landeshauptstadt München, 2012.

Groeben, Klaus von der. *Verwaltung und Politik 1918–1933 am Beispiel Ostpreußens* (2nd ed.). Kiel: Lorenz-von-Stein-Institut, 1988.

Gröning, Gert and Joachim Wolschke-Bulmahn. *Liebe zur Landschaft. Arbeiten zur sozialwissenschaftlich orientierten Freiraumplanung, Teil 3: Der Drang zur Landschaft. Zur Entwicklung der Landespflege im Nationalsozialismus und während des Zweiten Weltkrieges in den "eingegliederten Ostgebieten."* Münster: Lit-Verlag, 1987

Grzimek, Günther and Rainer Stephan. *Die Besitzergreifung des Rasens. Folgerungen aus dem Modell Süd-Isar. Grünplanung heute*. Munich: Callwey, 1983.

Grzimek, Günther. "Friedhofskapelle in Weingarten / Württemberg," *Kunst und Kirche* 28, vol. 2. 74–76.

Grzimek, Günther. "Olympische Park-Ideen," *Garten + Landschaft* 103 (1993). 30–35.

Grzimek, Günther. Architekturwettbewerbe Olympische Bauten. Munich, 1972. 2. Special volume: Bestandsaufnahme Herbst 1970. 1–4, 18–21.

Grzimek, Günther. Architekturwettbewerbe Olympische Bauten. Munich, 1972. 3. Special volume: Bauabschluß Sommer 1972.

Grzimek, Günther. *Die Aktion "Sandfloh" der Stadt Ulm/Donau*. Munich: Callwey Verlag, 1957.

Grzimek, Günther. *Eine Geschichte der Parkanlagen aus aktueller Sicht*. Munich: Meyster Verlag, 1984.

Grzimek, Günther. *Eine Geschichte der Parkanlagen aus aktueller Sicht*. Naturraum-Reihe. AGG, TU München, Pfeffenhausen.

Grzimek, Günther. *Grünplanung Darmstadt*. Darmstadt: Eduard Roether Verlag, 1965.

Grzimek, Günther. *Grünplanung in Ulm*. Ulm: Stadtverwaltung Ulm, 1954.

Grzimek, Günther. *Hochschule für Bildende Künste Halle, Lehrstuhl für Landschaftskultur* (vol. 1968a). Munich: Callwey, 1968.

Grzimek, Günther. *Manieristensammlung der Familie Grzimek. Vom Aufgang der Neuzeit*. Ravensburg: Drexler, 1966.

Grzimek, Günther. *Menschenleben. Erinnerungen eines Urahns.* Dorheim: Podzun-Verlag, 1970.

Grzimek, Günther. *Spiel und Sport in der Stadtlandschaft. Erfahrungen und Beispiele für morgen.* Schriftenreihe der Deutschen Gesellschaft für Gartenkunst und Landschaftspflege, vol. 9. Munich: Callwey, 1972.

Heyne, Erich. "Stadion-Wettbewerb für München." *Baumeister* 5. 479.

Hochschule für Gestaltung Ulm. *Die frühen Jahre* (vol. 5). Ulm: Archiv der HfG.

Hoffmann, Lutz. "Aufstieg aus den Trümmern 1945–1960," in *München wie geplant. Die Entwicklung der Stadt 1158 bis 2008.* Referat für Stadtplanung und Bauordnung Landeshauptstadt München. Exh. cat. Stadtmuseum München. Munich: Schiermeier, 2004.

Höllerer, Joseph. "Der Schuttberg auf dem Olympia-Gelände." *Garten + Landschaft* 5. 148–49.

https://www.hu-berlin.de/de/ueberblick/geschichte/juedische-studierende/uni-im-ns/entfernung.

Hübner, Emanuel. "Olympisches Dorf 1936" (published on May 8, 2018). *Historisches Lexikon Brandenburgs.* https://www.brandenburgikon.net/index.php/de/sachlexikon/olympisches-dorf.

Hübner, Emanuel. *Das Olympische Dorf von 1936. Planung, Bau und Nutzungsgeschichte.* Paderborn: Schöningh, 2015.

Humboldt-Universität. "Chronik der Friedrich-Wilhelms-Universität zu Berlin 1937/38." https://www.digi-hub.de/viewer/image/1603980265057/1/LOG_0003/.

Humboldt, Alexander von. *Ansichten der Natur.* Ed. Christian Döring. Special printing of vol. 17 of the original edition. Berlin: Aufbau-Verlag, 2019.

Kaiser, Gerhard. "Grünpolitik muss bürgernah sein. FORUM Gespräch mit Professor Günther Grzimek." *Ulmer Forum* 57 (1981). 12ff.

Keller Landschaftsarchitekten. *Entwicklungsplanung Olympiapark 2018. Materialsammlung und Grundlagenworkshop.* Munich: Landeshauptstadt München, Referat für Stadtplanung und Bauordnung, 2008.

Keller, Regine. "Demokratisches Grün. Von der Besitzergreifung des Rasens bis zu Occupy." *Der Architekt* 2 (2014). 40–47.

Kellerhoff, Sven Felix. *Berlin unterm Hakenkreuz.* Berlin: bebra Verlag, 2006.

Kellner, Ursula. "Landschaftsbilder. Einfluss auf die Gestaltungen von Landschaft bei Heinrich Wiepking (1891–1973)." Lecture. Hannover.

Kellner, Ursula. *Heinrich Friedrich Wiepking (1891–1973). Leben, Lehre und Werk.* Disseration. Universität Hannover, 1997.

Krysmanski, Renate. *Die Nützlichkeit der Landschaft,* vol. 9. Münster: Bertelsmann Universitätsverlag.

König, Andreas. *Günther Grzimek.* Thesis. Technische Universität München-Weihenstephan.

Kreutzmüller, Christoph and Michael Wildt, eds. *Berlin 1933–1945. Stadt und Gesellschaft im Nationalsozialismus.* Munich: Siedler Verlag, 2012.

Kulturreferat Landeshauptstadt München. Milbertshofen - Am Hart. Kulturgeschichtspfad 11. Munich, 2015. 2nd 2017 edition. https://stadt.muenchen.de/dam/jcr:405464f7-a6c0-4fea-9910-9a93a3ea0739/KulturGeschichtsPfad-11-Milbertshofen-Am-Hart.pdf.

Landeshauptstadt München 2012. Schulze/TOPOS. Parkpflegewerk Olympiapark. *Amtsinternes Konzept.* Munich, 2012.

Landeshauptstadt München. "Referat für Stadtplanung und Bauordnung." *Stadtentwicklungsplanung: Zukunft des Olympiaparks. Leitlinien für ein visuelles Gesamterscheinungsbild.* Munich, 2012.

Lauterbach, Iris, "'Die Kunsthistoriker sind uns auf den Fersen!' Die Gartenkunst im Kontext und Wechselspiel von Praxis, Lehre und Kunstgeschichte in München, 1900 bis 1945." *Die Gartenkunst* 33 (2021), vol. 1. 68–90.

Löwenhauser, Paul and Werner Göhner. "Die olympischen Pläne und ihre Verwirklichung." *Münchner Leben* 13 (1968). Olympics edition. 22–36.

Mäding, Erhard. *Regeln für die Gestaltung der Landschaft. Einführung in die Allgemeine Anordnung Nr. 20/VI/42 des Reichsführers SS....* Berlin: Verlag Deutsche Landbuchhandlung, 1943.

Mäding, Heinrich and Wendelin Strubelt, eds. *Vom Dritten Reich zur Bundesrepublik. Beiträge einer Tagung zur Geschichte von Raumforschung und Raumplanung.* Leipzig, June 12–13, 2008. Hannover: Verlag der ARL, 2009. https://nbn-resolving.org/urn:nbn:de:0168-ssoar-284556.

Mazzoni, Ira. „… in die Jahre gekommen, Olympiapark in München." *db, deutsche Bauzeitung 142/9* (issue on *Draussen* (outside)). 57–62.

Meissner, Irene. "Der Umgang mit den Bauten des Nationalsozialismus." In Landeshauptstadt München, *Referat für Stadtplanung und Bauordnung Lokalbaukommission, Untere Denkmalschutzbehörde, Denkmalschutz in München*. 40 Jahre Bayerisches Denkmalschutzgesetz. Munich: Landeshauptstadt München, 2013 (3rd edition, 2018). 42–44.

Meyer, Konrad. "Siedlungs- und Aufbauarbeit im deutschen Osten." *Die Bewegung* 8 (1941). 71. https://www.agrar.hu-berlin.de/de/institut/profil/geschichte/profil/geschichte/leseprobe.

Moser, Eva. *Otl Aicher. Gestalter*. Ostfildern-Ruit: Hatje Cantz Verlag, 2011.

Mühlmann, Andrea. *Günther Grzimek*. Master's thesis. Technische Universität München, 2015.

Nachlass Otl Aicher. Findbuch 09. https://hfg-archiv.museumulm.de/wp-content/uploads/2020/06/09_aicher-neu.pdf.

Nachlass Wiepking. Dep. 72B, Nr. 116 (30.7.1933). Osnabrück Stadtarchiv, M. (1965). Stadtchronik. https://www.muenchen.de/rathaus/Stadtverwaltung/Direktorium/Stadtarchiv/Chronik/1965.html.

Nerdinger, Winfried. "Fatale Kontinuität. Akademiegeschichte von den zwanziger bis zu den fünfziger Jahren." In *Tradition und Widerspruch. 175 Jahre Kunstakademie München*, ed. Thomas Zacharias. Munich: Prestel, 1985. 179–203.

Olympiade München 1972/117. Aicher Olympische Spiele München.

Orzechowski, Lothar, ed. *Arnold Bode*. documenta Kassel. Kassel: Stadtsparkasse Kassel, 1986.

Pache, Jörg. "Die Entfernung unerwünschter Studierender, Uni im NS."

Pauli, Sarah. *Günther Grzimek. Architekt des demokratischen Grüns. Der Münchner Olympiapark als zeitlose Gebrauchslandschaft*. Munich: Grin-Verlag, 2012. https://www.grin.com/document/201990.

Peters, Paulhans. "Die Bauten für die Spiele der XX. Olympiade in München und die Stadt." *Baumeister, Zeitschrift für Architektur Planung Umwelt* 8 (1972). 338ff.

Poblotzki, Ursula. *Menschenbilder in der Landespflege 1945–1970, Arbeiten zur sozialwissenschaftlich orientierten Freiraumplanung 13*. Munich: Minerva, 1992.

Pres, Werner. *Der Olympiapark München 1972 und das Reichssportfeld Berlin 1936 unter Einschluss des Olympischen Dorfes bei Döberitz unter sporthistorischer Betrachtung*. Munich: Grin-Verlag, 2010.

Rathgeb, Markus. *Otl Aicher*. London: Phaidon, 2006.

Reichard, Christian. *Kurze Übersicht über die Entwicklung des Fachs Chemie an der Universität Marburg von 1609 bis zur Gegenwart*. Marburg: Philipps–Universität Marburg, 2020. https://www.uni-marburg.de/de/fb15/fachbereich/dekanat/chemie.pdf.

Retrospektive. documenta. https://www.documenta.de/de/.

Rückl, Steffen and Karl-Heint Noack. "Agrarökonomen der Berliner Universität 1933–1945. Von der Vertreibung unerwünschter Hochschullehrer bis zur Ausarbeitung des 'Generalplan Ost.'" In *Die Berliner Universität in der NS-Zeit*, vol. 2: Fachbereiche und Fakultäten. Ed. Rüdiger vom Bruch. Wiesbaden: Franz Steiner Verlag, 2005. 73–91.

Rückl, Steffen. *Verfolgte Hochschullehrer der FWU 1933 bis 1945. Wirtschafts- und Sozialwissenschaftliche Fachgebiete der Landwirtschaftlich-Gärtnerischen Fakultät der Humboldt-Universität zu Berlin*. Berlin, 2007.

Schiller, Kay and Christopher Young. *München 1972. Olympische Spiele im Zeichen des modernen Deutschland*. Göttingen: Wallstein, 2012.

Spieker, Elisabeth. *Günter Behnisch – die Entwicklung des architektonischen Werkes: Gebäude, Gedanken und Interpretationen*. Stuttgart: Universität Stuttgart, 2005.

Stadion-Wettbewerb für München. *Baumeister* 5 (1965). 28, 36.

Stauss, Kilian and Fritz Auer. *Olympiapark München. Gestaltungshandbuch 2015*. Munich: Landeshauptstadt München, 2015.

Stöbe, Sylvia. Arnold Bode – Künstler und Visionär. Kassel: Euregioverlag, 2021.

Stoffers, Henning. "Über den alten Zoo und was aus ihm wurde." Münster, Menschen, Geschichten und Erinnerungen. https://www.sto-ms.de/bildgeschichte/über-den-alten-zoo-und-was-aus-ihm-wurde/.

Szymczyk, Elisabeth. "Gartenkünstlerische Tendenzen der sechziger und siebziger Jahre." *Rheinische Heimatpflege* 50 (2013), no. 1. 81–90.

Valentien, Donata, ed. *Die Wiederkehr der Landschaft.* Berlin: Jovis, 2010.

Vogel, Hans-Jochen. *Die Amtskette. Meine 12 Münchner Jahre. Ein Erlebnisbericht.* Munich: Süddeutscher Verlag, 1972.

Vogel, Thomas. *Dem "Grab allen Anstandes" entstiegen. Ulm-Entwürfe im ersten Nachkriegsjahrzehnt.* Ulm: Archiv der HfG.

Wackerbarth, Horst, ed. *Kunst und Medien. Materialien zur documenta 6.* Kassel: Stadtzeitung und Verlag, 1977.

Wiepking-Jürgensmann, Heinrich. *Die Landschaftsfibel.* Berlin: Deutsche Landbuchhandlung, 1942.

Zutz, Axel. "Wege grüner Moderne. Praxis und Erfahrung der Landschaftsanwälte des NS-Staates zwischen 1930 und 1960." In *Vom Dritten Reich zur Bundesrepublik. Beiträge einer Tagung zur Geschichte von Raumforschung und Raumplanung.* Leipzig, June 12–13, 2008. Eds. Heinrich Mäding and Wendelin Strubelt. Hannover: Verlag der ARL, 2009. 107–48. https://nbn-resolving.org/urn:nbn:de:0168-ssoar-284556.

Author and Editor

Regine Keller, 2022,
photo: Ulrike Myrzik

Regine Keller was born in 1962 in Pirmasens. After studying art history and theater studies at Ludwig Maximilian University in Munich and working in the theater in Salzburg, Munich, and Schweinfurt, she completed an apprenticeship in garden and landscaping. In 1991 she began studying landscape planning at the Technical University of Munich (TUM), where she graduated in 1996. From 1996 to 2000 Keller was research assistant for Professor Christoph Valentien, chair of Landscape Architecture and Planning at TUM. In 1998 she founded the Büro Keller Landschaftsarchitekten office for landscape architects, today Keller Damm Kollegen GmbH. In 2005 she was appointed professor for Landscape Architecture and Public Space at the TUM. From 2006 to 2009 she was dean of studies at the faculty for Landscape Architecture and Planning; from 2009 to 2011 dean of the Faculty for Architecture, from 2011 to 2014 Vice President of the TUM, and since 2021 Head of the Department of Architecture at the TUM.

2003 Art Grant of the Bavarian Academy of Arts
2013 "Pro meritis scientiae et litterarum" prize from the Bavarian Ministry for Science, Research, and Art
2015 Bavarian Architecture Prize

Regine Keller is a member of the Architecture Consulting Committee of Berlin, Bavarian Academy of Fine Arts, Academy of Arts Berlin, the Goethe Institute and ICOMOS, Chamber of Architects, the Deutscher Werkbund, Deutsche Akademie für Städtebau und Landesplanung DASL, and Association of German Landscape Architects. She has belonged to the board of the Villa Massimo Grant from the Kulturstiftung der Länder since 2021.

Regine Keller lives and works in Munich.

Contributor

Anette Freytag was born in 1971 in Klagenfurt. She studied art history at the University of Vienna and received her PhD from ETH Zurich in 2011 with a thesis on Dieter Kienast. Since 2016 she has been a professor of landscape architecture at Rutgers, The State University of New Jersey. She is an author and the recipient of numerous awards and prizes.

Colophon

GRÜN
Günther Grzimek:
Planning – Design – Program

Editor and Author
Regine Keller

Concept and Structure
Otl Aicher, Günther Grzimek,
Regine Keller

Project Management, Hirmer Verlag
Cordula Gielen

Copyediting
James Copeland, Berlin

Translation from the German
Caroline Ahrens, Hamburg
David Sánchez Cano, Madrid

Design, Typesetting, and Production
Sabine Frohmader, Sophie Friederich

Prepress
Reproline mediateam GmbH & Co. KG,
Unterföhring

Paper
Garda Ultramatt 150 g/m²

Font
Rotis Semi Sans

Printing and Binding
Printer Trento s.r.l.

Printed in Italy

Bibliographic information published by the Deutsche Nationalbibliothek The Deutsche Nationalbibliothek lists this publication in the Deutsche Nationalbibliografie; detailed bibliographic data are available online at http://www.dnb.de.

© 2022 Hirmer Verlag GmbH, Munich; and the authors

ISBN 978-3-7774-4018-7 (English edition)
ISBN 978-3-7774-4017-0 (German edition)

www.hirmerpublishers.com

Cover: Based on the original design by Otl Aicher

Image Credits

We have made every effort to identify copyright holders. Any copyright owner who has been inadvertently overlooked is asked to contact the publisher. Justified claims will be settled in accordance with the customary agreements.

AGG: 8, 9, 14, 18l, 18r, 27, 37, 48, 53 © Karsten de Riese, 60, 61, 62, 63, 66, 68, 69, 132b, 164–176 © Karsten de Riese, 179t, 179b, 181; **AGG** FaszNr. F7: © Watter Helmut: 101t, 101b; **AGG** FaszNr. 12: 123, 124, 126t, 133tl, 133tr, 134r, 137, 138b, 141, 144, 145, 147; **AGG** FaszNr. 12, F1: 72t, 72b, 73, 74, 75, © Christian Kandzia: 126b, 129t; **AGG** FaszNr. 14: 111t, 111b, 112bl; **AGG** FaszNr. 17: 76, 77, 78, 79; **AGG** FaszNr. 19/20: 94, 95, 97; **AGG** FaszNr. 24–29: 107; **AGG** FaszNr. 388: 110, 113tl, 113tr; **AGG** FaszNr. 511 + 111: 102, 104, 105; **AGG** © Joachim Kimpel: 70, 71, 74, 75; **AGG** © Peter Prinz: 125t, 125b, 128t, 128bl, 128br, 129bl, 129br, 133b, 138tl, 138tr, 139t, 146; **AGG** © Walter Sack: 130b, 132tl, 132tr, 136; **AGG** © Horst-Jörg Schliep: 142, 143; **AGG** © Wolfgang Siol: 72t, 72b, 73, 86, 87; © **Archiv Alwin Seifert, TUM:** 198; **Archiv Stiftung Saalecker Werkstätten:** 197; **Archiv ETHZürich:** 199; **Barkenhoff-Stiftung Worpswede:** 197; **Bayerische Akademie der Schönen Künste**, München: 204; **Bayerische Staatsbibliothek München/Bildarchiv**, © Karsten de Riese: 46, 127, 140; **Becker**, Günther, © Hessische Heimat Zeitung: 39; **Berlin, Stiftung Stadtmuseum Berlin**, © Harry Croner: 24t; **Bundesarchiv:** 26l; Bundesarchiv/©Otto Hagemann: 22; Bundesarchiv / © Georg Pahl: 26r; **Coordes**, Gesa: 108, 109; **Enzwieser**, Hans, © Süddeutsche Zeitung, München: 43; **Huhle**, Kurt, © Süddeutsche Zeitung: 40; **Illustrierter Film-Kurier** Nr. 1836: 24b; **Internationales Olympisches Komitee (IOC)**, Lausanne: 25; **Keller**, Regine: 80, 81, 149; **Köln, Rheinisches Bildarchiv**, © Fritz Geus: 16; **Landeshauptstadt München:** 42, 139b; **Mechau**, Thilo: 198; **München, Stadtarchiv**, © Erika Groth-Schmachtenberger: 45; **München,** Stadtmuseum: 196; **Münchner Leben:** 118, 119; **Myrzik**, Ulrike: 215; **Nedden**, Beate zur: 198; **Pierre Mendell Design GmbH**, © Courtesy Die Neue Sammlung München: 162; **The Pk. Odessa Co** / Markus Lanz: back cover photo, 4, 5, 32, 33, 82–85, 88–93, 98, 99, 116, 117, 131, 150, 151, 153–155, 158–163; **The Pk. Odessa Co** / Sebastian Schels: 135, 152, 156, 157; **Rautert**, Timm: 59; **Ruppel**, Alexander: 112t, 115; **saai**, Archiv für Architektur und Ingenieurbau, KIT, Werkarchiv Behnisch & Partner: 100, 120l, 120r, 121r, 121l, 122, 130t, 134l; **Schulze**, Cordula: 34; **Ulm,** HfG-Archiv: 30, 31, 55, 57l; **Ulm,** Stadtarchiv: 28; **Zürich**, Museum für Gestaltung: 57r